Focus on Developmentally
Appropriate Practice

Equitable &
Joyful Learning
in Kindergarten

Eva C. Phillips & Amy Scrinzi, EDITORS

Susan Friedman, SERIES EDITOR

National Association for the Education of Young Children

Washington, DC

National Association for the Education of Young Children

1401 H Street NW, Suite 600
Washington, DC 20005
202-232-8777 • 800-424-2460
NAEYC.org

NAEYC Books

Senior Director, Publishing & Content Development
Susan Friedman

Director, Books
Dana Battaglia

Senior Editor
Holly Bohart

Editor II
Rossella Procopio

Senior Creative Design Manager
Charity Coleman

Senior Creative Design Specialist
Gillian Frank

Publishing Business Operations Manager
Francine Abdelmeguid

Through its publications program, the National Association for the Education of Young Children (NAEYC) provides a forum for discussion of major issues and ideas in the early childhood field, with the hope of provoking thought and promoting professional growth. The views expressed or implied in this book are not necessarily those of the Association.

The following selections were previously published in the specified issues of *Young Children*:

March 2018—Chapters 18; May 2018—Chapters 5 and 21; November 2018—Chapter 23; March 2019—Chapter 11; July 2019—Chapter 12; November 2019—Chapter 4; Fall 2021—Chapter 19; Fall 2022—portions of Chapter 17; Winter 2022—Chapter 8

Chapter 27 is excerpted from J.K. Adair & S. Sachdeva, "Agency and Power in Young Children's Lives: Five Ways to Advocate for Social Justice as an Early Childhood Educator," in *Advancing Equity and Embracing Diversity in Early Childhood Education: Elevating Voices and Actions,* eds. I. Alanís & I.U. Iruka (Washington, DC: NAEYC, 2021), 105–13.

Chapter 20 is adapted from S. Erdman & L.J. Colker, with E.C. Winter, *Trauma and Young Children: Teaching Strategies to Support and Empower* (Washington, DC: NAEYC, 2020).

Portions of Chapter 17 are adapted from M. Fine, "A Jungle Gym for Snails: Joyful Learning in the Kindergarten Classroom," NAEYC blog, January 25, 2018.

Chapter 1 is adapted from E.C. Phillips & A. Scrinzi, *Basics of Developmentally Appropriate Practice: An Introduction for Teachers of Kindergartners* (Washington, DC: NAEYC, 2013).

Permissions

The 6 Cs rubric on page 60 is adapted, by permission, from American Psychological Association, from R.M. Golinkoff & K. Hirsh-Pasek, *Becoming Brilliant: What Science Tells Us About Raising Successful Children* (Washington, DC: American Psychological Association, 2016), Fig. 1.1. © American Psychological Association. No further reproduction or distribution is permitted.

Chapter 15 is reprinted, by permission, from J. Harris, "Centers in Kindergarten: When Do You Have Time for That?," in *Milestones: A Publication of the North Carolina Association for the Education of Young Children,* Spring 2015, 19–22.

Reproduction of painting on page 99 is reprinted, by permission, from Miyuki Tanobe.

"'Look-Fors' When Implementing Play-Based Learning" on pages 128–129 is adapted, by permission, from M. Bhansali, M. Hillegass, & E. Mei, "Guidelines for Play in Kindergarten: What You Should Look for in Your School as You Implement Play-Based Learning" (Teach Plus, 2022). © Teach Plus.

"Phonemic Awareness Routine" on pages 139–140 is adapted from *The Reading Teacher's Top 10 Tools* and used by permission from 95 Percent Group. © 95 Percent Group.

NAEYC accepts requests for limited use of our copyrighted material. For permission to reprint, adapt, translate, or otherwise reuse and repurpose content from this publication, review our guidelines at NAEYC.org/resources/permissions.

Photo Credits

Copyright © Getty Images: cover, xii, 15, 20, 74, 114, 133, 145, 160

Courtesy of the authors: 23, 48, 69, 92, 96, 101, 108

Library of Congress Control Number: 2023916039

ISBN: 978-1-952331-34-3

Item: 1173

Contents

About the Editors

Volume Editors

Eva C. Phillips, EdD, is dedicated to teaching and advocating for young children and early childhood educators. Throughout her almost 40 years of service to North Carolina, she served as a kindergarten teacher, a state-level Title I preschool and kindergarten consultant, an assistant professor and Birth-Kindergarten Education Program Coordinator, and a district-level program manager for early learning. She has collaborated on numerous projects supporting developmentally appropriate practices and was cocreator and cofacilitator of North Carolina's Power of K Teacher Leader Initiative while at the North Carolina Department of Public Instruction. Dr. Phillips also served as president of the North Carolina Association for the Education of Young Children from 2009 to 2013. After retiring from the state in 2017, she began a consulting business to support early learning educators through professional development, consulting, and coaching. She is coauthor of the book *Basics of Developmentally Appropriate Practice: An Introduction for Teachers of Kindergartners* and the white paper *Children Come First: Ensuring School Policies, Practices, and Strategies Lead to Positive 3rd Grade Outcomes*. She is dedicated to working with educators in their pursuits to provide the most authentic, appropriate, engaging, and challenging experiences for all young children.

Amy Scrinzi, EdD, is an accomplished educator with extensive experience in the field of education spanning more than 30 years. She is an assistant professor of child development at Meredith College in North Carolina. In addition, she serves as the coordinator of the birth-to-kindergarten licensure program, overseeing and guiding aspiring educators in their journey to become licensed educators. Dr. Scrinzi is a former classroom teacher of pre-K through third grade, having taught in several public school districts in North Carolina. She later worked at the state's Department of Public Instruction as a state-level early childhood education consultant, developing and facilitating projects that included coleading the state's Power of K three-year kindergarten teacher leadership initiative. She also served as a state-level K–2 math consultant, state lead for the North Carolina Kindergarten Entry Assessment (KEA), and state-level mentor for nonpublic pre-K teachers seeking a birth-to-kindergarten teaching license. She is coauthor of the book *Basics of Developmentally Appropriate Practice: An Introduction for Teachers of Kindergartners*. Her experience as a classroom teacher, consultant, mentor, and author has equipped her with a comprehensive understanding of early childhood education, and she remains dedicated to supporting teachers' use of effective practices that align with the developmental needs of young learners.

Series Editor

Susan Friedman is senior director of publishing and content development at NAEYC. In this role, she leads the content development work of NAEYC's books and periodicals teams. Ms. Friedman is coeditor of *Each and Every Child: Teaching Preschool with an Equity Lens*. She has extensive prior experience creating content on play, developmentally appropriate uses of media, and other topics for educators and families. She has presented at numerous educational conferences, including NAEYC's Professional Learning Institute and Annual Conference, the South by Southwest Education (SXSW EDU) Conference & Festival, and the School Superintendents Association's Early Learning Cohort. She began her career as a preschool teacher at City and Country School in New York City. She holds degrees from Vassar College and the Harvard Graduate School of Education.

Focus on Developmentally Appropriate Practice
Equitable and Joyful Learning Book Series

In this series, each book presents essential, foundational information from both NAEYC's position statement on developmentally appropriate practice and the fourth edition of *Developmentally Appropriate Practice in Early Childhood Programs Serving Children from Birth Through Age 8*. The books provide early childhood educators with the context and tools for applying developmentally appropriate practice in their work with specific age groups: infants and toddlers, preschoolers, kindergartners, and children in the primary grades. The foundational content is supported by examples of developmentally appropriate practice in real classrooms, illustrated through articles from NAEYC's books and periodicals, *Young Children* and *Teaching Young Children,* and through new material.

Developmentally Appropriate Practice

An Introduction

What Is Developmentally Appropriate Practice?

Developmentally appropriate practice is about effective teaching and joyful, engaged learning. It is a framework that guides the thinking and work of early childhood educators to create healthy, respectful, and responsive learning environments in which children thrive. It requires both meeting children where they are—which means that teachers must get to know them well—and helping them reach goals that are both challenging and achievable. NAEYC defines developmentally appropriate practice as "methods that promote each child's optimal development and learning through a strengths-based, play-based approach to joyful, engaged learning" (NAEYC 2020, 5). But no single method is appropriate in all settings or with all children. Educators use several sources of information to make intentional decisions about what's developmentally appropriate for *this* child at *this* time. These sources include what is known from research about child development, each child's individual characteristics, and each child's and family's context. Applying developmentally appropriate practice, then, means gaining the tools to build on children's strengths and knowledge so you can set goals and provide experiences that are suited to their learning and development.

Besides being an approach to teaching, developmentally appropriate practice is a position statement. Developed in the mid-1980s, NAEYC's original position statement on developmentally appropriate practice was a response to inappropriate teaching practices and expectations for preschool and kindergarten children. The statement has since been expanded to include children from birth through age 8. It remains focused on supporting equitable, high-quality learning experiences for all young children. The position statement emphasizes the need for teachers to have a foundational knowledge of child development and a wide set of skills to support children's learning. The position statement also calls for teachers to embrace children's cultural, linguistic, and racial and ethnic diversity as well as individual learning needs and development. Effective educators learn who their children and families are and recognize the unique, multiple assets each brings to the learning community.

The fourth edition of *Developmentally Appropriate Practice in Early Childhood Programs Serving Children from Birth Through Age 8* examines developmentally appropriate practice in more detail. That book expands on the important concepts of the position statement with contributions from early childhood experts and champions of high-quality early learning experiences. The book and position statement, along with the advancing equity position statement and the book *Advancing Equity and Embracing Diversity in Early Childhood Education: Elevating Voices and Actions*, present integrated resources for all early childhood educators, regardless of their role or the ages of the children they serve.

As an educator, use the position statement on developmentally appropriate practice and the accompanying resources to get an overview of the ideas and components of developmentally appropriate practice. Reflect on your current practice and develop goals to improve your practice so that you are responding to children's learning needs within the larger context of their culture, language, racial identity, and other social identities.

Using the Three Core Considerations to Make Teaching Decisions

Effective early childhood educators use three core considerations to make decisions about curriculum and teaching: commonality, individuality, and context.

Here we briefly outline each of these and provide some examples to help you connect the core considerations to your work.

Commonality

Research on how children learn and develop provides several principles of human development and learning that are true for all children (see "Principles of Child Development and Learning," below). Teachers need a clear understanding both of how children learn and develop and what teaching practices are effective. However, learning is also greatly influenced by culture, experience, and individual characteristics. Within general progressions, development will look different for each child. For example, play is a foundational way children learn, but it can look different based on a child's culture and experiences. While children of various social, cultural, and linguistic backgrounds develop similarly in many ways, their specific identities and the history around those identities help shape their development and learning. It is important to understand the common characteristics of children's development and learning and how they may take unique forms.

Individuality

Each child is a unique individual but also a member of family and community. Effective educators get to know each child and family. They see individual differences—including children's personalities, abilities, knowledge, interests, cultural and social identities, home languages, and approaches to learning—as assets to build on. For example, Francisco is a dual language learner who speaks Mixtec and Spanish. He is learning English as a third language. Knowing this about Francisco helps his teacher make decisions about how to effectively support his learning. Understanding each child and their individual characteristics will influence your planning, instruction, and assessment.

Context

To fully support each child's development and learning, teachers consider the children's and families' social and cultural contexts, as well as their own. As an educator, you might hold certain biases (whether known or unknown) based on your own upbringing,

your personal experiences, and your identities. Be reflective about your practices to ensure that you are not teaching and making decisions from a deficit perspective based on stereotypes and misinformation about certain groups. For example, Elijah might arrive in your classroom speaking a common dialect of English called African American Vernacular English (AAVE), sometimes negatively referred to as Ebonics or even "bad English." Although Elijah's standard English skills are still developing, his AAVE skills are strong. Educators should not let deficit assumptions about home language and other characteristics influence their beliefs about children's behavior or their emerging skills.

As you learn more about each of these core considerations, you will understand how they work together and how to balance them as you plan and teach. You will begin to make decisions based on your knowledge of child development; effective educational practices; and the family, societal, and cultural values and priorities in your program's community.

Principles of Child Development and Learning

Developmentally appropriate practice is based on several principles of child and family development that have emerged from decades of research. The principles inform teachers' planning, instruction, and assessment. They also describe the importance of culture, context, and relationships for children's development.

1. Development and learning are dynamic processes that reflect the complex interplay between a child's biological characteristics and the environment, each shaping the other as well as future patterns of growth.

2. All domains of child development—physical development, cognitive development, social and emotional development, and linguistic development (including bilingual or multilingual development), as well as approaches to learning—are important; each domain both supports and is supported by the others.

3. Play promotes joyful learning that fosters self-regulation, language, cognitive, and social competencies as well as content knowledge across disciplines. Play is essential for all children, birth through age 8.

4. Although general progressions of development and learning can be identified, variations due to cultural contexts, experiences, and individual differences must also be considered.

5. Children are active learners from birth, constantly taking in and organizing information to create meaning through their relationships, their interactions with their environment, and their overall experiences.

6. Children's motivation to learn is increased when their learning environment fosters their sense of belonging, purpose, and agency. Curricula and teaching methods build on each child's assets by connecting their experiences in the school or learning environment to their home and community settings.

7. Children learn in an integrated fashion that cuts across academic disciplines or subject areas. Because the foundations of subject-area knowledge are established in early childhood, educators need subject-area knowledge, an understanding of the learning progressions within each subject area, and pedagogical knowledge about teaching each subject area's content effectively.

8. Development and learning advance when children are challenged to achieve at a level just beyond their current mastery and when they have many opportunities to reflect on and practice newly acquired skills.

9. Used responsibly and intentionally, technology and interactive media can be valuable tools for supporting children's development and learning.

Guidelines for Developmentally Appropriate Practice in Action

These three core considerations and nine principles are a foundation for six guidelines for putting developmentally appropriate practice into action. The guidelines lead teachers as they make decisions in these areas:

1. Creating a caring, equitable community of learners

2. Engaging in reciprocal partnerships with families and fostering community connections

3. Observing, documenting, and assessing children's development and learning

4. Teaching to enhance each child's development and learning

5. Planning and implementing an engaging curriculum to meaningful goals

6. Demonstrating professionalism as an early childhood educator

These guidelines are the principles in practice and form the structure of each book in the series. The star graphic below illustrates how each guideline represents one aspect of what teachers do to effectively support children's learning. Each guideline is critical to the overall practice of teachers. The guidelines all work together to create practices that are developmentally, culturally, and linguistically appropriate for all children. They are described in greater detail throughout each book.

1 Creating a Caring, Equitable Community of Learners

2 Engaging in Reciprocal Partnerships with Families and Fostering Community Connections

3 Observing, Documenting, and Assessing Children's Development and Learning

4 Teaching to Enhance Each Child's Development and Learning

5 Planning and Implementing an Engaging Curriculum to Achieve Meaningful Goals

6 Demonstrating Professionalism as an Early Childhood Educator

Developmentally Appropriate Practice in Kindergarten

"I teach kindergarten!" teachers proudly respond when asked what they do for work. In this exchange, they are often met with responses of delight and respect—as well as comments that highlight the challenging work of a kindergarten teacher. Teaching kindergarten *is* hard work, *and* it is extremely rewarding. This book was created with you, the kindergarten teacher, in mind. Focusing on the unique joys, needs, challenges, and opportunities that occur in working with kindergarten children, it shares ideas and key concepts outlined in NAEYC's position statement on developmentally appropriate practice through a kindergarten lens. This book also models practices that you can adapt to use in your own program to enhance children's learning and well-being.

Typically, children arrive in kindergarten having met only one requirement: age. Therefore, children come to you from a variety of cultures with a wide array of experiences. Some children have had many experiences interacting with other children; others have had few opportunities for such interaction. Some children have received early interventions that supported their growth and development; some arrive with unforeseen challenges that require further investigation. Some children have experienced a language-rich environment, in which storytelling, books, singing, and interactive dialogue have been part of their everyday lives. Other children arrive with similar experiences in a language other than English. Some children have benefited from a safe and healthy home environment; some children come from trauma-based environments in which basic physiological needs such as food, shelter, and clothing have not been a constant. Children are unique, and effective teachers both value each child for what they bring to the kindergarten classroom and seek to understand how to provide what each one needs in order to thrive.

You, too, are unique! You come to the teaching of kindergarten students with your own set of experiences, training, skills, hopes, and aspirations. Your knowledge of child development and your teaching philosophy about how young children learn, grow, and develop guide the many decisions you make each day. You strive to build on the children's strengths and provide engaging, meaningful learning opportunities that are designed to move each and every child forward to the best of their ability. What a wonderful—and important—job you have!

Our hope is that this book affirms, inspires, and challenges you as you strive to provide the best kindergarten experience for each of the children. You will see examples of nurturing environments in which the social and cultural contexts of children and families are supported and how teachers foster trusting relationships and teach, model, and support prosocial behaviors so that children are better able to solve social conflicts, build friendships, self-regulate, and manage strong emotions in a healthy way. The chapters also provide examples of how teachers value families as members of the kindergarten team and use strategies for capitalizing on opportunities to learn from and partner with them. Authentic assessment practices are highlighted as they are shown being integrated within daily learning experiences and used to inform decisions. The authors share insights about providing integrated learning opportunities that you can adapt to create a robust, rigorous learning environment that is play oriented, where children touch, hold, and manipulate objects; predict; observe; and explore concepts with wonder, excitement, thoughtfulness, curiosity, and questioning. You will see examples of how teachers offer choices and use strategies that help children to develop a sense of agency while also meeting required mandates and expectations.

The chapters provide multiple examples of how purposeful play is integrated throughout the day, illustrating how play is not a *break from* the curriculum but rather the *best way to implement* the curriculum (Tepperman 2007; Zosh et al. 2022). You will read about selecting teaching strategies and making curriculum decisions that are "just right" for each child—in which they are challenged to achieve at a level just beyond their current mastery with opportunities to reflect on and practice newly acquired skills. Last, you'll be inspired to further your own professional growth as an advocate and leader by reading about various roles and activities that kindergarten teachers like you have embraced.

Educators do not teach in vacuum. Having an administration that supports and prioritizes play-based learning and other facets of developmentally appropriate practice is a critical piece of implementing it in the classroom. Recognizing that not all educators have this support, we encourage you to examine your own context—what you *are* able to do and the support you have or potentially could grow in your school and greater community—as you consider this book and the strategies illustrated. Use and adapt what you read here to your own context; band together with others who are invested in this work; and develop your ability to advocate for practices and environments that facilitate equitable, joyful learning for all kindergartners.

What Is in This Book?

Each of the six parts of this book highlights one of the guidelines for developmentally appropriate practice. The chapters have been carefully selected to reflect various aspects of the guidelines, including equity, inclusion, and instruction that is culturally responsive. The educators featured in these chapters have successfully implemented and strive to continue implementing the guidelines in their kindergarten classrooms. Although these chapters don't cover every topic in the position statement on developmentally appropriate practice, you'll find important ideas and strategies that you can integrate into your work as you support children and their families.

The introduction to each part discusses the guideline addressed in that part and includes overviews of each chapter. Although the guidelines are addressed in separate parts, you will find common themes across the six parts. The guidelines work together to support your use of developmentally appropriate practice. While the practices described in each chapter work well for the children in those particular settings, remember that developmentally appropriate practice is not a scripted, one-size-fits-all approach to early learning. Instead, use the material to reflect on the practices and approaches that could be effective with the kindergartners *you* work with. Be inspired to think about ways you establish goals and create experiences

that fit who and where the children are and that are challenging enough to promote their progress and further their interests.

Each chapter includes sidebars (identified by an icon) that connect to the position statements on developmentally appropriate practice and advancing equity and to the fourth edition of *Developmentally Appropriate Practice in Early Childhood Programs Serving Children from Birth Through Age 8*. Focusing on a certain aspect of developmentally appropriate practice and equity, each sidebar is intended to support your reflection on how that aspect relates to the chapter.

Throughout the book, we note the use of the guidelines of developmentally appropriate practice in action to illustrate how kindergarten educators can apply what is known about child development and learning to actual classroom practice. You will, however, want to spend some time reading more about the guidelines in the fourth edition of *Developmentally Appropriate Practice*. This will give you a richer understanding of child development and how you can best nurture and support each child.

Part 1: Creating a Caring, Equitable Community of Learners illustrates ways that teachers create caring and equitable classroom communities in which children have a sense of themselves and others as valued members, develop meaningful relationships, and gain competence and confidence to thrive as learners. Building such a community begins with creating smooth transitions to kindergarten, including examining school readiness and the many ways families can engage in their children's educational experiences. You'll read about that here, as well as ways effective teachers purposefully incorporate opportunities throughout the day for relationships to be developed between and among children and adults. You'll also read how teachers can explore race and gender topics in a way that leads to powerful conversations and discoveries as kindergartners focus on their own strengths and unique stories. In addition, the chapters explore ways to use children's literature to open a world that is diverse and as unique as each kindergarten child, expanding their awareness of the world around them.

Part 2: Engaging in Reciprocal Partnerships with Families and Fostering Community Connections demonstrates opportunities for kindergarten teachers to establish a meaningful and supportive partnership with families. Moving beyond a one-sided approach in which teachers focus solely on distributing information to families, the authors in this section discuss how reciprocal relationships can be formed and used throughout the kindergarten year to support children's learning and development. The authors also demonstrate strategies for how to support children's and families' home languages. Furthermore, you'll read about the importance of communication to develop trust when considering families' cultural perspectives on important topics such as play.

Part 3: Observing, Documenting, and Assessing Children's Development and Learning illustrates the careful decisions teachers make when choosing how and when to assess students' development and learning, including using a variety of authentic assessment strategies that are aligned to state standards. Instead of considering assessment as something that distracts teachers from teaching, the authors describe how assessment practices are actually part of the instructional experience. Here you will find steps for thinking through assessment practices. The chapters also provide examples of assessment tools, including teacher-created assessment tools, along with strategies for using them throughout the day during play-based experiences to collect reliable and valid information.

Part 4: Teaching to Enhance Each Child's Development and Learning discusses intentional, research-based teaching practices that support each child across all domains of learning and development. The authors of these chapters highlight the understanding that play is an essential way for children to learn. Strategies for individualizing learning experiences by using a variety of instructional practices that are play based, including the use of play as a healing agent for children with trauma, are discussed. The chapters describe the use of learning centers, storytelling, mentor texts, and inquiry-based investigations as effective ways to support children's diverse learning needs while addressing curriculum mandates. In addition, the delicate art of scaffolding is described and illustrated through vignettes and is unpacked for you to further your reflection on the topic.

Part 5: Planning and Implementing an Engaging Curriculum to Achieve Meaningful Goals highlights the ways teachers make curriculum choices that are developmentally appropriate as they juggle mandates and expectations that may or may not be in the best interests of young children. The chapters explore the use of self-directed learning, inquiry-based instruction, effective questioning techniques, integrated units of study, and intentional opportunities to support rich vocabulary development. The authors also stress the importance of deepening your own understanding of content and how children learn so that you can teach rich content in meaningful, developmentally appropriate ways. Throughout, you will also read about ways the authors find and cultivate joy in teaching and learning despite setbacks and frustrations.

Part 6: Demonstrating Professionalism as an Early Childhood Educator articulates the importance of being an informed professional and passionate advocate for promoting responsive educational practices. As you continue to learn and grow as a professional, the chapters in this part provides steps for you to identify and work against biases and injustices that your children and families may be facing. This part also recognizes your role as a teacher-researcher and provides insight into how you might conduct your own research as an effective professional development experience. In addition, you'll read about the impact that teacher leadership opportunities had on a group of kindergarten teachers and will be inspired to further develop your own professional practices within your own context.

We would be remiss if we did not stress the critical role of self-reflection in your daily practice. As you read and reread these chapters, use the reflection questions in the introduction to each part to engage in thinking and conversations with colleagues and families. Consider how your work is developmentally, culturally, and linguistically appropriate for each child in your learning environment. As a lifelong learner, use the many tools and resources NAEYC offers and encourage others to do the same so that you support each and every child to achieve their full potential. (Visit NAEYC.org/dap-focus-kindergarten for additional material related to this book.)

PART 1

Creating a Caring, Equitable Community of Learners

RECOMMENDATIONS FROM THE DAP POSITION STATEMENT

Developmentally appropriate practice takes place within a community of learners: a group of young children linked in relationships with one another and with one or more teachers, learning and developing together in partnerships with families. Children learn and develop best when all participants in a community consider and contribute to one another's well-being and learning and are valued for the strengths they bring.

Alaia arrives at her classroom door on her first day of kindergarten both excited and a little nervous. Although she already met her teacher, Mrs. Fraser, a few weeks before during a home visit, Alaia is reassured when she sees Mrs. Fraser's smiling face at the door. Mrs. Fraser walks Alaia to her cubby, helping her unload and hang up her backpack. Alaia is excited to see her name and photo on the cubby, letting her know this is her own special space. Alaia remembers she brought a photo of her family, as Mrs. Fraser had asked her to do during her home visit. Mrs. Fraser helps her add it to a shelf with the photos of the other children's families. Mrs. Fraser invites Alaia to choose an activity to do as the other children arrive. Alaia joins Holden at the Lego table, and as they build Mrs. Fraser hears Holden compliment Alaia's structure. After all the children arrive, Mrs. Fraser asks them to join her on the carpet to greet each other. Then they sing songs, dance, and read the book *All Are Welcome*, by Alexandra Penfold, which follows children through a school day and repeats the message that no matter their race, family makeup, clothes, religion, or ability, everyone belongs here. The children in Mrs. Fraser's kindergarten class, too, feel welcomed and cared for as they see themselves reflected throughout the room. The teacher intentionally chose the greeting activity and this particular book

to read as a way to begin to lay the groundwork for Alaia, Holden, and their peers to feel that they are a part of this new community and that they all belong.

Community is the foundation for learning. When planning for building a community of kindergartners that supports children's development and learning, teachers consider two important characteristics: caring relationships and equity. All significant learning occurs within the context of positive and supportive relationships. In early childhood classrooms, equity is "the practice of consistently viewing each child as an individual and customizing one's treatment of them to increase access and remove barriers to classroom resources" (NAEYC 2022, 112). Effective teachers ensure that young children feel a sense of belonging and feel valued for who they are and what they bring. In the vignette above, the educator actively developed a caring and equitable community of learners through her interactions with children and families, her selection of classroom materials, and her attention to children's ideas and feelings.

A caring community such as this provides a foundation for children's future experiences and attitudes about school and learning. Early positive relationships predict a wide array of later positive outcomes, including social skills, success in relationships, and enhancements in cognitive skills such as thinking and reasoning (Center on the Developing Child 2004). To build and maintain these relationships while supporting children's growing independence and their ability to become responsible members of the community, effective teachers consistently and purposefully do the following:

> Create a welcoming environment for young children and families that represents and reflects the diverse backgrounds, experiences, and cultures within the community of learners

> Engage in authentic conversations with children

> Work to build a strong sense of group identity

> Observe, identify, and build on children's strengths

> Use culturally responsive teaching practices

> Learn about and incorporate children's interests into learning experiences

> Provide meaningful opportunities for children to practice regulating their own bodies, feelings, and actions

> Allocate time for children to become deeply engaged in meaningful exploration (NAEYC 2022)

> Provide opportunities for children to take responsibility for the care of the classroom and support each other

When children feel safe, valued, and seen within their kindergarten community of learners, meaningful learning occurs—great things are possible!

READ AND REFLECT

As you read the chapters in this section, consider and evaluate your own classroom practices using these reflection questions.

"Successful Transitions into and out of Kindergarten: Supporting Children and Families" highlights challenges and opportunities for making the transitions to and from kindergarten more seamless and successful for children and families. Focusing on collaboration at the classroom and wider system levels, the chapter offers strategies that build on children's experiences to ensure a successful kindergarten year. **Consider:** What challenges do you see when children begin kindergarten in your room? What ideas in the chapter might make the transition less challenging for them and their families?

"Routines, Rituals, and Mantras for Building a Joyful Classroom in Kindergarten: Reflections from a Small Mountain Community Classroom" describes joyful everyday practices the authors have used with kindergartners and the power of those practices for building and sustaining a caring, equitable learning community. **Consider:** What routines, rituals, and mantras contribute to the development of your own community of learners? What additional practices can you employ? The authors found home visits to be helpful in beginning to establish a reciprocal relationship with families. For families who may not feel comfortable with home visits, what are some alternative ways to get to know families and children before school begins?

"Supporting Self-Regulation and Autonomy in Kindergarten: One Teacher's Journey" describes the changes a teacher made as she moved from controlling her students' learning environment to providing a child-centered, teacher-facilitated one in which children have opportunities to develop executive function skills

and autonomy. **Consider:** What opportunities do you provide students to develop executive function skills? In what other ways does this chapter inspire you to support children's autonomy?

"How Do I See Myself? How Do Others See Me? Exploring Identity in Kindergarten" shares one teacher's approach to exploring self-identity with young children, with strategies for engaging in conversations with and providing appropriate, meaningful experiences for kindergartners. **Consider:** In what ways do you already explore similarities and differences with kindergartners? How can you dig more deeply into the topic of self-identity with your students?

"Becoming Upended: Teaching and Learning About Race and Racism with Young Children and Their Families" shares powerful stories about, and strategies for, talking with young children about race and racism and responding to families' feelings and concerns within trusting relationships—strategies supported by research. **Consider:** What feelings arise when you dig deeper into your own experiences with racism? How can you use your experiences, feelings, and new knowledge to have honest, though potentially difficult, conversations with children and families?

NEXT STEPS

1. List the ways in which you intentionally support positive relationships with your students and their families as well as relationships between students. Think about the impact of those strategies on your students' success. What areas are strong? Which may need improvement? What additional strategies can you implement?

2. Read NAEYC's position statement on advancing equity (NAEYC.org/resources/position-statements/equity) to learn more about identity, race, and racism and explore your own understandings, experiences, and emotions. What biases do you have based on your own experiences, and how do those biases affect your interactions with young children? Which specific ideas challenge your thinking? Are there areas in which you would like to change, and how could changes impact your practice? Talk to a trusted colleague or friend and journal your thinking as you explore these topics.

3. Implement a new routine, try a different ritual, or create a new mantra with your students. How is this practice supportive of children?

References for the chapters in this part can be accessed online at NAEYC.org/dap-focus-kindergarten.

CHAPTER 1

Successful Transitions into and out of Kindergarten
Supporting Children and Families

Eva Phillips and Amy Scrinzi

For many children, two of their most dramatic education transitions occur around kindergarten—their first participation in an elementary school setting and, at the end of kindergarten, entry into the primary grades. When children enter kindergarten, they essentially become citizens of two cultures—home and school. They must learn to navigate the new etiquette, rules, and conditions of the classroom, which are often different from those at home and in other familiar settings. While this is true regardless of ethnicity or cultural background (Lam & Pollard 2006), it is especially so for children whose home cultures are different from the school's. When all adults caring for a child—teachers, family members, care providers—work together to create positive, communicative relationships, the child and the adults will have smoother, less stressful transitions.

Factors Affecting a Child's Experience of the Kindergarten Transition

A transition is defined as a passage from one place or stage to another. The transition to kindergarten affects all aspects of a child's life: where they spend time during the day, who they interact with, what they feel, and how they behave. As active, participatory learners, kindergartners learn to make sense of and adapt to the new environment in creative and dynamic ways; some children do so more quickly and easily than others. This depends on many factors, including a child's individual characteristics and cultural experiences, whether or not they have delays or disabilities, and the child's experience or lack of experience in an early childhood setting. For adults and children alike, change is stressful. But it can be especially unsettling for young children with limited experiences and few well-developed coping strategies.

Chronological or developmental age at kindergarten entry also greatly affects children's transition. The variation found in a kindergarten classroom can be huge. In a typical kindergarten classroom, there could be a spread of 2 to 2½ years in age—from about 4¾ to 7½ years old. This is a result of varying cutoff dates for kindergarten entry, children being held back a year—a practice called "redshirting," a trend that lacks evidence of a relationship to long-term academic success, including for dual language learners and children with disabilities (Range, Dougan, & Pijanowski 2011; Sands, Monda-Amaya, & Meadan 2021; Sucena et al. 2020)—and a small percentage of children who are repeating their kindergarten year (another practice that has no research base to prove its long-term effectiveness). In reality, no matter the cutoff date, kindergarten classrooms are likely to include children whose ages vary by as much as 12 months or more. Classrooms will always include children who come to kindergarten ready for challenges as well as those who need more support. "Kindergarten is a time of change, challenge, and opportunity. Because of the great individual variation among kindergartners and the wide age range of kindergarten children, teachers must be responsive to developmental, individual, and cultural variations" (NAEYC, n.d.).

Teachers must also be aware of the different personalities of the children in their kindergarten classrooms, including those who are slow to warm up and those who are flexible and easygoing. Providing support for those children and all those in between is critical to smooth transitions. These factors deeply influence children's ability to transition from one setting to another, which is another important reason teachers and families must work together to support young children through these transitions. Adult relationships (between teachers and families and among teachers, especially kindergarten teachers and the preschool or prekindergarten teachers who taught children the year before they entered kindergarten) will make a great difference in how children experience the transition.

Supporting the Transition to Kindergarten

Transitions are not one-time events that only happen on the first day of kindergarten. They begin before children enter school and continue throughout the year. All parties, including the preschool setting and elementary school, play important roles in creating a successful transition for children and families. The importance of a strong relationship between the educators in those two programs within the community cannot be overstated. The transitional period will be more seamless for children and families when there is communication, collaboration, and alignment among preschools, child care programs, family child care programs, and the elementary schools in the community. "To promote ongoing learning and build upon early successes, both ECE providers and K–12 local education agencies (LEAs) must consider each other's roles and coordinate their efforts . . . through alignment of transition goals, approaches, and practices" (Erlich et al. 2021, vii).

For example, if the kindergarten teacher understands the schedule, routines, and amount of time spent in uninterrupted play-based learning experiences in the typical community preschool, they are better able to mirror that at the beginning of the kindergarten year. The same is true when children transition from kindergarten into first grade. By ensuring some similarities in the schedule, routines, and learning activities, educators will help children feel more at ease. This critical alignment between programs greatly enhances the transition experience for children, families, and teachers.

It is also essential to remember to include special education administration, staff, and related service providers in transition conversations to maximize the positive experiences in the regular classroom

and minimize the time a child with a disability will be removed from classroom routines and activities. Administrators need to be proactive in determining how and when specialized services and specially designed instruction can be embedded into what is already happening.

Successful transition practices support children's development of self-esteem, self-confidence, and independence. Creating culturally and linguistically responsive environments that incorporate families' cultural and linguistic resources is crucial. All families will feel better prepared and more able to support their children if they know what is expected—within the context of and in relation to what happens at home—and that their traditions, culture, language, and expectations are valued (Rhodes, Enz, & LaCount 2006). A teacher's understanding of children's and families' funds of knowledge not only strengthens their relationships but also enhances the instructional practices and transition experiences for all children. A child's funds of knowledge can be described as

> Academic and personal background knowledge

> Accumulated life experiences

> Skills and knowledge used to navigate everyday social contexts

> World views structured by broader historically and politically influenced social forces (OSPI, n.d.)

Teaching and learning are directly related to funds of knowledge:

> Gaining a better understanding of a student's funds of knowledge can enhance classroom practices for both teachers and students. Using a funds of knowledge approach to understanding students' overall sets of abilities and experiences can help teachers draw on these skills in classrooms to enrich their understanding of academic content while also motivating them during classroom activities. (OSPI, n.d.)

Good teacher-family relationships have endless benefits for children, including making the transition into school easier.

 Help families understand the importance of maintaining their home language as English is introduced at school.

Advocating for Effective and Supportive Local Transition Policy

by Laura Bornfreund

Family visits, information nights, questionnaires, and beginning-of-the-school-year activities can help children and families adjust to new kindergarten classrooms. The behind-the-scenes work, however, matters most when creating seamless transitions for children and families as they move in and out of kindergarten. This work includes cross-grade-level planning and collaboration, relationship-building among elementary school principals and directors of early childhood programs, and better alignment of what happens in early childhood programs and the early grades of elementary school.

Think of a 4-year-old boy—let's call him Isaac—who attended a high-quality preschool. His day included both child-initiated and adult-guided experiences in literacy, math, science, and social studies learning. He had ample time to explore his interests, play with his friends, and engage in pretend play. Isaac's teacher helped him work through his emotions during a rough day and understand when a peer was having a difficult day as well. His teacher engaged the children in lots of hands-on learning in small group activities. He did very few worksheets.

When Isaac starts kindergarten, his day looks very different. While the content areas are the same, he often sits in his seat or with the whole group on the carpet. When he uncrosses his legs or gets wiggly, his teacher corrects him in front of everyone. The teacher expects him to work silently for much of the day. He has 20 minutes of recess every day after lunch—as long as he follows the rules. Sometimes, he has to sit out.

While some might think it is best for kindergartners to learn through more didactic methods such as whole-group instruction and worksheets rather than through active, hands-on play-based experiences, research does not support this (Barker et al. 2014; Yogman et al. 2018). We must address the chasm between what many children experience in preschool programs, Head Start, and other early learning experiences and the typical kindergarten classroom. Making meaningful change and narrowing the chasm requires a dedicated team of educators, staff, and school, district, and community leaders who are responsible for developing a kindergarten transition plan, reevaluating it, and making sure that every part of the school (curriculum, instruction, assessment, family engagement, professional development, and so on) aligns with what science says about how young children learn and develop.

As a kindergarten teacher, you are at the center of these critical transitions for children, *and* you need other partners, including your colleagues and administrators, to make these transitions as successful as possible. In some school districts and states, school administrators are realizing the value of building their understanding of early childhood and developmentally appropriate practices. The National Association of Elementary School Principals and the National P–3 Center have spurred some of these efforts to strengthen early learning leadership with their publication "A Principal's Guide to Early Learning and the Early Grades" (Kauerz et al. 2021). The competencies described in this publication address areas important for enabling seamless transitions in your school and community. You can encourage your principal to access this guide and other resources designed for administrators, such as the early childhood and learning toolkit from AASA (The School Superintendents Association) (AASA Early Learning Cohort 2022), and offer suggestions for creating more successful transitions.

Principals and other building and school district administrators are essential for establishing the conditions that make seamless transition and developmentally appropriate practices more possible. In my visits to pre-K, kindergarten, and first grade classrooms across the country, I learned how some leaders are doing this. In Washoe County, Nevada, for example, one principal shared that she worked with her first grade teachers to ensure they were engaging students in the same kinds of choice time and center activities as kindergarten. That same school principal shifted class sizes around, slightly increasing upper elementary classroom numbers to keep kindergarten class sizes smaller like in pre-K. In Ferndale School District in Washington state, all pre-K and kindergarten teachers include what district leadership calls an hour for uninterrupted work time that is not at the end of the day. They call it this to build educators' understanding that in pre-K, kindergarten, and the early grades, children's play is also their work—and a time when a lot of meaningful learning happens. During the uninterrupted hour, children choose from a teacher-curated list of activities that typically include dramatic play, art, blocks and other building toys, sensory table, and games. Sometimes teachers also set up activities that connect with something the children are learning about. In one classroom I visited, the teacher put items in the sensory bin with the direction for children to create a desert habitat. The Ferndale district is working to extend this practice into first grade classrooms too.

These are just a few ways school leaders can promote alignment across classroom environments and activities, enabling smooth transitions for students as they move in and out of kindergarten.

Laura Bornfreund is a senior fellow and advisor on early and elementary education with the Education Policy program at New America.

Strategies to Support Smooth Transitions

Schools and families can work together to ensure smooth transitions to kindergarten. Here is just a sampling of effective strategies:

Prior to Kindergarten Entry

> Consider your school's transition team. Ideally, schools would have in place an organized community transition team consisting of preschool and kindergarten teachers, community child care representatives, pediatricians, special education personnel, administrators, and families to develop a community-wide strategic plan for transitions for the children and families. If such a team is not in place, discuss with your school administrator how to connect with children's families and preschool teachers before the start of school.

> Discuss and review with preschool teachers any shared individual portfolios, which may include work samples, assessment data, and information about each child's interests and learning levels as well as strategies that have been effective with the child.

> Invite the preschool teachers and children to visit the local elementary school to see a kindergarten classroom and to meet the teachers. Schedule time to visit the preschool classroom to see what the children are experiencing, as well.

> Share thoughts and ideas with families about ways they might support their children's transition into kindergarten, and ask them how you can best support their children.

> Adapt or create a family survey to find out about family language, children's interests, and parents' hopes and wants for their children.

> Determine if you need interpreters for families whose home language is not English.

> Create documents in families' home languages and terms they understand that provide information about programs, services, and school policies (Alanís, Arreguín, & Salinas-González 2021).

> Plan and invite families to attend orientation activities and special events. Consider families' work schedules and modes of transportation when determining the time of day and location for these activities.

Improving transitions for children and families requires careful planning, effective policies and practices, and sustainable funding. Educators can establish practices that put families more at ease, but the planning must begin well before the first day of school. On day one, teachers and schools should already have enough information to begin tailoring instruction, strategies, and environments to meet the needs of every student. (Bornfreund et al. 2022)

At the Beginning of the Kindergarten Year

> Consider implementing a staggered entry plan for incoming kindergartners. Although there are many ways to do this, typically, small groups of children come to school each day for the first few days. This allows for a smaller teacher-child ratio so teachers can provide more individualized attention, support, and guidance.

> Send a personal letter, postcard, or e-card in each family's home language to all incoming kindergartners welcoming them to your class.

> Initiate home visits if the family is willing, allowing an opportunity to meet each child and family at their home or another convenient location to begin establishing a partnership with one another in a one-on-one manner.

> Provide families with an orientation packet of important information about the school and classroom, including a description of a typical day, school and classroom policies and procedures, and information related to learning standards and expectations. Have these available in families' home languages; if necessary, identify a translator to create these documents.

> Use questionnaires or surveys to gather information from families about their children's home language, favorite books and songs, interests, fears, health, and so on. This will help you get to know the children and align instructional activities with children's funds of knowledge, strengths, and needs.

> Provide multiple avenues, such as a classroom message board, email, or interactive journal, for families to ask questions, share information, and give input on their child's education. Gather information about families' hopes and expectations.

> Ensure that your classroom library includes a variety of books related to starting kindergarten and the variety of feelings associated with starting something new.

> Make sure that the books and materials in your classroom offer a sense of belonging for children and their families by representing their cultures.

> Provide opportunities for children to express their feelings about beginning kindergarten, including puppet shows, dramatic play center experiences, drawing, and writing.

> Participate in common planning time (same-grade and cross-grade) on a regular basis to provide children with what they need to learn, grow, and flourish in an aligned system from preschool or pre-K through first grade and beyond.

Find the preceding transition strategies and many more in the resources listed in the sidebar.

When teachers and families develop respectful, reciprocal relationships founded on strong communication, they can work together effectively to make transitions smooth and help children adjust to their learning environment.

Kindergarten Transition Resources

Articles and Web Resources
> North Carolina Ready Schools Toolkit. www .smartstart.org/ready-schools-toolkit

> "North Carolina Prekindergarten and Kindergarten Transition Planning: Guiding Principles and Practices." https://docs.google .com/document/d/1jsv0ftX3Ns-je8fZJfK _9HecHCSGlDaljCwnh-ABwSg/view

> "Supporting the Transition to Kindergarten in Nevada: A Guide for Ensuring Equitable, Coordinated, and Sustainable Programming for Young Children Entering Elementary School."

https://webapp-strapi-paas-prod-nde-001 .azurewebsites.net/uploads/nevada_kindergarten _transition_guide_63118a9fb3.pdf

> "Toolkit for Using Policy to Enable Effective and Supportive Transitions for Children, Families, & Educators." www.newamerica.org/education -policy/reports/toolkit-for-using-policy-to-enable -effective-and-supportive-transitions-for-children -families-educators

> *Transitions and Alignment from Preschool to Kindergarten* by Bruce Atchison & Sarah Pompelia (2018)

> "Transitions to Kindergarten" by Marie Kielty, Angèle Sancho Passe, & Sherrie Rose Mayle (2013)

> *Transitioning to Kindergarten: The Why, What, and How of this Important Milestone for Connecticut Students.* https://portal.ct.gov /-/media/sde/essa/transitioningtokindergarten _whywhathow.pdf

> "Transition to Kindergarten." https://eclkc.ohs.acf. hhs.gov/transitions/article/transition-kindergarten

Books
> *Is Everybody Ready for Kindergarten? A Toolkit for Preparing Children and Families* by Angèle Sancho Passe (2010). Appendixes available here: www.redleafpress.org/Is-Everybody-Ready-for -Kindergarten-A-Tool-Kit-for-Preparing-Children -and-Families-P2462.aspx

> *Reaching Standards and Beyond in Kindergarten: Nurturing Children's Sense of Wonder and Joy in Learning* by Gera Jacobs and Kathleen Crowley (2010)

EVA C. PHILLIPS, EdD, supports early learning educators through professional development, consulting, and coaching.

AMY SCRINZI, EdD, is assistant professor at Meredith College and coordinator of its birth-to-kindergarten licensure program.

CHAPTER 2

Routines, Rituals, and Mantras for Building a Joyful Classroom in Kindergarten

Reflections from Our Small Mountain Community Classrooms

Lee Messer and Marylee Sease

Joy in a kindergarten classroom has a look and feel all its own: Talk and laughter—always a hum. The sound of children talking and reacting to a new noticing. The look of accomplishment when a child is able to figure out why their structure keeps toppling over—and fixes it—or reads a Just Right book for the first time. And the quiet that occurs when children are listening, thinking, planning, and reflecting—listening and thinking during a first read of *A Letter to Amy* (by Ezra Jack Keats); planning across the pages of a book at the writing center; reflecting on why the pet tarantula is suddenly more active now that spring is here.

Joy in a kindergarten classroom is also a sense of community. It is about having and belonging to a group, about being a working, contributing member of a classroom family. Children learn not only to care about their teacher but also to develop caring and empathy for each other. This sense of community doesn't occur because of the size of your classroom or the materials you have or anything in the physical environment alone. It is about the intentional actions and interactions of educators, administrators, and children and families. There is a real joy in being a part of a kindergarten classroom family.

We (the authors) taught kindergarten side by side for more than 30 years in a small mountain community in North Carolina. We found value in building relationships with our students and families through particular routines, rituals, and mantras, which helped everyone understand that "we are all in this together" (Holland 2018). These consistent practices helped us to build and sustain an equitable classroom community, year after year. Routines, rituals, and mantras helped foster deeper relationships that allowed us to better meet the individual needs of each child. In this chapter, we share some of our most treasured of these practices.

> According to the *Oxford English Dictionary*, *routine* is defined as a sequence of actions regularly followed, like a daily classroom schedule, while a *ritual* is more of a ceremonial action, such as singing the same song to call children to group time. A *mantra* is a guiding principle that is frequently repeated to encourage oneself and others, such as "We're all working on something."

Establishing Routines and Embedding Rituals

As educators, we always knew it was important to establish and sustain routines in our classrooms so that our students knew what to expect during each part of the day. Some routines were more for management, such as how to pack up when it was time to go home. Other routines had value in establishing community and learning—for example, circle time. This time was a part of our morning daily routine and it was meaningful, because it not only provided structure but also provided the opportunity to embed rituals and mantras that we highly regarded.

In our routines we embedded daily classroom rituals that evoked emotion and understanding of each other. As the children became invested in these practices, their learning was deepened. Some examples of daily rituals during our group time were classmates greeting each other as the "leader of the day," reading the name cards, wishing absent children well, and celebrating the reader with a reader cheer. The children anticipated these practices and felt valued through them. They were motivated to read their classmates' names, and when an absent child returned to school, that child wanted to know if they had been wished well!

Getting to Know Families

One of the most powerful ways we began building community each year was with the ritual of the home visit, which helped get the school year off to a positive, collaborative note. Part of the ritual was that first phone call to each family saying "I am so excited! Your child is going to be in our classroom family!" That expression of genuine feeling helped to instill a sense of trust in the family. We assured the family that the child's best interests were first and foremost. A feeling of teamwork developed as we began building the relationship. We were intentional in developing a good rapport with each family. When families felt that they mattered and were respected, they felt more comfortable sharing events that could affect their children's learning. It was worth every minute of time on the phone, gas in the tank, and family couch that we sat on with a child, snuggled together as we shared a read-aloud and made those earliest connections. Families appreciated the effort teachers made traveling the long-winding roads and steep terrain of our mountainous community, as it made them feel valued and connected. Creating rapport with the child and family was the cornerstone of a positive, trusting classroom community.

One of our goals of those initial home visits was to learn about each family and develop our knowledge of what each child would need for a smooth, successful transition to kindergarten. This knowledge drove decisions we made for any accommodation we thought children might benefit from as they began school.

During the home visits, we provided a picture frame for each child. When a child walked through the door on their first day, they brought the frame containing a photo of their family or those important to them—a piece of home. This keepsake helped the child with the transition to school and provided a springboard for discussion about how we were all alike and how we were all different. Artifacts from the home visit—children's drawings and photographs—were also on display in the new environment, welcoming all to the classroom.

We invited families to accompany their kindergartner to the classroom in the morning, especially during the first few weeks of school. This gave them the opportunity to meet classmates and families and to see their child developing independence as they prepared for the day. Families began building connections as they got to know each other, building a network that strengthened their support systems.

Families want their children to feel safe at school and happy in their relationships. They want them to learn. These initial rituals of home visits and welcoming families and children to the classroom contributed to each child feeling safe, happy, and a valued member of the learning community.

EQUITY Creating a sense of belonging for each child and their family begins with building a strong, nurturing relationship and creating a culturally responsive environment in which young children see themselves in materials, books, and experiences.

Greeting Children

A sincere welcome or greeting got a child off to a good start each day. Using what we knew about each child and taking the time to assess individual needs determined our first intentional act of differentiation. Some children were ready to jump in and be with their friends; others may have needed a quiet moment with a book as they transitioned to the classroom. Our responsiveness to children as they entered the classroom mattered. Authenticity was always important when interacting with a child, but especially during the first contact of the day. When a good rapport was established, a child was more likely to reveal their feelings, which enabled us to be more responsive and helped the child to be more settled and ready to learn. According to Becky Bailey (2000), an expert in early education and developmental psychology, meaningful rituals support optimal brain development, increase attention span, and amplify cooperation, in addition to several other positive outcomes. When we really listened to children, we were also modeling for them how to seek to understand others. This added to the foundation we were building for a caring community of learners.

Morning Gatherings

The tradition of gathering for circle time, or morning meeting, was another way to start the day as a caring community of learners. Many rituals were associated with this important group time. There was always a call to gather, greetings, movement, and celebrations. Supporting children as they thought about what it looked like to be safe and happy and to listen and think was a powerful way to begin the day. What did it mean for the children to be responsible for their actions and learning? These were things to ponder and talk about as a group to support our community of learners. One way to end our time together was by asking "How will you make this a great day?" This set the tone for the expectation of working toward having a good day. It provided opportunities to plan and to articulate and take ownership of one's role as a member of the classroom community.

Using Children's Names

Names are powerful! "Honoring all students' names is a building block in creating welcoming, inclusive classrooms. This is about making sure every student knows they are important" (Walker 2021). Rituals connected to children's names offer unparalleled learning opportunities that also build connections and enhanced relationships. One of the first goals of our kindergartners was to learn the names of their classmates. Their friends' names became the most important words in their vocabulary. The names also were important environmental print for young readers because they appeared throughout the classroom and were incorporated into other rituals and routines. We used children's names in class books, individual books, and the daily calendar. As children went home and shared stories about what happened at school, families also became familiar with the names of their children's classmates. This broadened the stakeholders included in "we're all in this together."

Purposeful Uses of the Calendar

Teaching children about the calendar has been a long-standing tradition in kindergarten. Although understanding the passage of time and the true purpose of a calendar is a difficult concept for young children to grasp, and traditional calendar time often lasts far too long for young children to benefit from it, using the calendar to find out who the day's class leader will be or who might be having a birthday that day are authentic, meaningful, and purposeful uses of a calendar. In our classrooms, everyone wanted to know who the class leader was each day. The leader's name was then used as the focus of literacy connections and mathematical thinking. We called this ritual "Name Work." Children were engaged because they knew the person behind the name, and that person was important to them. They were also eager for their turn when their own name was highlighted. The leader followed up by reading the names of their classmates, and the children all exchanged greetings and well wishes.

> One morning, Eli and Braxxton race to the calendar in the circle time area. Eli points to Braxxton's name and declares, "See. You're the Lucky Leader today. There are your two *x*s." Braxxton responds, "I told my mama I had to be here early today 'cause I was the Lucky Leader." Mrs. Messer smiles and says, "So that's why you were the first one at kindergarten today. We walked in together." Eli leads Braxxton to the jumbo magnetic letters so he can begin to build his name for the Name Work ritual as part of the circle time routine. "I see you located your uppercase *B*. Circle time will begin in five minutes," announces Mrs. Messer.

Read-Aloud Rituals

Circle time often drew to a close with the ritual of the read-aloud. Intentionality went into each book selection. Our goal was to balance the reading of books that built on things that were already familiar in the children's rural community and to also expose children to people, places, and ideas that may not have been familiar, provoking critical thinking. Multiple readings of favorite texts were as much a part of building a caring community of learners as anything else that was done, and this occurred often throughout the kindergarten day. Bringing children close and having them lean in as they listened to a story became a classroom family experience and a recurring talking point. They would refer back to these stories in conversations and lessons throughout the year. Making the time to read aloud good, quality literature and to talk about it built and deepened classroom community. Children got to know characters and saw how they were relatable. They shared a common bond with their classmates and the characters in the story. Extensions of these stories were often acted out in dramatic play and the block area where the kindergartners were developing self-awareness. The children took these same books home to share the stories and characters with their families.

> *Shortcut* by Donald Crews is a favorite text in Mrs. Sease's classroom. The children lean in one day as Mrs. Sease reads, "Should we run ahead to the path home or back to the cutoff?" The children call out, "Go back! Go back!" Veronica adds, "They'd better stick together." Josie and Hayden cling to each other as the train in the book draws closer and closer to the characters the children have grown to love. The group gasps as Mrs. Sease turns the page and reads, "THE TRAIN! THE TRAIN! GET OFF! GET OFF! GET OFF THE TRACKS!" Isaiah, able to reference other parts of the story because he has heard it many times, calls out to the characters, "Don't worry about them snakes! Just get off the tracks!" As Mrs. Sease wraps up the story, Isaiah says to her, "Remember when you came to my house and saw that snake that I found in my yard? My daddy says it's the good kind of snake. You think those were good snakes down there?" Mrs. Sease realizes that Isaiah is making a connection between the events in the story and her earlier visit to Isaiah's home.

 The curriculum should provide mirrors so that children see themselves, their families, and their communities reflected in the learning environment, materials, and activities. The curriculum should also provide windows on the world so that children learn about peoples, places, arts, sciences, and so on that they would otherwise not encounter.

Mantras: A Foundation for Shared Classroom Values

Once school began, the most important thing we taught, modeled, and reinforced, before any academics, was classroom values about how we treat ourselves,

each other, and our classroom. We embedded these in all of our routines throughout the day. We taught them as mantras, but we also put them into action. For example, we would say, "If you play, you clean," and then we would ask, "Why is that important and what does that look like in our classroom?" We talked about it, and then we modeled it over and over again until it became an understanding and children began practicing this idea of playing and cleaning. Alfie Kohn, educational theorist and author, said, "In an effective classroom, students should not only know what they are doing, they should also know why and how" (Mintz 2021). We taught the why and the how; the mantra was that simple, verbal connection to remind the children of this understanding.

Children find true joy in being in charge of their own actions and their learning in the kindergarten classroom. This was accomplished through daily opportunities to employ self-regulation as they practiced the classroom values through routines where choice and decision making were encouraged. Infusing the learning environment with the mantra "We are all working on something" led children to take ownership of what they were working on. For instance, one child might have been working on holding back their words instead of interrupting while another was working on recognizing the letters in their name. It was important for everyone to realize that we all had strengths and we all had areas that needed work. It can be comforting to children when they discover that even their teacher is working on something! Appreciating their differences led our kindergartners to understand how they could help each other work toward their goals and monitor their progress. When children communicated what they were working on to their families, it helped the families put learning into perspective: it was not about being perfect, but about making a mistake, realizing it, working toward fixing it, and learning and growing from it.

When we took the time to discuss and model these concepts to support children as they practiced them, classroom management was more authentic. Children became more aware of how behavior affects learning and began to take more responsibility for managing their own behavior. They developed a desire to work toward self-regulation as a member of the community. Self-management is a necessary life skill. Young children need to put energy into figuring out answers to "What am I working on?" and "What do I do to practice and improve?" They also need support

and scaffolding from adults and peers. This practice and reflection was so much more meaningful and productive for the children in our classrooms than worrying about where they fell on a behavior chart at the end of the day.

Supporting Partnerships Among Children

The joy of collaborating through partnerships took the children's thinking and relationships to a whole new level in our kindergarten classrooms. As a sense of community was established and children took ownership of classroom values, they naturally began to collaborate. We built on this natural collaboration by teaching children skills for working together. Purposeful partnering helped develop the skills that were needed to enhance and extend thinking, understanding, and creating. For example, knowing the routines and rituals of reading workshop (Teachers College 2023), as well as the mantras to support and encourage a partner, empowered children to be not just learners but also teachers. Because the routines and rituals were explicitly taught, the children could focus on reading and on supporting each other rather than on procedures. Partnering furthered the connectedness within the classroom and facilitated appreciation for another's perspective, prompting questions like "Why do you think this?" During the knee-to-knee portion of the reading workshop routine, when partners sit facing each other and take turns talking, children could go deeper with comprehension of a text together (Moore 2019).

What is the role of the teacher in creating and sustaining collaborative partnerships? First and foremost, teachers need to accept the value of such partnerships. Children learn from adults, and they learn so much from each other (Center on the Developing Child 2004). By allowing and providing time for children to work collaboratively, you give them the opportunity to learn from each other. You can scaffold each partnership by teaching children how to ask questions and how to give feedback to support their partner.

Providing Supports for Learning to Engage in the Classroom Community
by Christan Coogle and Heather Walter

When kindergartners begin their adventure into school, they all need some scaffolding to learn what it means to be a part of this new community. As routines and communities are built, some learners may need more explicit environmental and instructional supports to become engaged citizens in the community, such as visual cues, adaptive seating, or visual supports.

One important skill area that is still under construction in young children is their ability to navigate social situations and to understand and regulate their emotions. Supporting this development through role plays or show-and-tell opportunities can help a child who would benefit from guidance on how to join others in play or how to share and take turns with others. For example, use visual cues, gestures, and words while role-playing how to ask a group if you can play with them in the block area. Use emotion cards (pictures of children's faces expressing sadness, anger, joy, and so on) to help children to understand how others may be feeling. Build classroom rules and expectations together with the message that, in this classroom community, "We are all working on something." This can provide the space for children to receive support and understanding from peers when challenges arise, whether they are academic or social.

Along with role playing, visual supports help all learners to engage effectively in routines. A visual support could be a picture that represents each step in the arrival sequence to support a child's use of target skills. During classroom activities such as circle time, center time, and self-directed play, adaptive seating can facilitate attention and engagement for students who are a bit wiggly, need additional boundaries to help with personal space and concentration, or require physical support. Providing differentiated supports to help all children succeed will help children learn and grow together.

"There is probably nothing more important in early childhood education and for human beings than relationships" (Erdman & Colker, with Winter, 2020, 50). Relationships with children and families were a key component to joyful learning in our kindergarten classrooms. Knowing the children and their families created a dynamic that led to a lifetime of loving to learn. If children know what to expect and feel they are an integral part of the classroom community, they are more likely to be engaged, be attentive, and learn new knowledge (Ostrosky et al., n.d.). Rituals can assist children in times of stress, unite people, create memories, and strengthen the bonds of school family (Bailey 2000). Routines, rituals, and mantras each have their place in helping to ensure equity and joy in kindergarten classrooms.

LEE MESSER, MAEd, serves as an instructional coach for pre-K–first grade teachers in North Carolina and is co-owner and lead consultant of Early Learning Specialists. She taught kindergarten for more than 30 years and served as clinical faculty at Western Carolina University. She was also a North Carolina Power of K teacher leader and a kindergarten demonstration classroom teacher.

MARYLEE SEASE, MAEd, is co-owner and lead consultant of Early Learning Specialists and an instructional coach for pre-K–first grade teachers. She retired after 30 years in the classroom and served as a North Carolina demonstration classroom teacher. She was clinical faculty and instructor at Western Carolina University and a North Carolina Power of K teacher leader.

CHAPTER 3

Supporting Self-Regulation and Autonomy in Kindergarten
One Teacher's Journey

Amy D. Blessing

Control and classroom management: two things often thought of as synonymous. At least they were for me in my early years of teaching. I felt that the more my classroom ran like a well-oiled machine, the better my classroom management was. That the more I controlled every detail, the better my children would behave, and the more they would learn. That without this level of control, the classroom would end up in chaos. I now know the opposite is true.

As Maya Angelou has been credited with saying, "Now that I know better, I do better," my own growth and learning has allowed me to make changes to my teaching practices that have had a lasting impact on my students' experiences. I have discovered that when I empower my students to make choices and learn to take responsibility for their own learning, the result is not chaos as I had feared. It is something profoundly more powerful. My students strengthen their executive function skills, gain independence, and become each other's cheerleaders along their learning journeys.

A Peek Inside My Micromanaged Classroom

If you had visited my kindergarten classroom in my first four to seven years of teaching, you would have seen several efficient, strategic systems of management in place. No longer a beginning teacher, I had gained enough experience to fine-tune my systems. My young students knew exactly where to be and what they should be doing at all times. They did what I told them to do. They had assigned seats; each table was a different color, with matching table baskets, morning journals, and name tags of the same color.

The students came in every morning and went to their table, sitting with the same classmates daily. They worked in their morning journals until it was carpet time. Then they came to the carpet and sat on their designated squares in nice, neat rows. During literacy and math stations, students stayed with their assigned groups and rotated through the stations throughout the week, following the designated rotation plan. These assigned table seats, reading, and math groups were carefully designed, ensuring I could make each group compatible. Personalities fit with each other, or students of similar strengths and abilities worked together. In other words, I tried to avoid any potential conflicts between children.

After station time came what should have been child-led center play time. I felt I was giving my students choice by implementing a color-coded ticket system. Centers around the room were designated by a different color: the block center was red, dramatic play was green, and so on. Each student had a collection of colored tickets to match each center. They could "choose" where to work that day by using their corresponding ticket, but once they used it, they did not get it back until they had used all of their other tickets. It did not matter if their block structure was unfinished. It would be a week or more before I allowed them back to the block center. Chances were, their block structure was no longer there, or their plan for building was a long-forgotten thought. And if they wanted to work with a specific friend, they were out of luck if that friend did not have the same tickets remaining.

I cringe even now as I write this, almost 20 years later. While my intent was to ensure that my students experienced all of the learning opportunities I provided, I was actually hindering their development and learning. The students only had to blindly follow this system without taking any ownership of their learning. My efficient, extremely micromanaged system did not give them a chance to develop and strengthen the skills that arguably were the most important: their executive function skills.

Reading, Writing, Math, and . . . Executive Function Skills?

What are executive function skills, and why do they matter? Harvard University's Center on the Developing Child (n.d.) explains executive function and self-regulation skills as

> the mental processes that enable us to plan, focus attention, remember instructions, and juggle multiple tasks successfully. Just as an air traffic control system at a busy airport safely manages the arrivals and departures of many aircraft on multiple runways, the brain needs this skill set to filter distractions, prioritize tasks, set and achieve goals, and control impulses.

These skills are exactly what we all need to succeed in school and beyond. Children who have not yet developed these critical skills typically struggle in the classroom environment; self-regulation skills allow children to remain focused and persist through daily challenges in a rigorous classroom (Oertwig & Holland 2014). Educators generally have a clear plan for developing literacy and math skills but not

DAP 4TH ED The importance of possessing strong executive function skills is one of the keys to success. The development of self-regulation is without question a critical piece of the kindergarten year. Understanding the complex and unique nature of development of the students within a community of kindergarten learners is necessary as teachers provide meaningful opportunities for the children to practice managing their emotions and behaviors and communicating effectively with others. See more in "Understanding the Role of Self-Regulation" in Chapter 6 of *Developmentally Appropriate Practice in Early Childhood Programs Serving Children from Birth Through Age 8,* 4th ed., page 117 (NAEYC 2022).

often for self-regulation and executive function skills. Yet research indicates that "children aren't born with these skills—they are born with the potential to develop them. Some children may need more support than others to develop these skills" (Center on the Developing Child, n.d.). Research shows that self-regulation abilities are strong indicators and predictors of future success in school and life (Ritchie, Maxwell, & Bredekamp 2009). It is the job of educators to provide that support for development.

Empowering Young Learners—The Power of Choice

High-quality professional development experiences centered on brain research and child development pushed me to take a closer look at my teaching practices. As I realized how my emphasis on control was hindering my students from developing autonomy and regulation skills, I began to make changes. Letting go of control and empowering students did not create a free-for-all, as I had feared. I found that the more responsibility I gave my young learners, the more they rose to the challenge. They were eager to develop their independence and help each other along the way. Behaviors and conflicts between children seemed to decrease, or perhaps the children were better equipped to handle them. Class meetings allowed for modeling and role-playing different scenarios that my students faced as they were given more independence and choice. We created a class plan with agreed-upon behaviors and expectations that every student signed. Our plan was posted in the room and referred to throughout the year. Previously, I had tried to prevent any conflicts through seating arrangements and groupings, which did not allow children the ability to develop problem-solving strategies when conflicts did arise.

My students now experience a wide range of learning opportunities and settings, working with all of their classmates throughout the day or week. I set my goals and objectives for the week and carefully plan intentional learning opportunities using a variety of materials and methods. Students then make choices regarding learning activities and materials, following their own interests and building on their strengths.

Students have ample time to revisit learning activities where they feel successful, which builds the confidence they need for more challenging tasks. They recognize and celebrate each other's strengths, often working in mixed-ability groups. Organization and structure are still evident in my classroom, but that structure now supports student choice and self-regulation.

Classroom Foundations for Executive Function Skills

Three factors support children's development of executive function skills: positive relationships; scaffolded learning opportunities that focus on all areas of development; and a safe, joyful learning environment (Center on the Developing Child 2012). I am intentional about all three of these factors in my classroom.

Developing and building a strong classroom community lays the foundation for positive peer relationships and relationships between children and adults. In my classroom, we believe in a growth mindset and the power of "yet." The children remind each other that they may not know something "yet," that the more we practice, the stronger we are, and that we have the strength to learn new skills. They celebrate when a classmate achieves a goal.

I design activities and learning opportunities to support the children's executive function skills. I make sure to include experiences that encourage social connection, support creativity and child-directed play, are scaffolded for individualized learning, and encourage children to learn from each other (Center on the Developing Child 2012).

Classrooms are where children spend most of their time during the school week. These places must provide a sense of safety and joy. They must be places where children are assured that mistakes are part of everyone's learning journey and are not to be feared, that we are all in this together, and that each of us is working on learning or achieving something. Classrooms should be places of joyful learning, allowing for creativity and exploration.

Getting Started: Strategies for Developing Self-Regulation and Student Choice

Changes in my teaching practices did not happen overnight. Letting go of control as a teacher can be intimidating. If you recognize yourself in the description of my early practices and want to make changes, give yourself grace as you move forward in your own learning trajectory. Here are some practical changes that made a difference in my classroom. Decide what works for you with the particular children you work with as a place to begin. As you see the power of student choice in your own teaching, you will develop your own strategies to further incorporate into your practice.

> **Unassign seats.** The use of assigned seats and carpet spots provided structure for behavior control and smooth routines in my classroom, but it created unintended conflicts. Instruction was often interrupted as children complained that someone was "in their spot," when in fact it was simply that their classmate's toe had crept over the carpet line into their assigned space. Now we have a solid color carpet without any designated spots and children sit where they feel comfortable. Through modeling and guiding, instead of the whining tone of "You're in my spot," I now hear children saying, "There's room here, sit with me" or "Can you move over a little bit? I'm squished." They demonstrate respect for each other as they respond to their classmates' requests. They are developing body awareness and ways to solve problems, both important life skills. Flexible seating around the rest of the room provides opportunities for children to work with materials in a variety of settings and with different classmates. They are no longer bound to their assigned seat. They group themselves based on activities and materials. For example, our morning routine when the children arrive used to consist solely of journal writing at their assigned tables. Now children select their morning work from a number of choices before we begin our morning meeting together. They can read books in the classroom library center, work on a Chromebook,

play a partner math game, complete a puzzle with a friend, or make a book using the art and writing center materials. Within a structure and routine, there is plenty of choice available.

> **Offer a variety of ways to work.** Flexible seating means more than unassigned seats. It provides opportunities for students to work in different positions around the room. Our classroom, for example, includes low tables for sitting on the floor, tables to stand at, lap desks, floor cushions, window seats, wobble stools, and traditional tables and chairs. Each learning space has clear expectations and guidelines on how to use the area. Giving children the opportunity to explore these different learning spots allows them to develop their preferences and understand how each option makes them feel. I have students who prefer the wobble stools while others prefer the chairs. Some love to work at the standing tables while others like to kneel at the low table. They are regulating themselves when they make these choices, often choosing to work where they know they have the most success.

> **Provide open access to materials.** Students have access to materials they may need in different resource stations around the room. They know where to find glue, scissors, staplers, tape, dry erase markers and erasers, pencils, and so on. They know how to choose and get what they need to complete a task. By providing them independence in gathering materials, I am helping them develop the ability to plan and complete a task. Art materials are also set out in a way that encourages the development of self-regulation skills; for example, instead of carefully pouring each color of paint into individual cups ahead of time, I store the paint in condiment squeeze bottles, and children choose their own colors to squeeze into ice cube trays. I no longer worry that they might mix the colors; instead, I share their excitement when they discover new colors—because they were given autonomy in the art center.

> **Add tools for easy cleanup.** Materials are also available for children to take care of their workspaces. Children use small dustpans and brooms to clean up snack crumbs or art center sequins. Baby wipes are perfect for wiping up

spilled paint or juice. With tools that are easy to use, children are better equipped to find solutions to problems. They jump in to help each other take care of the classroom spaces and materials.

> **Personalize spaces for saving work.** Planning and goal setting take time. I want children to be able to set goals that extend beyond one day of learning. I think back to when I did not allow my students to return to a center until the following week. Why would they ever have planned beyond that day? Now my students can save and return to their work, day after day, until they feel they have accomplished their goals. The block center always has structures up so children can return and continue building. We clean up only when it is agreed that everyone is done working on the structure. Lego structures are kept on trays with names on sticky notes so children can add to them over time. Students have their own art drawer where they keep any unfinished drawings or artwork, a work folder for their literacy station work, and a writing folder for writer's workshop pieces. They know that their work is valued and respected. They know how and where to find their work to return to and continue their plans. Reluctance to clean up and transition to new activities, which can often result in disruptive behaviors, is lessened when children trust that cleanup does not mean the loss of their unfinished work. We rarely hear "But I'm not done!" anymore.

> **Provide choice even in "must-do" tasks.** Our daily schedule includes both open-ended, child-directed play (centers like blocks, dramatic play, and art) and more closed-task, teacher-directed activities such as literacy and math stations. Allowing student choice even in these teacher-directed activities increases students' engagement in the activities and continues to support their self-regulation skills. Student choice during these times does not necessarily include the choice to *not* complete the task, but rather when and in what order they will complete the tasks. Tasks may be checked off a job choice board as they are completed. This also allows me to present a variety of activities that address one specific skill. For example, if we are working on the math skill of counting on, I can teach and present multiple partner games that incorporate this same skill. My students can choose which game they would like to

play, even if they make the same choice each day. No matter which choice is made, I know all of them will practice the targeted skill.

Conclusion

A strong classroom community where children are empowered, have continuous opportunities to develop their self-regulation and executive function skills, and experience the celebration of their strengths is actually the "well-oiled machine" I was striving for all those years ago. More than 275 teachers and administrators have observed my demonstration classroom over the years, and these visitors often express amazement at my students' independence. They notice the high time on task and deep student engagement. But most of all, they observe the power of joyful learning. Let's strive for that to be the case for all children.

AMY BLESSING, MEd, NBCT, is a kindergarten teacher in eastern North Carolina. She has taught kindergarten for more than 24 years and has worked with statewide professional development initiatives as well as national organizations to effect change for children.

CHAPTER 4

How Do I See Myself? How Do Others See Me?

Exploring Identity in Kindergarten

Doriet Berkowitz

One winter my teaching intern and I launched a self-identity unit with our 26 kindergartners. Unlike the more typical "How are we the same? How are we different?" units I had shaped and implemented in previous years, we planned this unit with the knowledge that our classroom community included at least one child who is transgender and at least one child with a family member who identifies as neither male nor female. We also had several students who did not follow gender-normative fashion and others who reacted by voicing traditional ideas about how girls and boys are supposed to dress. Seeing a need to bring up gender expression and identity in an intentional and age-appropriate way, we also hoped the unit would inspire ongoing conversations and cultivate more perspective taking. We wanted all of the children to understand the many ways individuals present themselves to each other and how they might wish to be seen by others in our community.

I was working at a public charter school where our shared vision was "to eliminate the predictive value of race, class, gender, and special abilities on student success in our school and in our communities, by working together with families and community members to ensure each child's success." With this vision guiding my teaching, I was not only permitted but *expected* to use time and resources to grow and foster the social and emotional understanding, confidence, and sense of community among the children in my classroom each school day. Much of our practice was grounded in the anti-bias framework of Learning for Justice (formerly Teaching Tolerance) (Van der Valk 2014), and we aimed to shape our social studies curriculum from these social justice anchor standards and domains of identity, diversity, justice, and action. I felt aligned with and inspired by Teaching

Tolerance blogger Becki Cohn-Vargas's (2015) call to "help students feel secure in their identities and free to be who they are and thrive at school."

This chapter outlines the different focuses, experiences, and conversations we held as a kindergarten community during our self-identity unit. It provides guiding questions, read-alouds, visual prompts, and conversation starters meant to facilitate deeper and more critical thinking for kindergartners as they investigate who they are, how they are connected to each other, and how they want to be seen. This unit can also be adapted for older students and has the potential to be a catalyst for ongoing, daily anti-bias education and inclusive community building.

 By recognizing that children's experiences may vary by their social identities, with different and intersecting impacts on their development and learning, educators can make adaptations to affirm and support positive development of each child's multiple social identities.

Parts of Who I Am

As part of a larger investigation into their self-identities, the children began by representing people, hobbies, sports, animals, objects, and memories that are important to them as parts of a mobile to hang outside our classroom. This was a comfortable place to start because they are experts on themselves and could choose what was most important about themselves that they wanted to share. This initial project took place alongside work they had done illustrating their own heart maps, which are drawn and labeled depictions of special people, pets, places, collections, and memories that they could tell true stories about.

We launched this self-identity unit with the mobile and heart map projects because they focus on celebrating children's strengths and unique stories. They highlight that every child is part of a family, friendship, or group in which others care for them. These initial projects also show that each child's identity is not identical to friends' or classmates' identities—that their hobbies, favorite foods, experiences, and dreams can be different. Making and presenting the mobiles and heart maps fostered a space in which kindergarten community members could feel a sense of significance and a connection to themselves and each other—a "true belonging" with authenticity at its core that "doesn't require us to change who we are" while attending to the multiple perspectives and life stories of their classmates (Brown 2021, 158).

Differing Perspectives

Once the children were comfortable and familiar with exploring the question "How do we see ourselves?" my intern and I helped them think about how *others* might see them and how they *want to be seen*. She and I asked the kindergartners to name a word they wanted other people to say about them. From this, several examples of discord emerged. One student shared, "I want people to think I eat healthy food, but some people say I don't eat healthy food." Another said, "I want people to say I'm cool, but they say I'm nothing."

Building on the children's comments, we explored this statement: "The way we see ourselves and the way others see us do not always match." We began to identify different types of toys we like to play with or wish we could play with. Then we thought about certain hobbies we feel afraid to do or toys we feel afraid to play with because of what other people might

think. Students used several enlarged illustrations from the book *Who Are You? The Kid's Guide to Gender Identity* (by Brook Pessin-Whedbee, illus. by Naomi Bardoff), to identify and circle a variety of items and toys they enjoyed using or wished they could use more confidently. (At this point in the unit, we used the first half of this book as a resource, but I did not read aloud the whole book.) They named reasons for not choosing a particular activity or toy they enjoyed, such as feeling afraid that others might laugh at them or think what they've made is "not good." As we shifted to similar questions regarding clothing and accessories, another idea that emerged was that some people might think someone who is "supposed" to "wear the leotard" or "carry the purse" doesn't belong to their own group.

Embedded in this study was a deeper study of our relationships with each other and an understanding of where ideas about identities come from. Knowing that many people feel safe with family but less comfortable out in public increases children's awareness of different audiences and perspectives. For example, children grappled with what it means if someone feels safe to carry a purse at home but not when walking around town.

The Images in Our Minds

To prompt further discussion about the mismatch between how we might want to be seen and how we are actually seen, I integrated several read-alouds into the unit. One was *Amazing Grace*, written by Mary Hoffman, which is about a young girl who wishes to be Peter Pan in a school play. A student in our class exclaimed, "But she doesn't look like the real Peter Pan!" In response, we examined where the picture in their heads of Peter Pan comes from and whether there is only one possible version of Peter Pan.

I found a variety of images of Peter Pan, including actors from several stage productions and movies, and then followed up by asking students, "What do you notice?" The following observations were shared:

Doriet (teacher): If you had a picture of Peter Pan in your head before we started reading *Amazing Grace*, raise your hand if I point to the picture.

Students: (*Most raise their hands when I point to the Disney cartoon version.*)

Doriet: I want to show you some other pictures of Peter Pan from movies or plays. What do you notice?

Children: (*Point to different images as they share their thoughts.*)

Jazz: He's fighting Captain Hook.

Atti: I notice this Peter Pan has blood.

Damond: I notice he's smiling like he helped someone beat the bad guy.

Anais: Parts of this one look like a girl.

Doriet: What parts?

Anais: I don't know.

Sal: This one is on a mountain.

Frannie: This looks like the Peter Pan from *Lost Boys*. This one has blond hair, but he usually has red hair. He looks like a really little boy, like our age.

Jeff: I notice that this Peter Pan has lots of people behind it, and it has yellow clothes.

Doriet: (*Points to an image of an adult male actor as Peter Pan.*) I'm wondering about this picture. It seems different.

Roland: (*Points to a cartoon image and to a still image from a recent film.*) I've seen the movie of both of these.

Doriet: (*Points to the cartoon image.*) Do you think that the play *Peter Pan* that will be showing in our town theater, that we will go to see together, will have a Peter Pan that looks exactly like this one?

(*Some students shake their heads while others nod.*)

Not long after this discussion, I read aloud *Red: A Crayon's Story* (by Michael Hall). A crayon labeled "Red" turns out to be wrapped in red paper on the outside but made of blue wax on the inside. Everything it tries to color turns out to be blue, much to the surprise, frustration, or disappointment of other crayons. The discrepancy highlights the idea that there can be differences between what people outwardly present—or what others project onto them—and how they see themselves on the inside. Bridging the two, and finding acceptance and validity, became another source of reflection among our students. Michael said,

"It isn't Red's fault that they can't color strawberries red. It's the factory's fault." Frannie added, "But once purple crayon could see that Red wasn't really red, she helped Red show its true color."

Assigning Labels Versus Asking About Preferences

Author and activist bell hooks states that "when we hear another person's thoughts, beliefs, and feelings, it is more difficult to project on to them our perceptions of who they are" (hooks 2000, 49). By discussing how we refer to each other, we became more aware of moments when we assigned labels, including genders, to people, whether or not those people had voiced their preferences. Preparing to read the picture book *We're All Wonders* (by R.J. Palacio), the children and I examined the book's front cover and thought about why Auggie has only one eye showing. As ideas were shared, some students referred to Auggie as "he," while a few students pointed out that we don't know if Auggie is a "he" or "she" because the book doesn't say. Here is how the conversation unfolded:

Doriet: (*Holds up the cover of the book.*) What might Auggie want to be called?

Frannie: It.

Jemma: He.

Josh: The.

Damond: Sami. It's a name my parent uses because they don't prefer the gender pronouns "he" or "she."

Jeremy: They.

Peter: We could call him a medium because maybe he could be a he and a she.

Roland: It looks like a boy and some boys have an eye like Auggie.

Atti: He looks like a pirate because he has no eye there. He's wearing an eye patch behind his skin.

The thoughts that the children shared about how to refer to Auggie introduced new language for us to consider. The conversation served as a very natural, child-led way to discuss and use pronouns; this continued in the future when we read and talked about

book characters as well as when we discussed real people in our lives and community. This moment of deciding what to call people provided an opportunity to name in gender-informed and sensitive terms and to counteract our own previous, less thoughtful naming conventions used by default. When we explore counternarratives, they "encourage us to see the other possible realities. They encourage people to challenge the unquestioning acceptance of cultural norms that have become more or less invisible over time" (Lewison, Leland, & Harste 2014, 92). In our school, we push ourselves and our students to disrupt our "default" language, reexamine our assumptions about others, and consider how and why we assign particular labels to ourselves and others.

My goal as an educator is to stretch my students' perspectives (and my own) to appreciate the complexity of who we are in relation to each other. This means that it becomes necessary to seek and create opportunities that highlight the multilayered messiness of who we are rather than the simplicity of who we "should" be. I also introduce children to the concept that gender is a social construct, and that "in their creativity, in their complexity" they can challenge their "outmoded thinking about gender as immutable" (Ehrensaft 2016, 7). If not carefully considered, that thinking is likely to be "imposed by society, reinforced by parents, and ultimately perpetuated by children themselves" (Bryan 2012, 42). Recognizing that students benefit from seeing themselves reflected in curriculum, as well as seeing others represented within their educational dwelling, my intern and I worked to stretch students' thinking by offering a wide spectrum of voices and perspectives. It is critical to identify groups in the classroom "that consistently benefit less from the way things are" (Minor 2019, 32) and to launch courageous conversations that result in some dissonance and new consideration for children and teachers.

Our efforts appeared to be paying off when our class had the following conversation in response to concerns from a student about comments that his shoes were "girl shoes."

Doriet: What does it mean that shoes are "girl shoes"?

Ben: I like to wear sparkly shoes. That doesn't mean that they're "girl shoes," or that only girls can wear them.

Josh: I think they're pretty.

Miranda: There's no such thing as girl shoes or boy shoes.

Manuel: I think you should wear them if they're your favorites.

Doriet: How would you feel if someone told you that you couldn't wear your favorite shoes to school?

Dana: I would be sad if someone told me I couldn't wear my favorite shoes.

As a teacher, I was stretched into reexamining gender-embedded words I myself was using freely with my students that unintentionally excluded at least one family member in our classroom community. After posting a morning message survey question asking "How many moms, dads, and siblings live at home with you?" I realized there was a parent in our classroom who identified as gender nonbinary—neither a mom nor a dad. The following day, I rephrased my morning message to ask "How many parents and siblings live at home with you?" Changing the word "mom" or "dad" to "parent" helped me change my message in a fundamental way. It became more inclusive, providing an opportunity for all students to participate in answering the question and for all family members to feel cared for in how they identify themselves and wish to be seen. Reflecting on this morning message yet again, I intend to ask, "How many family members live at home with you?" to be even more inclusive. Although all my current kindergartners live with at least one parent, it is not uncommon for children to be raised by grandparents or other family members.

What I Want You to Know About Me . . .

About a month after launching this unit, we returned to *Who Are You? The Kid's Guide to Gender Identity*, focusing on the second portion about gender identity. The book lists a variety of words related to gender that different people like to be called to match how they see themselves. After finishing this book, and hearing the choices of language beyond binary "boy" or "girl" language, we moved into a slightly higher level of awareness of gender expression and identity. Students explicitly stated what they wished to be

called. While most kindergartners wanted to be called what we had called them before, two kindergartners asked to be called "they" rather than "he" or "she." (See "Guiding Questions to Initiate Identity Exploration with Children.")

Guiding Questions to Initiate Identity Exploration with Children

1. What do you love about yourself? What makes you special?

2. Can you name a few positive character traits you possess? How do you show or demonstrate them to yourself? How do you show or demonstrate them to others?

3. How are you the same as other people in your community (friends, classmates, family members, sports teams, and so on)? How are you different?

4. Which different groups in your community are you a part of?

5. How do you want other people to see you? What do you want them to say about you?

6. What is a word you hope others use to describe you?

7. What parts do match and what parts don't match between how you *want* to be seen and how you are *actually* seen by others? Why do you think that is? What can you do about it?

8. If someone had the wrong idea about you—about your identity—what are you prepared to say to them?

9. What are some questions you can ask with curiosity if you are confused or do not understand how someone wants to be seen, or what they want to be called?

10. Name a book whose character(s) reflect you in some way. Name a book whose character(s) provide you with a different perspective and experience from your own.

Ultimately, this self-identity unit became about caring for each other, paying attention to the language we use to talk about each other, considering the ways we perceive each other, and wondering how those perceptions match or disrupt our preexisting assumptions. In caring for each other, we embraced all definitions of caring—thinking about others, looking after others, and taking on others' troubles. This particular unit emerged and evolved over the course of six weeks, with read-alouds and conversations woven through our morning meetings and afternoon project time several hours each week. Over the span of it, we also recognized that "caring is a burden, a commitment, hard work. When we teach children to care, we ask them to accept this burden, to commit themselves to the hard work of caring" (Charney 2002, 22–23).

The lasting effectiveness of this self-identity unit was and will continue to be measured by the level of self-correction we employ when we find ourselves making assertions based on inaccurate assumptions and the careful and sensitive attention we give to imagining perspectives and experiences different from our own. While gender awareness, expression, and identity were explored in this unit, there are so many other critical components of how we identify ourselves and the groups we belong to that should not be neglected in this process. In this unit, identity issues related to family structures, skin color, nationality, stories of origin, and adoption also emerged. We gave each similar attention when it came to naming experiences and what we want to be called. In exploring these subjects, and in learning to continually reflect and self-correct, we move closer to the world we envision, one in which each person we encounter in our families, schools, and communities feels seen, valued, and understood, and one in which every young child has opportunities to reach their fullest potential.

DORIET BERKOWITZ, MEd, served as an elementary and inclusion teacher for grades K–5 at the Bloomington Project School, a public charter school in Bloomington, Indiana. She has developed curriculum for young children that promotes their social, emotional, and academic growth and well-being.

CHAPTER 5

Becoming Upended

Teaching and Learning About Race and Racism with Young Children and Their Families

Kirsten Cole and Diandra Verwayne

Children's awareness of racial differences and the impact of racism begins quite early (Tatum 2003; Winkler 2009). Multiple studies document the ways that young children take notice of racial differences and note that as early as preschool, children may begin excluding their peers of different races from play and other activities (Winkler 2009). Many argue that creating safe spaces for children to explore these topics is more important than ever, given the political and cultural climate in the United States, where these issues are highly visible (Harvey 2017; Pitts 2016; Poon 2017). As such, parents and teachers have an obligation to teach and learn with children about these critical and complex issues (Delpit 2012; Derman-Sparks, LeeKeenan, & Nimmo 2015; Ramsey 2015).

This chapter documents how one kindergarten teacher, Diandra Verwayne (the second author), worked with the parents in her classroom to grow *together* in their understandings of the role we all must play in talking with young children about race and racism. In addition, the chapter offers curricular and pedagogical resources for adults who are committed to engaging with young children in this crucial work.

One Teacher's Work

Ms. Verwayne taught kindergarten at a racially and economically diverse public school. Born in Guyana, she moved to the United States at the age of 6 and recalls that when she entered school, she was made to feel like an outsider because of cultural differences. When she was in elementary school, she felt like she had to hide her culture so that she could be accepted by the masses. As an educator, she didn't want that to happen within her classroom. She wanted her students

to be able to recognize who they are. Ms. Verwayne was committed to affirming children's racial and cultural identities throughout the year.

In her planned curriculum, Ms. Verwayne began by offering learning experiences that allowed children to observe and celebrate their unique identities. She also acknowledged the need for teachers to reflect on potential questions and concerns to prepare (as much as possible) for unplanned teachable moments. While she knew that some adults may resist addressing topics like identity, race, and racism with young children, she remained committed to the idea that these issues were an essential part of the early childhood curriculum. Musing about this tension, she asked herself these questions as she designed curriculum:

> If I do talk about race, will it offend anyone? How do you talk about it in a way that doesn't offend people? I think a lot of teachers will just choose not to address it because if you don't address it, you're not offending anybody. I think this is the problem that we have in our country . . . we never have an honest, open discussion about race *ever*.

Considering that racism and racially motivated violence in the United States are visible to adults and children, Ms. Verwayne felt the stakes were too high to ignore this topic in her classroom.

Responding to Families' Anxiety

Ms. Verwayne believed it was important to discuss families' concerns about these topics. Two parents whose children were enrolled in Ms. Verwayne's kindergarten classroom were interviewed by Kirsten Cole (the first author) about the curriculum. Fabiola is a Haitian American mother of two. Ellie is a White mother of two. Both mothers' first-born children were in Ms. Verwayne's class.

After moving to the United States at the beginning of kindergarten, Fabiola was frequently the target of racial epithets and other acts of racism. Fabiola described the painful consequences of having internalized these oppressive messages, in large part because as a child she did not have the opportunity to process these experiences with her parents or teachers. As a parent, Fabiola has prioritized giving her children many opportunities to celebrate their racial identity and making space for their questions about race and racism. Nonetheless, Fabiola recognizes the potential for some families, particularly White parents, to feel uncomfortable with such a curriculum.

Ellie, in contrast, expressed some initial resistance to having her daughter participate in open discussions of racial differences. Ellie grew up in the Midwest in mostly racially homogeneous environments. As is the experience for many White children, Ellie recalled that race was never discussed. Echoing the "colorblind" view that many White families espouse, Ellie recounted, "I don't think I thought about it much. I always thought, 'Everybody's wonderful. Everybody's the same.'" When her daughter began to attend public school, Ellie and some of the other White parents discussed their concerns about Ms. Verwayne's curriculum. Ellie recalled,

> They did a worksheet for social studies about identity. The worksheet asked them to note their physical traits: eye color, skin color, hair color, hair texture, things like that. . . . I was thinking, "What is this? This is ridiculous. There's no reason that 5-year-olds should be doing this sort of exercise. This is futile. Why should my kid be having to say that she's White?"

In recalling how she felt at the time of this incident, Ellie articulated a stance many White people are raised to adopt: claiming to not see color as the most equitable way to approach teaching and learning about race.

Many scholars have questioned the presumed benefits of the colorblind approach (Husband & Escayg 2022; Pollock 2005). As society is not equitable and racial bias does exist, the colorblind approach denies children the validity of their experiences of the world. Because the impact of racial bias is visible, not allowing children to process this injustice is confusing, and it denies them the opportunity to see themselves

as agents of change to resist injustice. Colorblindness fails to acknowledge the impact of racism on all people and, further, does not push White people to do the important work of reckoning with the legacy of white supremacy in their lives (Derman-Sparks, Ramsey, & Edwards 2011; DiAngelo 2012).

During her weekly family engagement time, Ms. Verwayne asked if anyone had any questions about the curriculum. Ellie responded, "Actually, there was a worksheet that came home, and I don't think this is a useful thing. I think it's really hurtful, because it makes them identify things they haven't even realized about each other." Ms. Verwayne was surprised by Ellie's reaction to the assignment, but she was grateful to have the opportunity to open a dialogue about their different views. She later explained to Kirsten, "I needed to understand where that parent was coming from, and that parent needed to understand where I was coming from." For her part, Ellie had the opportunity to hear both Ms. Verwayne's intentions and also other parents' perspectives on the curriculum. Ellie recalled,

> Fabiola responded, "Well, as a Black woman, we take a lot of pride in who we are and we want to talk about it a lot." As soon as she said that I realized, "Oh, of course. You're proud of your race. And I am not." For Ellie, this exchange offered a genuine turning point in reckoning with her own racial identity.

Ellie's reflection on this experience revealed another tension the colorblind view often masks. In naming the root of her discomfort, Ellie illuminated one of many challenges teachers face when doing this work in schools. The false premise of colorblindness is often deployed to obscure the discomfort White people have with confronting ongoing and historical racial oppression and injustice (Harvey 2017). As Fabiola noted in a later interview, "I think it's really detrimental to tell children they don't see what they're seeing and they're not feeling what they just felt—that they can't trust their eyes and they can't trust their gut."

While Ellie had entered the conversation seeking to maintain the colorblind view, she suddenly realized that not speaking about race with children does not protect them. Having had the opportunity to see the issue from another perspective, Ellie reported being transformed. Reflecting on this incident in a later interview, she recalled,

> It was just totally eye-opening. It upended me. Ever since then I just thought, there are so many parents of both Black and White kids and kids of every race

that need to have those conversations about these differences, and that the differences are good. I realized that it has to be talked about.

This transformation—this "upending"—would not have been possible had Ms. Verwayne not opened this potentially challenging dialogue with families.

Particularly in early childhood, it is essential to build trusting and respectful relationships with families. Not all families will be receptive to a curriculum that addresses these issues, nor will all families be as open to being transformed in their thinking as Ellie was. For early childhood teachers seeking to do the critical work of teaching about race and racism, it is important to be prepared to address families' myriad responses, including being ready and willing to create space for conversations many of us have been taught to avoid. While some families may never be open to a new way of thinking, teachers who model this openness will set the tone for approaching disagreements respectfully. As Fabiola noted, the hesitation that many White parents have stems from adults' issues rather than any difficulty children may have in exploring the topic (DiAngelo 2012). She mused,

It's not a scary thing. It may be uncomfortable, but it's a good thing to be having this conversation at this stage. And it was fine. We pass on these anxieties to our kids. The more anxious we are in talking about it, the more anxious they feel. They think that there's something wrong with what they're saying.

It may be surprising that children are ready for us to facilitate these learning opportunities. As parents and teachers, it is critical that we make *ourselves* ready for planned and unplanned opportunities to learn about race and racism.

Following Children's Leads

Teaching and learning about race should begin with children's observations. Children notice differences and need to feel safe and supported in asking questions about what they notice. Fabiola explained that her daughter's learning about race "has been very child directed. . . . If she asks a question, more times than not it's just an observation of something. So I acknowledge the fact that she's absolutely right. She's noticing differences." Ms. Verwayne concurred; she liked to follow children's leads and design projects, activities, and read-alouds that emerged from their questions

and concerns. She emphasized that children's innate sense of justice and fairness created opportunities for them to wrestle with these questions. She explained to Kirsten, "Their questions mean that they're seeking an answer about this topic. And they have a lot of curiosity and wondering, and they need a way to figure out that answer." As with other inquiry-based learning experiences, a curriculum that emerges from the children's process of making sense of the world often yields the most engaging opportunities for learning.

Considerations for Beginning to Address Race and Racism with Young Children

When planning to implement a curriculum that addresses issues of race and racism, consider the following:

> Identify colleagues who are also committed to a racial justice curriculum and work together. Alternatively, seek out communities online to support your teaching practice. Remember, you are not alone!

> Anticipate the kinds of concerns or misconceptions that children and families might have, and prepare in advance some strategies for responding.

> Recall experiences that have expanded your own thinking about these issues, and consider sharing the story of how your perspective has grown and changed.

> Make yourself available, either in person or over the phone, to communicate with families about their perspectives on the curriculum. Email communication can often amplify disagreements, so try to keep communication face to face, if possible.

> Model a stance of respectful openness. Even if you disagree, strive to set a tone that maximizes the possibilities for considering different viewpoints.

> Recognize that we—children, families, and colleagues—are all on a journey of growth with respect to these issues. Draw upon the ways that you scaffold children's learning in other areas and apply these skills when supporting others' growth.

While some of children's observations and questions about racial differences may be straightforward, at times children echo harmful biases they have heard elsewhere. Ms. Verwayne recalled an afternoon when her class returned from lunch in a state of distress. One of her students, a girl who is Black, had told another child, "I don't like White people." At the time, the nightly news was full of reporting about police brutality against Black Americans, so Ms. Verwayne suspected that the child was repeating something she had overheard an adult say. Though math was on the schedule for the afternoon, Ms. Verwayne asked the children to join her in a circle on the rug. Drawing upon strategies she had learned in Responsive Classroom workshops, she reminded the children of their classroom norms that create space for each child's voice, such as using accountable talk grounded in their experiences and listening to each other with care. As they shared their feelings about what had happened at lunch, Ms. Verwayne prompted them to reflect on the sense of community and friendship they had cultivated together in class. They concluded that, while some people of any race may "not always be nice," we cannot draw conclusions about a whole race based on the actions of individuals.

Planning for Learning Through Children's Literature

For parents and teachers wishing to open a dialogue about racial identity and racism, children's literature provides an excellent starting point. Well-written children's literature allows children to identify with and develop empathy for characters, particularly those who may be different from themselves. Stocking the classroom library with children's books that represent a diversity of experiences is essential (Sims Bishop 1990). Especially when children are beginning to do the challenging work of learning to read, it is important for them to be able to select books that allow them to feel a connection to the content. If children do not see their lives and interests reflected in the books in your library, they may feel that reading is not for them.

Fortunately, excellent resources exist to guide teachers and families in creating such libraries (see "Resources for Stocking Your Library with Equitable and Inclusive Children's Titles"). Strive to provide a balance between books that celebrate the accomplishments of seminal

figures in the fight for racial equality and those that represent diverse characters engaged in ordinary, everyday experiences.

Resources for Stocking Your Library with Equitable and Inclusive Children's Titles

> Lee & Low Books. www.leeandlow.com

> We Need Diverse Books. https://diversebooks.org

> Social Justice Books. https://socialjusticebooks .org/booklists

> Raising Race Conscious Children. http:// raceconscious.org/childrens-books

---

Once you develop a classroom library that addresses issues of race and racism from many perspectives, prepare yourself to respond to children's questions as they arise. Ms. Verwayne recalled that when reading about the life of Dr. Martin Luther King Jr. and the topic of segregation, her students asked, "But why would people do that?!" Ms. Verwayne was glad that she had anticipated these questions and was able to provide context by talking about Jim Crow and how it institutionalized racial bias and made it the law of the land.

Developing Strategies for Responding to Teachable Moments

In addition to planning a curriculum that addresses issues of race and racism, Ms. Verwayne described how she often needed to think on her feet in responding to children's natural curiosity about race and difference. Teachers may have a desire to address these topics but feel unprepared to respond when the issues arise in their classrooms. In an era when many educational reforms have argued for standardization and "teacher proofing" the curriculum, the work of responding to complex issues requires that teachers have the training and time to reflect on and discuss them, and that they are able to ground their responses in the deep knowledge they have of their classroom communities.

As described earlier, Ms. Verwayne used protocols and practices offered by the Responsive Classroom to facilitate a complex conversation about racial bias.

By developing these routines, Ms. Verwayne asked the children to join her in taking ownership of creating the kind of classroom in which they all felt included. These pedagogical strategies were supported by the content of her social studies curriculum, which explored the meaning of community.

A number of organizations have created forums for the exchange of social justice curriculum ideas (see "Preparing for and Responding to Teachable Moments"). Responding to teachable moments is never one size fits all, but resources that provide candid and thoughtful sharing of teacher knowledge can provide teachers with models of practices and strategies. Even pedagogical models that do not explicitly address race and racism, such as the practices offered by the Responsive Classroom, can be adapted to create a framework for talking about race in the classroom.

Preparing for and Responding to Teachable Moments

> NAEYC's anti-bias resources. NAEYC.org /resources/topics/anti-bias

> *Anti-Bias Education for Young Children and Ourselves,* second edition, by Louise Derman-Sparks & Julie Olsen Edwards, with Catherine M. Goins (2020)

> *Don't Look Away: Embracing Anti-Bias Classrooms,* by Iheoma Iruka, Stephanie Curenton, Tonia Durden, & Kelly-Ann Escayg (2020)

> *Rethinking Early Childhood Education,* by Ann Pelo (2008)

> *What If All the Kids Are White? Anti-Bias Multicultural Education with Young Children and Families,* second edition, by Louise Derman-Sparks & Patricia G. Ramsey, with Julie Olsen Edwards (2011)

> Center for Racial Justice in Education. https://centerracialjustice.org

> Learning for Justice. www.learningforjustice.org

> Raising Race Conscious Children. https://raceconscious.org

> Responsive Classroom. www.responsive classroom.org

Committing to Teaching for Equity and Justice

Young children are ready for us to join them in this important work of healthy racial identity development. Doing this work effectively, however, requires adults to commit to talking to each other about topics we have often been taught to avoid.

Many White adults avoid conversations about race and racism because we have been taught to believe the myth that being colorblind and "colormute" (Pollock 2005) will erase the oppression that the system of white supremacy perpetrates. People of color must talk to each other for survival in a society that harms our bodies, wellness, and livelihoods, as is poignantly illustrated by Gandbhir and Foster's (2015) short documentary *A Conversation with My Black Son* (available at www.youtube.com/watch?v=lXgfX1y60Gw). White fragility (DiAngelo 2018) often results in White people responding to discussions of race and racism in ways that further harm people of color.

As we consider the need for families and teachers to be able to talk to each other across spaces of racial difference, we know that this necessary work resides at the nexus of this complexity and pain. This is further complicated by the fact that White educators make up more than 80 percent of the teaching workforce and that many of them have not had the kinds of life experiences and education that prepare them to do this work well (Schaeffer 2021). We all need to commit to doing this important work *now*.

What can White educators do? Those of us working with children of all races must commit to unlearning the harmful myth of colorblindness. We need to do this without placing a burden on people of color to teach us. When we do engage with people of color, let's listen with humility and care and not let our fragility do further harm. Discounting the perspectives of people of color deepens the trauma. Fortunately, there are many resources to support our learning and growth. Oluo's 2018 book *So You Want to Talk About Race* is a generous and accessible text, while Bell and Schatz's 2022 *Do the Work! An Antiracist Activity Book* offers readers an interactive workbook format for active reflection. White female educators may wish to review Jackson and Rao's 2022 book *White Women: Everything You Already Know About Your*

Own Racism and How to Do Better. White educators can also seek out journalistic sources and film, such as NPR's *Code Switch* podcast, that document experiences and perspectives that we may have not had exposure to if we live and work in predominantly White spaces. Educating ourselves will better prepare us for engaging with families and colleagues in this essential work.

 Educators monitor their own behaviors for potential implicit biases or microaggressions. When they inadvertently engage in behavior that hurts or undermines an individual's self-worth, educators model how to manage negative emotions and to repair relationships.

What can educators of color do? As the experiences of people of color are not monolithic, we can access the resources listed previously to expand our view. Research has demonstrated that young children and families of all races need educators of color in the workforce (Cherng & Halpin 2016), so we need to take good care of ourselves. To do this, we can prioritize having a support system in place to sustain us when this work takes a toll.

All early childhood educators will benefit tremendously by studying NAEYC's 2019 position statement on advancing equity in early childhood education. We can organize reading groups to review the equity statement together to identify actionable steps we can take to put these commitments into practice in our classrooms and schools. Concrete suggestions to support the ongoing self-reflective work that is required to grow as an anti-racist educator are offered in Allen and colleagues' *Teaching Young Children* article (2022), "Creating Anti-Racist Early Childhood Spaces."

As Ms. Verwayne's experiences illustrate, this work is both challenging and essential. However, we also see practicing anti-racism in early childhood as joyful work. There is a powerful sense of solidarity and energy to be found in working together to take steps toward fostering a more just and loving world.

Concluding her reflections on her own experiences with Ms. Verwayne's kindergarten, Ellie emphasized, "In a school where you don't have the kind of diversity we have, [this work] might be even more important." Early childhood educators spend much of their time

and energy nurturing children's capacity for kindness and respect. Helping children see their role in fostering equality and inclusion through racial justice is a critical piece of this project.

KIRSTEN COLE, PhD, is a teacher, researcher, and parent from Brooklyn, New York, and an associate professor of early childhood education at the Borough of Manhattan Community College, The City University of New York (CUNY). Additionally, she has chaired the equity, diversity, and inclusion committees for both of her children's public schools.

DIANDRA VERWAYNE, MS, is a 23-year veteran of New York City public schools. She taught for more than 15 years in Brooklyn and served on her school's diversity committee as a teacher representative. Currently she works as an instructional coordinator for the New York City Department of Education's Division of Early Childhood Education.

PART 2

Engaging in Reciprocal Partnerships with Families and Fostering Community Connections

RECOMMENDATIONS FROM THE DAP POSITION STATEMENT

Developmentally appropriate practice requires deep knowledge about each child, including the context within which each child is living. Educators take responsibility for forming and maintaining respectful, reciprocal relationships with children's families, and families' expertise about their own children is sought out and valued. This approach gives educators the knowledge and insights they need to provide learning experiences that are fully responsive to each child's needs and experiences.

Ms. Cole, in her first year of teaching kindergarten, anxiously greets the first family to come for a conference. The father stands with his arms crossed. "Ms. Cole," he announces, "we didn't appreciate the parent questionnaire that you sent home in September." Shaken and confused, Ms. Cole realizes that she needs to deviate from the script she had prepared and listen to the family's concerns.

"Please tell me more," she says, motioning for them to come in. "We felt like the questions were very intrusive," the mother states. "Oh, please let me explain," says Ms. Cole. "I sent the questionnaire to better understand each child's strengths, interests, and family background and to answer any concerns or questions. Do you mind sharing which question or questions you are referring to?" The parents, visibly more relaxed, explain that the questions related to family makeup and family situations upset them. They are in the process of separating and did not feel comfortable sharing that in the survey. Ms. Cole listens carefully. When she feels they could move to another topic, she talks about

their child's strengths and needs and the strategies she is using in the class to support his learning. She also mentions the availability of school resources, such as meeting with the school counselor, if they feel it would be beneficial. Later, Ms. Cole uses the parents' suggestions to add a sentence to the instructions of the questionnaire explaining that completing it is optional and offering to meet with families individually. (Adapted from Steen, in Mancilla & Blanco 2022, 155–56)

You have a very important job! You have the responsibility to welcome all families and children into kindergarten, which is most often their first formal school experience. From the moment teachers know which children will be enrolled in their classes, they work hard to establish a relationship with each child, provide an environment in which all families feel seen and heard, and help the families form a connection with the school. To do so requires knowing each child as an individual. Kindergarten teachers acquire much of this knowledge from the children's families. Because the relationships between children and the adults in their lives are critical to children's success, educators invite families to share information about their children's interests and strengths, goals they have for their children, and any fears or concerns they may have.

Rather than begin the year with an arbitrary list of skills and dispositions they hope all children can do independently when entering kindergarten—many of which favor White, English-speaking, middle-class families—effective teachers reflect on their own beliefs and assumptions about school readiness and challenge potential bias by asking themselves, "Am I ready to serve this child and family?" By learning each family's beliefs about their role in their children's schooling, teachers can respond to these families in a sensitive and supportive way, as Ms. Cole did. To gain further insight, you can learn about each family's past relationships with other educators and school experiences—not to stereotype them or to find out what you're "in for," but to identify practices and methods of communication families feel comfortable using. This solid groundwork paves the way for the development of a reciprocal partnership that helps to deepen your knowledge about children's learning and development.

In this important partnership, you provide ongoing information about the child in the context of school. The child's family members share their own observations of their child's learning and development, as you respectfully listen and seek clarification. You then combine your knowledge and wisdom together with that of the family to make decisions together that are in the best interest of the child.

Teachers welcome families to be partners in their children's learning experiences in a variety of ways, considering each family's preferences, availability, language, and interests. You might invite families to share relevant hobbies, interests, and skills with the children throughout the year, such as donating items to the classroom for exploration; talking with the children in person or via video conferencing about a particular topic; serving as a chaperone on field trips; or helping to plan for, set up, and/or participate in a culminating event in which children's learning is celebrated.

Regardless of the strategies you use in your classroom, the message is clear: families are valued members of your school community.

READ AND REFLECT

As you read the chapters in this section, consider and evaluate your own classroom practices using these reflection questions.

"Developing Culturally Responsive Family Partnerships in Kindergarten: Communicating About the Value of Play and Honoring Families' Funds of Knowledge" explains the importance of trusting relationships between educators and families and offers strategies for how kindergarten teachers can develop mutual trust with families. **Consider:** Are your current relationships with families built on trust? How might these strategies help you to improve this important component of your partnerships?

"Family Math Stories: Math for Cross-Cultural Connections and Community" describes the process of creating and using a Family Math Book to collect stories from families about mathematics. **Consider:** How might this strategy enhance what you are already doing to incorporate family's culture, knowledge, and experiences in your curriculum?

In "Exploring Families' Language Practices Through a Social Studies Inquiry in Kindergarten," two bilingual teachers share how they worked together to plan and implement an integrated unit of study about families to support all learners in their bilingual kindergarten classrooms in New York City. **Consider:** What practices described in this chapter could you use in your own classroom?

"Being the Bridge: Strategies for Supporting the Families of Kindergartners Whose Primary Language Is Not English" captures a conversation between a kindergarten teacher and an early childhood educator focused on the author's experience and strategies for working with children and families whose first language is not English. **Consider:** How might you incorporate some of the strategies described to ensure that you are meeting the needs of your bilingual students and their families throughout the school year?

NEXT STEPS

1. Make a list of the strategies you use to engage families. Which of those strategies help you establish trusting and respectful relationships? Consider how you might improve your approach based on the chapters. Next, identify strategies that are founded in the traditional perspective of "parent involvement" or "parent education." Choose one of these strategies and talk with colleagues about how you could change this practice to support the development of reciprocal relationships with your families.

2. Ask families whose children were in your class in the past to highlight aspects of their experience with you that they found particularly helpful, welcoming, and/or productive. Invite them to offer suggestions and ideas that you—or your grade level or school—could implement to improve partnerships between families and teachers.

3. Work with your kindergarten team to identify specific strategies for the team to implement that build trust and respect with families. Begin by identifying idea(s) presented in these chapters. Talk with preschool and kindergarten teachers in your area, or via a trusted platform, to learn about additional strategies. Create a written plan and seek input from families. As you implement the ideas, make notes of what worked, what didn't, and new ideas that you may discover.

References for the chapters in this part can be accessed online at NAEYC.org/dap-focus-kindergarten.

CHAPTER 6

Developing Culturally Responsive Family Partnerships in Kindergarten

Communicating About the Value of Play and Honoring Families' Funds of Knowledge

Iris Chin Ponte and Yvonne Liu-Constant

Mr. Klien, a kindergarten teacher, had worked to adopt a play-based approach to learning in his curriculum planning. He had gained the support of the school's principal, but in conferences he was surprised and felt overwhelmed by families' perspectives and concerns about play and content learning. One family pressed for more rigor and academic learning: "When I ask my child what she did at school, all she says she does is play! I send her to school to learn to read, write, and do math, not to play. She can play at home. I don't want her to get behind in her learning." Others demanded *more* time for play and expressed concern that their children not be pushed into academics too fast: "They say kindergarten is the new first grade—and I don't agree with that. My top priority is for my child to learn to be a good friend and enjoy school. And I want him to use his imagination. Teaching reading, writing, and math can wait till first grade." Mr. Klien shook his head as he shared these comments with the principal, Ms. Ross. "I know that families have different values around education, and I respect that. But how do we reassure them that we all want similar things for their children and meet everyone's expectations?"

Integrating play and learning is an ongoing challenge for many kindergarten teachers who understand the strong connection between the two but must also address the academic expectations of formal schooling. Gaining principal support is critical to successful implementation of a play-based approach in the classroom. Even with this support, as Mr. Klien found,

it can be challenging for families and educators alike when there are dissimilarities between families' beliefs and values and the expectations of the school.

Families' views on the role of play in learning are not only individually determined but also influenced by culture. For example, while children all over the world play, where, when, how, and with whom they play as well as when or if there is an age to stop playing is culturally determined (Mardell et al. 2023). Views on school as a place for playing are also culturally influenced; in some cultures, school is considered a place for serious, rigorous, and orderly learning, and play happens only during recess. Other cultures value exploration and open-ended thinking, and not only tolerate but appreciate the messy, unruly process of playful learning at school. Even within the educational system in the United States, the pendulum of national trends swings from skill-based to play-based learning and back, and varies greatly from school to school and even from classroom to classroom.

The tension between playing and learning is felt nowhere more than in kindergarten, as kindergarten is the introduction to formal schooling for children and families. Kindergarten teachers who strive to engage students in playful learning understand the connections between play and learning and are able to articulate these connections to families while being responsive to families' values and cultures. How? It begins with building trust.

Trust is a critical component of collaborative partnerships. Trusting, open partnerships between educators and families establish a foundation for each child to thrive in school. Teachers can develop a mutually respectful relationship with families by employing a culturally responsive family engagement approach. This approach involves "practices that respect and acknowledge the cultural uniqueness, life experiences, and viewpoints of classroom families and draw on those experiences to enrich and energize the classroom curriculum and teaching activities, leading to respectful partnerships with students' families" (Grant & Ray 2013, 4).

Two frameworks that are particularly helpful for addressing families' viewpoints about playful learning in a culturally responsive way are the funds of knowledge approach (Moll et al. 1992) and the practice of finding the third space in anti-bias education (Derman-Sparks et al. 2015).

Funds of Knowledge

Early childhood educators should see families as experts on their children and value their personal and cultural knowledge and experiences—what Luis Moll calls the families' *funds of knowledge* (Moll et al. 1992). The key idea of this concept is that teachers learn *from* and *with* families and incorporate families' knowledge into classroom experiences. The funds of knowledge approach "reframes family-school relationships to make communication, interactions, and curriculum development a two-way process" (Weiss et al. 2005, xxii). This is consistent with the emphasis on engaging in reciprocal partnerships with families that is a foundation of developmentally appropriate practice (NAEYC 2020).

When teachers have a better understanding of the occupations and daily routines of the families within their communities, they can develop school activities and projects that are connected to the families' lives. For example, Mr. Klien might learn that many families in his school community love to garden and cook with fresh produce. Mr. Klien might design a playful community gathering connected to gardening, reading, and a math-based cooking project. Insights into what is meaningful in a community can have a direct impact on educators' success at connecting play and learning.

 DAP Educators make meaningful connections a priority in the learning experiences they provide each child. They understand that all learners, and certainly young children, learn best when the concepts, language, and skills they encounter are related to things they know and care about, and when the new learnings are themselves interconnected in meaningful, coherent ways.

Finding the Third Space

As the opening vignette demonstrates, it is not unusual for families and schools to have different perspectives about educational practices, policies, and learning goals. Often the child is caught in the middle. Conflict is often viewed as something to avoid; however, disequilibrium, tension, and conflict can be when real learning occurs. The goal of addressing conflicting views is not to have a winner or loser but to manage the conflict in a way that is inclusive.

Productive handling of differences begins before an actual conflict occurs. From the beginning of your relationship with a family, you should be building trust, working intentionally and proactively to create a climate in which disagreement is acceptable and problem solving supports positive outcomes. It is also essential to recognize that there are no perfect solutions for all situations. Some ambiguity and uncertainty are an inevitable part of this process. Rather, look for specific solutions for conflict episodes that make sense in terms of your program's values and context (Derman-Sparks, LeeKeenan, & Nimmo 2015).

In *Leading Anti-Bias Early Childhood Programs*, the authors discuss an approach called *finding the third space*. The third space is the intellectual and emotional place where people in conflict can come to a mutually decided agreement that goes beyond their initial viewpoints. Three steps can help you reach a third space: acknowledge, ask, and adapt (Derman-Sparks, LeeKeenan, & Nimmo 2015):

Step 1, Acknowledge: Recognize that a problem exists.

Step 2, Ask: Gain clarity about where each person stands on the issues and their desired outcomes. Respectfully share your own views and what you hope for. Be sure that everyone feels heard.

Step 3, Adapt: This is the solution step. Together, look for common ground and consider alternative ways to solve the problem.

Here is how Mr. Klien used these steps to work toward a third space with the families of his students, also incorporating their funds of knowledge.

> Ms. Ross acknowledged that Mr. Klien raised an important issue: differing views on play and learning in kindergarten. These views reflected not only different opinions of the families in his class but also diverse values in the community. In some situations, these perspectives were in contrast to the school's views and practices. *(acknowledge)*
>
> Ms. Ross encouraged Mr. Klien to consider the perspectives of the families from a strengths-based position and to find out more from them. How do they play and learn at home? What is familiar to them in their upbringing and cultural contexts? How can their knowledge and experiences contribute to the community of learners in his classroom? *(ask)*
>
> To discover more from the families and explain his own approach to playful learning, Mr. Klien planned a math event for the families of his students. Families joined their children in the classroom one morning to learn about the math curriculum by engaging in activities together. Supported by Ms. Ross to make playful learning the focus, Mr. Klien selected some of the children's favorite math games from the curriculum, and the classroom was filled with excitement and laughter as the children and their families played together. Mr. Klien scheduled the event so that the children went to art class afterward, allowing him to discuss the experience with the families, share the key learning concepts, and answer questions. When Mr. Klien met with the families, he asked, "Did your children have fun? Did you have fun?" and more important, "What did your children learn?" Mr. Klien noted that the children enjoyed their learning because it was engaging, meaningful, active, iterative, and joyful (Zosh et al. 2022). The families identified many math concepts embedded in the games and recalled what their children said that showed their math understanding. As parents spoke, Mr. Klien wrote all the math concepts on chart paper and then showed how they matched the standards in their state math curriculum framework. *(ask)*

> Mr. Klien took the discussion one step further to connect to the families' funds of knowledge and asked, "Did you play any games like these growing up, where you were learning and playing at the same time? What did you play?" This question prompted the sharing of many fond memories of favorite games from childhood—card games, board games, hopscotch, hand games, double Dutch (jump roping), and many others. Mr. Klien again took notes and concluded the meeting with an open invitation for the families to come into class and teach the children their favorite games. In addition to families who volunteered, Mr. Klien followed up on his notes and reached out to Imani's father to teach mancala, Chong-min's mother to teach Go, and Lorenzo's grandfather to teach dominoes. *(ask, adapt)*
>
> As the families shared their games, the children proudly took on the role of expert and led their peers in playing. After each new game was taught, Mr. Klien discussed with the children what they learned, which often extended beyond math. These wonderful discussions were shared in newsletters to families. At the last family conference of the school year, many families shared anecdotes of their children playfully learning different subjects—math, literacy, science, history—at home, in the grocery store, and during family outings. "Many of them finally see that it's not play versus learning, but play *and* learning!" Ms. Ross said to Mr. Klien. "I learned so much from the families, and so did the children!" *(ask, adapt)*

Conclusion

"Effective parent involvement programs match the needs of school and community in creating a positive school climate" (Barrera & Warner 2006, 73). Trusting relationships are the foundation for developing culturally responsive partnerships between families and schools. When differences in values arise, honoring families' funds of knowledge while actively seeking the third space enhances trust in the relationship, opens genuine learning possibilities for both families and educators, and advances the mission and goals of the school and community.

Tips for Communicating the Importance of Playful Learning to Families

1. Display a chart in the room for visitors listing 10 things children learn from play. Share these in a newsletter or online. Reinforce the connections between center/station activities and learning.

2. Offer opportunities to illustrate the connections between play and learning.

3. Post images of children playing and learning—both indoors and out. Label them with information about what the children are learning.

4. Provide time for families to observe and engage in playful learning, ask questions, and reflect on play and learning together.

5. Become more comfortable talking about play and learning. Practice with a colleague.

Adapted from L. Bongiorno, "Talking with Parents About Play and Learning," *Teaching Young Children* (August/ September 2018), 18–20.

IRIS CHIN PONTE (she/her), PhD, is director and classroom teacher at the Henry Frost Children's Program in Belmont, Massachusetts. A former Fulbright Scholar, she has taught and conducted extensive school research in the United States, the United Kingdom, Taiwan, China, Japan, and Newfoundland.

YVONNE LIU-CONSTANT (she/her), PhD, is an early childhood educator who loves teaching children as much as she loves working with teachers. She is the practitioner specialist at the Pedagogy of Play, Project Zero, Harvard Graduate School of Education. She also teaches at Lesley University and Boston Teacher Residency and is trained as a cultural researcher.

CHAPTER 7

Family Math Stories
Math for Cross-Cultural Connections and Community

Hannah Kye

At the beginning of the school year, I sent a letter to the families of my kindergarten students, inviting them to bring a family treasure, or a picture or drawing of one, to share about during back-to-school night. The invitation was inspired by Roessingh's (2012) dual-language family treasure project, which helped connect children and families across linguistic and cultural backgrounds. My class was diverse, with several families speaking home languages other than English.

On the night of the event, families arrived and sat at their children's tables. After a brief introduction, I shared my family treasure, and then families took turns sharing theirs. Sunghui's mother said,

> My mom told me this story, but I haven't told it to Sunghui before. My grandfather was a carpenter. This is his tool, a hand plane. When a war started in his country, he had to leave on a long journey. Along the way, he was often stopped by soldiers. He would show them this tool to show that he was not dangerous, just a humble carpenter. They let him pass, and he found a safe place to live and later came to America to start a new life. Because of this tool, Sunghui could be born here and come to school here with you.

Around the classroom, family members shared about a blanket, a bread pan, and photographs. I thanked the families for their stories and displayed a slide on the projector with this question: Where does mathematics live in our stories?

I said that tonight we would make a family math book to keep in the classroom, a book that our class would use throughout the school year as we explored math concepts. Families could contribute one or more pages about their family treasure to the book. I asked the families to find the math in their stories, whether the ages of loved ones; the time of day when the treasure was often used; or a measurement, shape, or pattern.

I encouraged the families to use their home language or a combination of languages on their pages. On the children's tables were materials to make a book page: blank paper, pencils, markers, and stickers. The stickers included numbers, shapes, and algebraic symbols. At a back table were math tools for exploration: rulers, timers, scales, measuring cups, and measuring tape. The materials were selected to encourage adult family members to use math language in their stories.

The room filled with conversation and laughter as families created and showed their pages to one another. Lilah's father showed her how to line up a ruler at the edge of their photo album, while Ben and his older sister bounded to the back table to take and return tools. As families left, they used a magnet to secure their book page to our whiteboard. Sunghui and her mother's page read,

> This is my great-grandpa's hand plane. The top is a rectangle. It looks like a wood block, but do not play with it. It is sharp. It is six inches long. He carried it for thousands of miles. One time, he made a bookcase for my mom with three shelves. He woke her up at 6:00 a.m. making the bookcase.

Classroom Context

One of my goals for inviting families to participate in making the family math book was to build a foundation of trust and partnership as these families made the transition into kindergarten. Research shows that children reap social, behavioral, and academic benefits from their families' involvement in school (NASEM 2016). The transition to kindergarten is a golden opportunity to begin building trust and set a strong foundation for family engagement (Hoffman et al. 2020).

Establishing trust between school and home is particularly important for families from underrepresented cultures, who may feel uncomfortable, underprepared, or unwelcome in schools (Ishimaru 2019). On their introductory surveys, seven families in my classroom noted that they used a language other than English at home. There were students whose families had emigrated within the past generation from Mexico, Puerto Rico, Korea, Japan, and Kazakhstan. Since the nineteenth century, schools in the United States have been a tool of assimilation to the dominant language and culture at the expense of families' ways of being (Hinitz & Liebovich 2023). In my classroom, I strive to implement culturally sustaining pedagogy (Paris & Alim 2014), which works against this cultural separation and instead affirms the value of family histories and resources. Culturally sustaining teachers are purposeful in making linguistic and cultural pluralism the norm in the classroom, including in math teaching and learning.

Family Math as Culturally Sustaining Pedagogy

Despite decades of research showing the academic and social and emotional benefits of family engagement, family math has only recently gained limited attention (Eason et al. 2020). Families are often overlooked in children's math learning, yet research shows that involving families offers a path to strengthening children's math identities. Children's positive math identities have been linked to later persistence, interest, and proficiency in math (Williams 2020). Family math engages families in children's learning in ways that honor and build on their backgrounds, knowledge, and experiences. These connections help children feel seen, see others, and connect math learning to their own heritage and community practices (Paris & Alim 2014). In addition, family math encourages parents to incorporate math learning opportunities in the home, which has been shown to increase children's math knowledge and later math proficiency (Eason et al. 2020). New models of teaching and learning are necessary to set the foundation for family math engagement and children's development of strong math identities. The family math stories created by the families of my students was a step toward such a model.

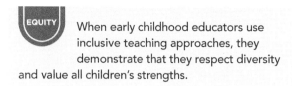 When early childhood educators use inclusive teaching approaches, they demonstrate that they respect diversity and value all children's strengths.

Culturally relevant and culturally sustaining pedagogies (Ladson-Billings 2014) call on teachers to learn about and work to improve issues of equity and diversity in schools. These asset-based pedagogies involve connecting curriculum to community histories and sustaining families' cultural and linguistic practices. Based on research on these pedagogies, there are three principles to carry forward from the family math stories that can strengthen connections between families' experiences and children's math learning, heightening children's interest in engaging with math.

Center Family Math Practices

Math education has a history of being abstract, cold, and detached from social contexts (McLeod 1992). By providing opportunities for the children's families to contribute their language, stories, and ways of doing math to the curriculum, math became a means of connecting people across generations and cultures. In the month after our back-to-school night, I frequently read the family math stories to the children, including the words in their home languages. While the children often wanted to hear the entire book, we also used individual pages in our classroom learning. For example, after Rie brought a folded paper crane to school, several children began gathering at the back table to fold paper during choice time. When introducing origami paper and books to the art area, I read the page Ben had made with his mother and sister, which had instructions on how to fold and tie his grandmother's scarf. Rie folded three colorful miniature scarves using the instructions, and as she helped her classmates, she recalled Ben's mother's demonstration: "First she set it down. Do you remember? And she folded it to a triangle like this. Corner to corner." Geometric ideas from the book, such as folding a square into a triangle, engaged children's spatial reasoning and introduced math vocabulary. Another time, as we explored measuring tools, Sunghui proudly made a connection to her great-grandfather, who was adept at using measuring tools along with his hand plane.

The family math book served as a touchstone that kept families at the center of our math curriculum. Each time the children read the pages on their own or spoke about the stories, they were acknowledging the value of their classmates' "memories, traditions, legacy, and ancestral connection" (Roessingh 2012, 135). The stories provided context for learning, helping us see our family members, including Ben's grandmother and Sunghui's great-grandfather, as people who used the same math ideas as we do.

Leverage Opportunities to Connect with Families

The back-to-school event where families shared their math stories was an annual school event during which teachers typically spoke about the schedule, curriculum, and expectations. Families received a district-recommended parent roadmap, which listed home math activities and examples of math learning in kindergarten, first grade, and second grade. These communications involve one-way information sharing, suggesting to families that professional knowledge is most valued. One-sided approaches like this also do not enable families to share knowledge and insights that could help teachers provide developmentally appropriate learning experiences for children (Mancilla & Blanco 2022). Thus, it was important to me that I clarify to the families of my students that their knowledge and practices would be central to our learning. I leveraged our time together for connecting and sharing stories rather than using it only to tell the families what I thought they should know about the coming year. After we made our book pages, I sent home examples of a parent email and note, so families had models of how to continue contributing to the curriculum and offering their expertise and feedback that we all could learn from.

Here are a few ways you can increase connection with families and contribute to remaking systems that better support culturally and linguistically diverse families:

> Turn one-way communication into two-way communication during family events, as I did on back-to-school night. This relational approach to teaching helps to create culturally relevant pedagogy (Ladson-Billings 1992).

> Expand single-language communications into multiple languages with the support of school translators, if available. When you email or text families, use the translation feature on your app, and encourage families to respond in their own language. Their communications can then be translated into your preferred language.

> Provide flexible options for participation. Families who could not attend our back-to-school night, for example, were able to contribute to the math book in the following weeks by sending their stories via email or in their child's backpack.

Sharing these strategies with colleagues and administrators can lead the way to strengths-based family engagement for everyone.

Diversify Sources of Knowledge in Math

Building one's cultural competence involves taking a stance of listening and learning. Teachers can ask themselves, "What are the sources of knowledge in this classroom? Who do we value and include in our curriculum plans?" This is particularly important because professional knowledge, including education research and its influence on mandated curriculum, has historically been based on a normative perspective of White, English-speaking children (NAEYC 2019a).

When seeking sources of knowledge for our math curriculum, therefore, I turned to families first. In the winter, our class began a math unit on recognizing, describing, and extending patterns. We returned to the family math stories to see if we could discover patterns in our family treasures. By this point, the children's ownership of the stories and vocabulary in the book was clear. When we reached the page with Mateo's blanket, the children shouted "las rayas" instead of "stripes." Mateo shared that he had more patterned blankets, and Lilah added that a room in her home "has stripes and birds on the walls." Via email and a letter sent home, I invited families to email or send in photographs, drawings, or descriptions of patterns from home. I asked, "When do you use patterns? It can be a pattern that you see or a pattern of sounds, motions, or time." The responses were posted on a bulletin board about patterns, and children's discussions about them included now-familiar characters from their family stories.

Next, recognizing that most instructional materials are not representative of diverse backgrounds, I brought in books that showed a variety of ways people and communities use math (see "Children's Books Showcasing Math"). The family stories ensured that each child felt ownership of their math learning and saw math in the context of their personal histories. The diverse children's books helped us use math to further understand other cultures and communities.

process rather than rote learning or repetitive practice, offering one model of math engagement for kindergartners and their families aimed at developing strong cultural and math identities. This can help children see the importance of math in their lives and believe they can succeed in math (Thomas & Berry 2019). The three principles explored in this chapter shed light on how teachers might use family math as part of culturally sustaining pedagogy and increase children's engagement in the math curriculum.

Children's Books Showcasing Math

The following children's books can be used in the classroom to show various ways people use math:

The All-Together Quilt (by Lizzy Rockwell)

Bracelets for Bina's Brothers (by Rajani LaRocca, illus. by Chaaya Prabhat)

A Day at Grandma's (by Mi-ae Lee, illus. by Yang-sook Choi)

Dumpling Day (by Meera Sriram, illus. by Inés de Antuñano)

Feast for 10 (by Cathryn Falwell)

Handa's Hen (by Eileen Browne)

Kiss by Kiss/ocêhtowina: A Counting Book for Families (by Richard Van Camp, trans. by Mary Cardinal Collins)

Lia & Luís: Who Has More? (by Ana Crespo, illus. by Giovana Medeiros)

Look, Grandma! Ni, Elisi! (by Art Coulson, illus. by Madelyn Goodnight)

Luna's Yum Yum Dim Sum (by Natasha Yim, illus. by Violet Kim)

Sometimes We Do (by Omo Moses, illus. by Diego Chaves)

HANNAH KYE, EdD, is an associate professor of interdisciplinary and inclusive education at Rowan University. Her research interests include family-centered curriculum and early STEM education with a focus on equity and diversity. She teaches preservice teachers and provides professional development for in-service teachers.

Conclusion

Collecting the stories shared aloud during back-to-school night through the family math book invited families into their children's school learning and formed the roots of our math curriculum. The stories featured family members as people who did math and showed mathematics as part of a natural

Exploring Families' Language Practices Through a Social Studies Inquiry in Kindergarten

Ivana Espinet, Maite T. Sánchez, Sabrina Poms, and Elizabeth Menendez

In a buzzing kindergarten classroom, children and their family members are seated at small tables. The class has collaboratively created a list of questions that children want to ask about cultural and linguistic practices valued and used by their families. The children take notes using drawings, invented spelling, and other forms of emergent writing as they speak to the adults.

Mr. Gomez is sitting next to his daughter, Amalia. He reads with her the list of questions: "¿Cuáles son algunas frases o dichos que usa tu familia con frecuencia?" (What are some sentences or sayings that your family uses frequently?) Amalia replies: "Te quiero mucho." (I love you.)

At the next table, Ms. Del Monte reads: "¿De dónde viene la familia?"—to which her daughter, Dalia, replies: "Nuestra familia viene de la República Dominicana." (Where does your family come from? Our family comes from the Dominican Republic.)

Carlos, a classmate, adds: "We are from Brooklyn because I was a baby in Brooklyn."

These conversations are examples of how Sabrina Poms and Elizabeth Menendez, two Spanish-English bilingual teachers (and the third and fourth authors of this chapter), engaged kindergarten children and their families during a family-focused social studies unit at their school. This chapter describes the collaboration between these teachers and Ivana Espinet and Maite T. Sánchez, two researchers from the City University of New York–New York State Initiative on Emergent Bilinguals (CUNY–NYSIEB) and the first and second authors. Together, the four designed a translanguaging space where bilingual children and their families could explore the linguistic and cultural practices that they engage in at home. This space was created within the context of a dual language bilingual education program and included a variety of activities through which children and families could learn from each other and about their active and dynamic language practices.

Sabrina and Elizabeth's inquiry work provides a model for working with multilingual families in both mainstream and bilingual early childhood settings. It exemplifies what García, Johnson, and Seltzer (2017) describe as a *Juntos* (together) stance; that is, designing asset-focused instruction in which families' language practices are at the forefront of family-educator collaboration and children's learning experiences. (See "Juntos in the Classroom" for more information about this approach.)

Juntos in the Classroom

García, Johnson, and Seltzer (2017) use the term *Juntos* to describe an educational approach that fosters collaboration among children, families, communities, and educators. The Juntos stance is informed by the following beliefs:

> Children's language practices and cultural understandings encompass those they bring from home and community contexts as well as those they take up in schools.

> Children's families and communities are valuable sources of knowledge and must be engaged in the education process.

> The classroom is a democratic space in which teachers, children, and families cocreate knowledge that can challenge traditional language hierarchies and work toward a more just society.

It also acknowledges young emergent bilinguals' dynamic language practices. We use *emergent bilingual* in this chapter to highlight a child's potential to becoming bilingual, rather than moving from speaking one or more languages other than English at home to solely speaking English.

Encompassing Diverse Language Practices in the Curriculum

In the United States, there are an increasing number of young children with home languages other than English who bring their rich linguistic and cultural knowledge and experiences to early childhood programs. However, unless these children are enrolled in a bilingual education program, the curriculum and teaching methods focus on supporting English rather than bilingual language development. Even in bilingual programs, home and school language practices are often treated as separate: children's language practices are seen from a monolingual lens, meaning educators view the children as two monolingual speakers in one (Grosjean 2010; Otheguy, García, & Reid 2019). This practice views each language as independent, rather than as an integrated, dynamic linguistic system. But young children growing up in bilingual or multilingual homes have a complex repertoire of language practices. They engage in *translanguaging* (Morell & López 2020)—or using more than one language to make sense of the world—by using all the features of their linguistic and multimodal communicative repertoires flexibly and dynamically (García 2009).

Research emphasizes the importance of supporting home language development in all early childhood settings by providing opportunities for children to continue their bilingual development instead of solely focusing on their shift to a monolingual, English-speaking reality (Tazi 2014). As such, it is essential that educators create a space in which young emergent bilingual children are able to leverage their ways of knowing, use language practices from their homes and in their communities, and feel socially and emotionally secure in their bilingual identities (García, Johnson, & Seltzer 2017; NAEYC 2019a, 2020).

However, schools do not always see families as partners in these efforts. Indeed, the language practices of language-minoritized communities have historically been stigmatized and devalued (Flores 2018; García & Otheguy 2016). While teachers and schools might invite families to participate in school events, they rarely view them as partners in instructional work and learning experiences (Espinet & Lê 2020). In contrast, developmentally appropriate practice advocates for teachers to celebrate and build on the funds of knowledge that children and families bring to the learning process (NAEYC 2020).

 EQUITY

Be curious, making time to learn about the families with whom you work. This includes learning about their languages, customs, activities, values, and beliefs so you can provide a culturally and linguistically responsive and sustaining learning environment.

The Context for a Social Studies Inquiry

One of the main goals of dual language programs is to develop students' bilingualism and biliteracy. Therefore, children learn all academic subjects in both English and Spanish. Sabrina and Elizabeth are coteachers at an integrated coteaching (ICT) bilingual kindergarten in an English-Spanish dual language bilingual public elementary school in New York City. ICT classrooms have two fully licensed teachers—one in special education (Sabrina) and one in general education (Elizabeth). Both teachers are bilingual. Together they plan the curriculum, teach the lessons, and support the learning and growth of all the children in the classroom.

During the 2018–19 school year, Sabrina and Elizabeth's school collaborated with CUNY–NYSIEB to design translanguaging spaces within the social studies curricula. (For more on this collaboration, see Espinet et al. 2020 and Sánchez, Espinet, & Hunt 2021.) Sabrina and Elizabeth's classroom consisted of 25 children, 9 of whom were classified as emergent multilingual language learners/English language learners. This is the official designation that the New York State Education Department uses for students who are not proficient in English, according to the

state's standardized assessment (www.nysed
.gov/bilingual-ed/emergent-multilingual-learners
-prekindergarten-programs). Many of the other
children who were identified as English proficient
spoke languages other than English at home—mostly
Spanish but also Hebrew, Italian, Mixteco, Russian,
and Swedish. In addition, approximately 40 percent of
Sabrina and Elizabeth's students had Individualized
Education Programs (IEPs), were primarily classified
as having speech and language impairments, and
received speech therapy to address specific needs.

Adapting the Curriculum

One of the units of New York City's social studies
kindergarten curriculum focuses on families and
explores the essential question "Why are families
important?" Because inquiry and project-based
learning are at the center of Sabrina and Elizabeth's
school's approach to teaching and learning, the school
has developed an "Inquiry Through Explorations
and Investigations" curriculum in which students
explore a question and then create projects or
presentations based on what they discover. Over the
years, the kindergarten classes have studied families
by doing multimodal projects, such as making family
crests that include images as well as words. As a
result of their collaboration with CUNY–NYSIEB,
kindergarten teachers adapted this unit to incorporate
a focus on how bilingual families use language. They
collaboratively designed classroom activities in which
family members would be active participants with their
children and in which the fluid language practices of
these families would be at the center of the inquiry.

Overall, the administration and the teachers in the
school emphasize the value of establishing positive
and trusting relationships with families and the
community. For example, the school has a policy of
conducting home visits at the beginning of the year
to learn from families before their children come to
school. It also has Family Fridays, during which time
family members are invited to visit classrooms and
participate in instructional activities with children. The
work shared in this chapter highlights how the school's
approach to collaboration with families drove and
enriched the design and implementation of the social
studies inquiry unit, which Sabrina and Elizabeth
continued to implement during subsequent years.

Using Language Fluidly, Like Families Do

Sabrina and Elizabeth's classroom had Spanish time
and English time, each separate. However, the design
of the social studies family unit was different in that
it aimed to highlight the dynamic bilingual practices
of children and families. At the beginning of the unit,
the teachers discussed with the children the languages
they spoke with their families and how they used those
languages at home. The children shared that, unlike
at school, at home there were generally no specific
times to speak one language or another. The teachers
explained that during the family unit's exploration
time, children and teachers would use language
fluidly rather than follow a strict separation. They
introduced the term *translanguaging* to describe how
multilingual families move fluidly between languages,
and they introduced a visual representation to the
classroom's daily schedule: a purple sign to indicate
that students could use all of their languages. (Spanish
time was usually in red and English in blue.)

Throughout the unit, children studied various aspects
of families, such as family traditions and how families
are composed. The teachers read several books that
featured different types of families, such as *Who Is
in My Family? All About Our Families*, by Robie
H. Harris, and *And Tango Makes Three*, by Justin
Richardson and Peter Parnell. The children also
worked in centers on different family-related activities.
These included creating family crests, building
wooden sculptures to show how families help each
other, making picture collages about their families,
designing house glyphs, and conducting book research.
Sabrina and Elizabeth encouraged children to use all
of their languages, and they adapted the centers and
family-related activities to help them take a closer
look at their families' linguistic practices. Children
and family members collaborated in this exploration
during Family Fridays.

Exploring Language Through Family Interviews

A family interview was the first Family Friday activity
that children did with family members. Before adults
came to visit, the children brainstormed questions
they would ask. These included general questions
about families, such as "Where does your family come

from?," "What does your family like to do for fun?," and "How does your family take care of each other?" Children also included questions about how their families use language, such as "What does your family like to say to each other?" and "What languages does your family speak?"

As seen in the opening vignette, children and adults felt comfortable translanguaging during this activity. The dialogues were fluid and used features of Spanish, English, and other home languages as children interviewed the adults and took notes. As children asked their questions and family members responded, the children constructed meaning, collaborated in building their family histories, and learned about language use in their families. The interviews also gave them space to use language flexibly and provided an opportunity for those who spoke languages other than Spanish and English at home to bring in and share their language practices. Children learned about who they are—and who their classmates are—as they shared their interviews with the class.

This activity leveraged the potential of asking questions to help develop children's oral language. For young emergent bilingual children to develop their communicative practices and repertoires, it is critical that oral language development occur in authentic social interactions that welcome children's flexible use of language (Souto-Manning & Martell 2016). Family interviews can be done in any early childhood setting, even if the teacher does not speak any of the children's home languages. This is because children and their families, rather than the teacher, guide the language use.

Exploring Language Use by Extended Family Members

Sabrina and Elizabeth wanted to expand discussions of how language is used in families beyond the immediate family unit. Knowing that each child had virtual or in-person contact with at least one grandparent, they asked the children to paint their grandparents' portraits. They then asked the children to label the portraits with the names they used for their grandparents. These included Abuelita, Lola, Bobo, and Grandma Candy.

After they finished the portraits, children worked with their families to record the words or phrases they shared with their grandparents. This activity was

critical because many grandparents lived far away or spoke languages other than English to the children. As members of transnational families, it is important that their cultural and linguistic connections to loved ones in other countries continue to be nurtured and shared with the classroom community. Recording the shared words and phrases also helped the children and their families think collaboratively about how they use language with their extended families, which might differ from how they speak with parents or siblings. This activity opened up space for children and family members to share stories and feel a connection with extended family, regardless of physical distance.

Exploring Language Through a Family Quilt

Sabrina and Elizabeth wanted their class to have a visual representation of these discussions. The family quilt was a medium to pair family voices with children's artwork. Each portrait of a grandparent was accompanied by a quotation of something the grandparent regularly said to the child or family. During one Family Friday, Sabrina and Elizabeth asked adults to talk about some of their family dichos (sayings), which they wrote along the outside of the quilt.

As part of the culmination of this unit, families participated in a class activity in which each child presented their quilt square and their grandparent's saying. Children began to recognize that, although families use language differently, many of their sayings had similar sentiments. As they read aloud the messages and dichos from their parents, some children recognized the sayings and said, "My mom also says that!" The portraits and accompanying words gave an intimate look into the language use of families in the classroom community.

Celebrating the Language Practices of Multilingual Families

In a Juntos stance, learning is a coconstruction of knowledge that involves children and their families. Each child and family member bring to the school a rich repertoire of cultural and linguistic resources, which are valued and leveraged for learning. Because families' linguistic and cultural practices are at the core of their relationships to each other and to the world, they need to be at the center of how educators plan and implement their work.

On the last day of the unit, families, teachers, and children reviewed the activities shared in this chapter as well as others they did together. As they looked back, they returned to the guiding questions they had explored, including "How do families use language?" The children and adults took notes about their observations.

In reviewing and analyzing what they had learned, both children and adults recognized the wealth of knowledge that families can bring to the classroom. They were also able to think about how families' individual experiences and differences are connected to a collective common experience: while individual families use features of different languages at home, all families translanguage as they use language fluidly among their members.

Tips for Partnering with Families

Consider the following when planning to partner with families to collaborate in learning experiences:

› Get to know the families so that they feel comfortable sharing their personal stories and information about their homes. Be sensitive, aware that some families may be hesitant to share information because, for example, they are undocumented or have fled horrendous situations in their home country.

› Invite children and families to discuss and analyze linguistic practices at home, in the community, and at school. For example, children and families can be invited to read books by authors who use translanguaging, then discuss how they use language at home (see Espinosa & Lehner-Quam 2019).

> Design activities in which children and adults collaborate in exploring questions and cocreating knowledge about their multilingual lives. These could include inviting children and families to cocreate linguistic maps (see Espinet et al. 2020).

> Use multimodal collaborative projects that engage family members to create together, such as making collages or recording stories together and sharing with the class.

Conclusion

Any educator who works with multilingual young learners in any setting can support children's multilingual linguistic and cultural identities and sense of belonging. The examples provided in this chapter can serve as inspiration to foster positive, reciprocal collaboration with families in exploring language use in their multilingual communities.

IVANA ESPINET, PhD, is a Latina, immigrant, bilingual scholar. She is assistant professor in the education program at Kingsborough Community College, CUNY. She is a former teacher and a former project director for the CUNY–NYSIEB.

MAITE T. SÁNCHEZ, PhD, is an assistant professor of bilingual education at Hunter College, CUNY. Her research focuses on language education policy and practice, translanguaging pedagogy, and bilingual teachers' preparation.

SABRINA POMS, MA, is a bilingual special education teacher at Dos Puentes Elementary School, a dual language public school in Washington Heights, New York City. Sabrina supports children with disabilities to access the general education curriculum and become bilingual and biliterate in English and Spanish.

ELIZABETH MENENDEZ, MS, is a first-generation Salvadoran American college graduate. She is a New York City Spanish bilingual teacher at Dos Puentes Elementary School in Washington Heights. Elizabeth has been a bilingual classroom teacher for 26 years.

CHAPTER 9

Being the Bridge
Supporting the Families of Kindergartners Whose Primary Language Is Not English

Laura C. Rodríguez-Pérez

So, if you want to really hurt me, talk badly about my language. Ethnic identity is twin skin to linguistic identity—I am my language. Until I can take pride in my language, I cannot take pride in myself.

—Gloria Anzaldúa, *Borderlands/La Frontera: The New Mestiza*

Volume editor's note: *This chapter relays a conversation I had with Laura C. Rodríguez-Pérez, a former kindergarten classroom teacher and currently a Peace Corps volunteer working in a primary school for the Deaf in Kenya. Laura's 14 years of experience working with children and families whose first language is not English offers many insights into providing the most effective and authentic support for these families. Building positive, trusting relationships with young emergent bilinguals and their families provides the foundation for Laura's work and is explored throughout the conversation. To read a Spanish version of this interview, visit NAEYC.org/dap-focus-kindergarten.*

—Eva Phillips

Why is it so important to build positive and trusting relationships with your kindergartners whose first language is not English?

When a child feels happy, loved, respected, and emotionally strong, then they are capable of learning, creating, and much more. Our role as early childhood teachers is to sow seeds of possibility in children. Going to school is one of the biggest transitions in their children's lives. Leaving their homes (what is familiar) and entering a new and unfamiliar system called "school" is an experience that changes their lives.

For many immigrant families, kindergarten symbolizes that first step toward the future, a future that entails many sacrifices and is full of uncertainty. That first interaction with the kindergarten teacher marks the future of a learner.

It is imperative to recognize that an emergent bilingual comes with a bank of enriching experiences, and it is necessary to create an inclusive school environment in which each child's cultural and sociolinguistic background is considered and celebrated.

Author's note

In this chapter I use the term *emergent bilingual* to refer to a child who is learning both their home language and English.

This new school environment designed for monolingual learners is sometimes intimidating and limiting for emergent bilinguals, as it sometimes requires them to put aside their identity and language in order to fit into the new school system. Accommodating the needs of adults or monolingual peers is required at such an early age. Monolingual teachers do not have the intention of excluding emergent bilinguals; however, in many situations, due to their unfamiliarity with the language acquisition process, monolingual teachers believe that emergent bilinguals' assimilation and absolute focus on the language of the school is the most efficient way for emerging bilinguals to perform like their monolingual peers. The intention may be good, but the method is incorrect. The role of teachers is to provide an emotionally safe environment in which *all* students can achieve their academic, social, and emotional goals. Emergent bilinguals are no exception.

As I mentioned earlier, emergent bilinguals bring a bank of unique experiences that will support and enrich the school experiences of everyone in your kindergarten classroom. Acquiring a second language is a unique process for each learner; however, teachers can create an inclusive environment in which children are an active and essential part of the school environment, dare to take risks, and share their history and their knowledge. Creating inclusive spaces requires consideration of the language, culture, and identity of your students. "From a social-justice perspective, educators should make every effort to communicate with language-minority families using layman's terms in the language(s) that they speak best" (Cuéllar 2018, 2).

Why is it so important to build relationships with the families of your students, in particular those whose first language is not English?

When you take the time to get to know the children's families and give yourself the opportunity to enter their culture, understand, and comprehend the world through their eyes, it allows you to break down cultural and language barriers. It is then that you can focus on your similarities and can learn and grow from your differences.

This opens up the opportunity for families to take an active role in the learning process, creating a special experience for families and providing them with a sense of ownership and empowerment. When families are authentically involved, you enter the most intimate part of a child's life, and because you enter into their world, you embrace it and accept it.

It is necessary that each family's cultural and linguistic identity be respected and valued and that teachers see it as a unique opportunity for growth for the entire school community.

What does the research say about the needs of emergent bilinguals?

Emergent bilinguals are students who are in the process of learning English in addition to their home language. While many emergent bilinguals are immigrants, the majority are born in the United States. Other names for this student population include *English language learners (ELLs), dual language*

learners (DLLs), and *bilingual/multilingual students.* One of the best ways to support the needs of our emergent bilingual students is through dual immersion programs, which refer to any "program that provides literacy and content instruction to all students through two languages and that promotes bilingualism and biliteracy, grade-level academic achievement, and sociocultural competence" (Howard et al. 2018, 3). Dual language programs create change and establish culturally and linguistically inclusive spaces. "Research also shows that ELs can benefit from continuing to learn in their native language, both academically and cognitively. . . . Oral proficiency and literacy in a student's first language, for example, can facilitate English literacy development" (Office of English Language Acquisition 2015, 1).

By encouraging parents to use their home language with their children, you help to ensure that children learn content knowledge and concepts. Research findings suggest that language skills in bilingual children are distributed across the two languages (Quiroga et al. 2001). In turn, this knowledge learned (in the home language) will transfer to the second language and ensures that emerging bilinguals create connections and a deeper understanding of the environment around them.

 Supporting the use of a child's first language is essential for successful development of a second language. When families are encouraged to continue using the child's first language at home and within their community, the learning of English at school is strengthened and enhanced. Embracing a child's culture, which includes their first language, strengthens the foundation of understanding, acceptance, and respect of the learners within the classroom community where all are seen as valued members of the group.

As I have mentioned, gaining proficiency in their home language is paramount for children. The following are activities that can be developed to promote this:

> Integrate into your routine familiar poems and songs in the children's home languages. Through music, students can learn literacy concepts such as phonemic awareness, rhyming, decoding, and reading comprehension (Hansen, Bernstorf, & Stuber 2014).

> Connect emerging bilinguals with other emerging bilinguals in the school.

> Promote reading and writing by encouraging the use of the home language at home.

> Encourage children to use their home language while playing and to express their thoughts and emotions.

> Support children to first learn concepts in their home language so they can transfer the concepts to English. Once they understand and conceptualize concepts, they should only focus on learning the new vocabulary and transferring between languages, thus increasing their linguistic repertoire. For example, once students understand that a cube has six square sides, they should be able to transfer that concept into the new language.

How do teachers build bridges with students and their families?

The first thing is to have a genuine desire to meet the families and see that through their experiences, stories, language, and culture you can create enriching environments for your emerging bilinguals. Families are complex and diverse; many of our immigrant families are made up of their extended families in the United States and their countries of origin. Understanding the essential role that the integration of families plays in children's learning process is critical. Not inviting or engaging families in this process is the missing piece in the puzzle, and without that piece, the puzzle will not be complete.

Vygotsky's theory teaches us that personal and social experiences cannot be separated. The world that children inhabit is transformed by their families, communities, socioeconomic status, education, and culture. Their understanding of the world comes, in part, from the values and beliefs of the adults and peers in their lives (Mooney 2000). These beliefs along with their language and identity serve as a compass for emergent bilinguals as they enter and navigate the school system.

"Strategies for Building Bridges with Families" shows several strategies that I have used to support and connect with families, especially those with a home language other than English.

Strategies for Building Bridges with Families

Be welcoming to all families.

> Conduct face-to-face, virtual, or hybrid meetings to establish expectations and roles (first or second week of school).

> Ask about language practices at home and the language goals and objectives of your families.

> Make an initial phone call.

> Conduct home visits, or suggest alternative places to meet if families prefer.

> Create a basic information questionnaire: identification, family composition, interests as a family, and talents and skills that parents would like to share in the class.

> Create an area or space in your classroom with photos of families, flags, and art or other meaningful cultural items from the countries of origin of the children.

View families as active partners with you in their child's education.

> Seek to listen and understand without judging.

> Be flexible and provide a variety of communication modes and times to communicate with families.

> Meet with families three to four times a year to exchange observations about children's strengths and needs. Ask questions and listen.

> Take photos and videos to document school experiences and share them with families on your communication platform.

> Provide times when most families can attend events.

> Attend family or recreational events within the community.

> Create workshops to share academic, social, and emotional strategies with families so that they can provide support at home. Ask families what topics would be most helpful to them.

Ensure that everyone can contribute in ways that they value and find meaningful.

> Invite family members to help organize the classroom, create materials, and work on an activity, either individually or in a small group.

> Appoint a student every week to invite their family to share anecdotes and experiences with the class. Make sure everyone has this opportunity.

> Invite each family and their student to document a family event, trip, or special celebration using photos or objects and share them in class. Provide them with a structure for the presentation.

> Integrate the diverse cultural experiences of children into your curriculum. Be sure to get families' input so you are doing this in ways that are meaningful to the children.

> Celebrate and integrate festivities or cultural events in class and invite families to share their experiences.

Agree on the most effective communication method with each family and ensure that communication is consistent and clear.

> Use newsletters, digital applications, emails, phone calls, and/or video calls to connect with families.

> Identify communication facilitators, such as interpreters and voice translation applications, among others.

Understand the importance of opportunities for families to share with each other and connect as a community.

> Establish activities that promote socialization between peers and families, such as going to the movies, the park to fly kites or play, the bookstore, a restaurant, a picnic, the local library, a museum, or other social activities in your community.

What else is important for kindergarten teachers to know about families and their partnership in the classroom community?

For many of the families of emerging bilinguals, this is their first school experience, and you have a unique opportunity to demonstrate to them the values that their children will acquire during their educational processes, such as empathy, fairness, responsibility, respect, higher academic expectations, and being a part of a new school and social community. Classroom communities are enriched when teachers value children and their families' identities, their importance, and their contributions through the exchange of their history and knowledge.

Being actively engaged in their children's school experiences is what families desire. Families want to be part of their children's lives, and sometimes they don't know how to do it in this new country with a new language and feel intimidated by it. Teachers can create a safe space where families feel welcome and can collaborate according to their abilities.

For example, encouraging families to enrich their children's linguistic repertoire by reading stories, telling stories, singing songs, and sharing nursery rhymes and poems in their home language supports oral language and comprehension development. Human beings are complex, and our identity is not limited to a geographical area, so it is extremely important to respect and give a voice to our identity.

Teachers and families are a team and together can successfully meet their children's needs. Kindergarten is the first step toward new adventures, enrichment, and possibilities. This experience is a secure bridge that connects emergent bilinguals, their families, and the school. When the school community celebrates and values each child's identity, it enriches their journey as a learner. In a safe and happy environment, all children can learn and enter this new stage of their lives.

LAURA C. RODRÍGUEZ-PÉREZ, MSEd, is a former kindergarten-to-second-grade dual language teacher in North Carolina and Puerto Rico, a mentor for beginning teachers, and currently a Peace Corps volunteer teaching literacy in a school for the Deaf in Kenya.

PART 3

Observing, Documenting, and Assessing Children's Development and Learning

RECOMMENDATIONS FROM THE DAP POSITION STATEMENT

Observing, documenting, and assessing each child's development and learning are essential processes for educators and programs to plan, implement, and evaluate the effectiveness of the experiences they provide to children. Both formative and summative assessment are important and must be conducted in ways that are developmentally, culturally, and linguistically responsive to authentically assess children's learning.

When Ms. Blessing asks Alonso, a dual language learner, about the three small structures he is building in the block center, he says, "They are the pig houses." Ms. Blessing realizes he is retelling the story from *The Three Little Pigs,* a book the class had been reading together. She observes Alonso as he uses small figurines to act out the story, completely in order, using simple, key phrases from the story. Ms. Blessing realizes that his receptive language skills are stronger than she had thought and that, while he is not yet able to successfully retell a story with many details in English (one thing her school's early literacy assessment measures), he does understand the story and has a concept of sequence. Ms. Blessing updates Alonso's learning target to "building vocabulary to retell simple stories," replacing the assumed learning goal of "sequencing stories." Because of her careful observations and recordkeeping of Alonso's engagement in play that is meaningful to him, Ms. Blessing can build on his existing knowledge and skills and is better able to address the next steps in his learning. (Adapted from "Assessment in Kindergarten: Meeting Children Where They Are," page 66)

This excerpt highlights the significance of authentic, observation-based assessment practices as the fundamental approach to understanding children's learning. At times, it might appear that assessment and teaching conflict with one another, competing for the precious time you spend with your kindergartners. Other times, it may be a smooth and enjoyable process, like in the example above, in which you capture assessment data authentically and use it to inform your next steps. Often, assessment decisions are outside of your control. Regardless, you can effectively support children's learning and development only when you understand what each child already knows and can do.

Developmentally appropriate kindergarten assessment

> Is integrated with teaching and learning

> Is purposeful and strategic

> Is appropriate for intended purposes and populations

> Is responsive to individual children and involves them

> Is inclusive of families (NAEYC 2022)

To make good decisions, you need good data, and you need to collect and analyze it often. Informal, observation-based assessment practices, such as anecdotal recordings, work samples, checklists, interviews, and performance tasks, "provide a well-rounded picture of development" and inform daily teaching and learning (NAEYC 2019a, 8). This includes data gathered from families, who are important partners in the assessment process. In addition, teachers use formal assessment practices such as screeners, diagnostic benchmarks, and summative assessments. By employing a balanced approach that combines formal and informal assessment methods, teachers can accurately track children's progress, identify learning gaps, and tailor instruction accordingly.

Teachers make the best decisions they can with the assessment data at hand. "Assessment results are estimates, at best. Teachers must regard them as tentative, subject to error, and subject to revision on the basis of additional information" (McAfee, Leong, & Bodrova 2016, 27). In the opening vignette, Ms. Blessing thought that Alonso was at one spot along a learning trajectory, but by observing him while working with blocks, she realized that he was further along. This isn't too surprising, since young children's development and learning proceed unevenly, often in spurts and regressions. Because Ms. Blessing carefully observed her children on a regular basis and collected data using a variety of methods, she was able to uncover this information about Alonso quickly and modify his learning goals.

There will be times when a teacher's own implicit biases cloud what they see and interpret. Generalizations are made based on personal experiences, beliefs, and values, often subconsciously (Gilliam et al. 2016). Reflective teachers recognize these generalizations and how they may be affecting their perception of a child—and seek to change their own behaviors first rather than expect a child to change (NAEYC 2019a). These practices are particularly important when working with children with disabilities, children who need extra challenges, and children whose social identities differ from the teacher's. Fair assessment practices help to prevent any unintended discrimination and ensure that major decisions are not based on limited data.

Thoughtful assessment practices not only inform teaching strategies but also promote a supportive, inclusive learning environment that nurtures the holistic development of young learners.

READ AND REFLECT

As you read the chapters in this section, consider and evaluate your own classroom practices using these reflection questions.

"Authentic Assessment and Playful Learning: Purposeful Assessment of Children's Understanding" describes the cyclical process of assessment and highlights the importance of children's active involvement in the assessment process. **Consider:** How might the methods described in this chapter support all learners in the assessment process?

"Observing, Planning, Guiding: How an Intentional Teacher Meets Standards Through Play" describes how observation-based assessment practices are incorporated in children's play and intentionally planned playful learning experiences. **Consider:** How might the

strategies shared in this chapter help you incorporate observation-based assessment practices within playful learning activities you already offer?

"Assessment in Kindergarten: Meeting Children Where They Are" offers specific strategies to collect authentic observation-based assessment data that is relevant, meaningful, and helpful to daily instructional decisions. **Consider:** What strategies described in this chapter are you using in your own classroom? What strategies might you consider incorporating?

"Assessing Young Children in the Inclusive Classroom: Using Data to Create Equitable and Joyful Learning Experiences for All" describes how assessment data are used to make instructional decisions, with particular emphasis on children with disabilities. **Consider:** How can the methods used in this chapter enhance how you use data to inform instruction in your classroom?

"Adding Play and Hands-On Learning into the Kindergarten Classroom: Balancing Mandated Curricula and Assessments with Developmentally Appropriate Practice" looks at the authors' struggles and provides strategies for bringing more balance to a potentially unbalanced system. **Consider:** What strategies presented might you use to provide additional balance to your own assessment program?

NEXT STEPS

1. Make a list of informal and formal assessment practices you use regularly. Do you consider your assessment system balanced, with more emphasis on authentic, observation-based practices? If not, identify a strategy to help you create a more balanced approach.

2. Identify three to five playful learning activities you use in your classroom. Consider how you can best capture authentic assessment data as you observe children engaged in those activities. Choose one of the activities and an assessment strategy, and prepare to gather data when you next introduce the activity.

3. How do you include children in the assessment process? Set a goal to increase children's involvement. Seek input from colleagues and gather feedback from the children and families.

References for the chapters in this part can be accessed online at NAEYC.org/dap-focus-kindergarten.

CHAPTER 10

Authentic Assessment and Playful Learning

Purposeful Assessment of Children's Understanding

Kimberly T. Nesbitt, Elias Blinkoff, and Kathy Hirsh-Pasek

What do we hope to learn when we assess young children? One purpose of assessment is to help educators determine if the children are really learning what they want them to learn. Unfortunately, the US education system has historically emphasized narrowly construed test scores that restrict views of child success. One consequence of this testing movement is that teachers narrow their focus on reading and math instruction aligned with annual tests (Berliner 2011). While reading and math are very important, it is critical to document children's knowledge and skills across an array of outcomes. In this chapter, we discuss authentic assessment, a broader, *whole-child* approach that recognizes children's social and emotional skills and mastery of academic content as complementary. Authentic assessment allows teachers to see the learning in children's everyday environments—at home, in school, and in the community—and enables children to show their learning in a variety of age-appropriate, culturally sensitive ways that reflect knowledge gained inside and outside the classroom. Authentic assessment is integrated into learning, not a separate activity. Through systematic, formative observations of learning as it occurs, teachers capture valuable, real-time information about children's learning processes (Scott-Little, with Reschke 2022).

Consider the example of kindergartners engaging in playful learning to create a veterinary clinic after staff from a local animal rescue organization visit their classroom. What might their teacher authentically assess while observing this play? Let's look at some of the skills and behaviors related to nationally recognized education standards that appear in these naturally occurring moments.

Playful Learning and Guided Play

Play lies on a continuum ranging from self-directed play (sometimes referred to as free or child-initiated play) to guided play to playful instruction. The distinction between these learning contexts is determined by whether an activity (1) has an explicit learning goal, (2) is initiated by children or an adult, and (3) is directed by children or an adult (Zosh et al. 2022). In self-directed play, children play together freely without constraints set by adults. In playful instruction, children complete an activity where the learning goal and process are determined and directed by the teacher. The children are not completely passive, but they are limited by the teacher's directions. Guided play lies in the middle. The activity is facilitated by a teacher to achieve an explicit learning goal. This may occur when the teacher sets up the activity, or when they support their students' deeper learning through questions or prompts. Throughout guided play, children maintain choice and agency to direct their learning (Weisberg et al. 2016). Evidence from the interdisciplinary science of learning indicates that guided play is uniquely suited to support children's academic achievement (e.g., Skene et al. 2022).

Children who are pretending to run a veterinary clinic are engaging in the following learning experiences, which are all aligned with existing content standards (National Council for the Social Studies 2010; NGA Center for Best Practices & CCSSO 2010; NGSS Lead States 2013):

› Collaborating to identify the resources needed to open their clinic requires children to

  • Participate in shared research and writing projects (Common Core W.K.7)

  • Follow agreed-upon rules for discussions (SL.K.1.A)

› Completing patient intake forms requires children to

  • Print upper- and lowercase letters (L.K.1.A)

  • Use words and phrases acquired through conversations and readings (L.K.6)

› Weighing animals requires children to

  • Describe measurable attributes of objects (K.MD.A.1)

  • Understand the relationship between numbers and quantities (K.CC.B.4)

› Identifying what the animals need to be healthy requires children to

  • Represent the relationship between the needs of different animals and the places they live (NGSS K-ESS3-1)

› Creating the clinic requires children to understand

  • The interactions among individuals, groups, and institutions and how people organize the production, distribution, and consumption of goods and services (National Curriculum Standards for Social Studies Theme 7)

Changing the lens on how you view naturally occurring moments in the classroom allows you to highlight real skills that children are learning—real skills that emerge in a well-defined context or theme. The authentic assessment in this example occurs within the holistic instruction of playful learning and guided play, permitting an equally broad evaluation of learning in action as it unfolds in context (for more information on playful learning pedagogy, see Blinkoff

et al., 2023; Hirsh-Pasek et al. 2020, 2022; Nesbitt et al. 2023; Zosh et al. 2022). When children engage in guided play, teachers observe and may capture an array of content outcomes, as demonstrated in the previous example.

 Authentic assessments seek to identify children's strengths and provide a well-rounded picture of development.

The *What of* Assessment: Measurement of the Knowledge and Skills That Matter

Content areas such as reading and math are important subjects to assess, but holistic instruction requires complementary holistic assessment (Darling-Hammond, Wise, & Klein 2019). Therefore, authentic assessment of children's learning should encompass social, emotional, physical, and cognitive development (NAEYC & NAECS/SDE 2003). The 6 Cs skills developed by Golinkoff and Hirsh-Pasek (2016)—collaboration, communication, content, critical thinking, creative innovation, and confidence—support this perspective (also see Hirsh-Pasek et al. 2020, 2022; Nesbitt et al. 2023). Informed by evidence from the science of learning, the 6 Cs encompass a breadth of skills that include, but go beyond, content mastery to help all students reach their goals, inside and outside the classroom (Golinkoff & Hirsh-Pasek 2016; Hirsh-Pasek et al. 2022). State education policy is now beginning to reflect this broader perspective on student outcomes, including social, emotional, and approaches to learning skills. For example, the Pennsylvania Learning Standards for Early Childhood—Kindergarten aim for children to

› Explore and ask questions to seek meaningful information (AL.1 K.A)

› Accomplish challenging tasks by employing familiar and new strategies (AL.2 K.C)

> Engage in reciprocal communication with adults and peers (16.2 K.C) (Office of Child Development and Early Learning 2016)

The *How* of Assessment: Developmentally Appropriate Assessment

What is assessed is critical. So too is *how* children are assessed. The world, including the United States, is a vibrant multiethnic, multiracial, multilingual, and multicultural setting. Since the goal of assessment should be to promote learning and growth for *all* children, assessments must be designed to yield information that is valid and fair without bias. Children need ample opportunities to learn and to demonstrate their knowledge through assessments that are relevant and meaningful to them (Nasir et al. 2021). It is essential that assessments be culturally responsive (Gay 2018; NAEYC 2019a) and accessible to all students across backgrounds. Teachers must be purposeful in collecting reliable and valid information about their students to minimize bias and ensure that they are effectively measuring learning and development.

 Recognize the potential of your own culture and background affecting your judgment when observing, documenting, and assessing children's behavior, learning, or development.

Quality education also extends beyond the classroom in multiple directions (e.g., Nasir et al. 2021). It is found in collaboration between children, educators, and families. Assessments derived through such collaborations are likely to be meaningful and relevant to all involved. Learning takes place within social, cultural, linguistic, and historical contexts that must be considered in assessment design and implementation (NAEYC 2020). For example, a dual language learner might show their understanding of a concept when evaluated through their primary language or nonverbally (e.g., by demonstration or drawing).

Teachers must synthesize information from multiple observations and contexts (e.g., multiple lessons of sorting and classifying objects), then evaluate

whether they have the information needed (e.g., did a child demonstrate their understanding of a functional pair?). While numbers gathered from individual tests, assignments, rubrics, and checklists are informative, they never offer a complete picture of students' strengths and needs unless they are considered together.

Summative and Formative Assessment

Assessment can be summative or formative. Summative assessments evaluate student learning and knowledge at the *end* of an instructional period. Formative assessments allow educators to gain information to shape students' *future* learning, measuring their progress toward goals. Because they assess learning through multiple lenses across multiple access points, both summative and formative assessments provide valuable information and should be used together to gain a comprehensive understanding of children's knowledge and skills (Black & William 2010).

Summative and formative authentic assessment can be carried out across all forms of instruction, including self-directed play (e.g., documenting a collaborative conversation between children as they build a block structure) and direct instruction (e.g., assessing and documenting how a student participates in a whole group read-aloud lesson on making predictions). However, authentic assessment is wonderfully applicable to guided play activities. As in the opening example of the classroom veterinary clinic, during these experiences teachers can step back and observe, employing authentic assessment of children's learning as it occurs.

The Cyclical Process of Formative Assessment

Formative assessment is an ongoing, cyclical process. First, educators design lessons that align with a clear set of objectives and goals, whether based on national, state, or district standards. In the example of the veterinary clinic, the goal could be for children to sort clinic supplies based on physical properties (e.g., size or texture) and then on functional properties (e.g., items for weighing or items for mending wounds) to meet the Common Core standard to "classify objects into given categories" (K.MD.B.3). During planning, educators also identify *how* to assess children's learning and progress toward established goals and objectives, including a breadth of skills beyond content (e.g., the 6 Cs). Assessments may include informal recording of moment-to-moment experiences or more formal assignments. For example, students may be asked to draw a pair of objects that are physically alike and another pair of objects that share the same function. With a clear vision of the goals and methods for assessing learning, the next step is to implement the lesson and observe and document students' learning, which is easier in guided play because the teacher can step back while the children direct the experience.

Finally, it is essential to share assessment findings with families, children, and other educators, highlighting children's growth and their future learning goals. This can be done through traditional approaches, such as report cards and conferences, but also through video clips and photographs. This technology gives families a near-real-time insight into their children's learning (e.g., a video of children working in the veterinary clinic). When families are included as partners in the interpretation of findings about their children's learning, they and their children's teachers can work collaboratively to reflect, plan, and make decisions about how best to support learning. Families also learn to see their children more fully when teachers enable them to see their children in varied contexts.

Types of Authentic Assessment in Kindergarten

Methods of authentic assessment include educators' anecdotal observations of students, systematic documentation of students' performance in classroom activities (e.g., through checklists), structured interviews, and collection of work samples in portfolios.

Anecdotal Records

One of the simplest authentic assessment methods is writing anecdotal records of children's behaviors. These brief notes on specific behaviors and language provide concrete evidence of a child's understanding. Take the experience of students working together to use standardized and unstandardized measurement tools (e.g., rulers and Unifix cubes) to compare three-dimensional objects found in their classroom. Simply saying that a student "worked effectively with others" does not provide details about the context, nor does it provide evidence for the statement. On the other hand, your observation that a child "worked with a partner to develop a solution to compare rectangles based on understanding that objects can be different sizes based on the side you choose" is concrete. Anecdotal records do not document everything; they focus on specific, relevant behaviors that align with the learning objectives of an activity. Consider using technology to supplement time-consuming note taking with videos or photos that offer a snapshot of the child's day, and share these with families.

Checklists, Frequency Counts, and Rubrics

When you identify a particular concrete skill or goal to measure, it may be helpful to transition from anecdotal records to more systematic data collection methods. These could include checklists, frequency counts, and rubrics. Checklists can be as straightforward as creating a predetermined list of concepts or objectives and indicating whether each one occurred. For example, you might use a checklist to track whether a child "continues a conversation through multiple exchanges" or "asks an open-ended question" (e.g., a child asks a peer, "How did you get that to work?"). Both items would document specific behaviors that demonstrate achievement of the objective. This approach can be extended to be a frequency count where the behavior is noted each time it is observed. Frequency counts are particularly helpful to document whether behaviors are increasing or decreasing over time.

Some child behaviors are important to document but may be too complex for a simple checklist or frequency count. In this case, consider using a rubric—a rating scale that is created to evaluate the quality of children's behaviors, responses, or products. Rubrics are also useful for documenting student growth. They usually contain evaluative criteria, quality definitions for those criteria at levels of achievement, and a scoring strategy (Herman, Aschbacher, & Winters 1992).

	COLLABORATION	COMMUNICATION	CONTENT	CRITICAL THINKING	CREATIVE INNOVATION	CONFIDENCE
LEVEL 4	BUILDING IT TOGETHER	TELL A JOINT STORY	EXPERTISE	EVIDENCE	VISION	DARE TO FAIL
LEVEL 3	BACK AND FORTH	DIALOGUE	MAKING CONNECTIONS	OPINIONS	VOICE	CALCULATED RISKS
LEVEL 2	SIDE BY SIDE	SHOW AND TELL	WIDE BREADTH/ SHALLOW UNDERSTANDING	TRUTHS DIFFER	MEANS-END	WHERE DO I STAND?
LEVEL 1	ON MY OWN	RAW EMOTION	EARLY LEARNING/ SITUATION SPECIFIC	SEEING IS BELIEVING	EXPERIMENTATION	BARREL ON

The 6 Cs. For each of the 6 Cs—collaboration, communication, content, critical thinking, creative innovation, and confidence—progress can be categorized within four distinct levels, with level 4 being the most advanced. The 6 Cs represent a dynamic system that permits students to exhibit different levels of skills in different learning environments.

Adapted, by permission, from Golinkoff & Hirsh-Pasek (2016).

The figure above provides a sample rubric developed to capture the dynamic 6 Cs skills (Golinkoff & Hirsh-Pasek 2016; Hirsh-Pasek et al. 2020). The first level of collaboration, "On My Own," would be assigned if a child takes action "without paying attention to others, seeking out help, or noticing if [they] receive help" (Hirsh-Pasek et al. 2020, 21). Each level from 2 to 4 includes a similar definition (see Hirsh-Pasek et al. 2020). This rubric is easily adaptable to track students' skills across activities and learning environments.

Structured Interviews

Engaging in a structured interview, or a one-on-one conversation, with a child offers more information on how that child understands content. It is important not only to know that a child is able to identify a viable solution or come up with the correct answer but also to understand *how* they came to their conclusion. Some children excel in math but cannot show you how they got the answer. Understanding the steps that lead a child toward a goal enables you to help them transfer this learning to new, more complex problems. Asking a child "Tell me how you figured that out" gives insight into their thinking.

Portfolios

Portfolios offer yet another way to capture children's learning that fits with playful learning. A thoughtful collection of children's works over a specified period of the year, sometimes referred to as *journey books,* can document growth and inspire students to take pride in their work. Selecting portfolio content should occur collaboratively between educators and students, leverage a variety of media to document learning and development, and serve as a record of what a student has learned and how the learning occurred. Children can engage in portfolio construction and presentation across subject areas.

Conclusion

Authentic assessment supports and extends kindergarten children's learning. Playful learning, and particularly guided play experiences, provide a unique window within which this assessment can occur. The approach enables ongoing, formative assessment to shape instruction, which should be considered in conjunction with summative assessments to ensure that you gather appropriate, meaningful examples of growth and learning in young children. *Regardless of the authentic assessment approach used, it is important to promote children's active involvement in the process.* Conversations and portfolios provide explicit opportunities for children to contribute to the assessment process, either by providing insights about their understanding and thinking or by helping identify works to be included in portfolios. The greater the opportunities for children to make their learning visible, the more invested they will be in the process and the more they will understand how assessment is a method for helping them and their teachers recognize their growth.

KIMBERLY T. NESBITT, PhD, is an associate professor in the Department of Human Development and Family Studies at the University of New Hampshire. Her work focuses on young children's cognitive development, with a particular focus on identifying instructional practices that enable young children from diverse backgrounds to learn and achieve in early education environments.

ELIAS BLINKOFF, PhD, is a postdoctoral fellow in the Department of Psychology and Neuroscience at Temple University. His research explores the intersection between the science of learning and educational practice and policy.

KATHY HIRSH-PASEK, PhD, is the Lefkowitz Faculty Fellow in Psychology at Temple University and a senior fellow at the Brookings Institution. Her research examines the development of early language and literacy and the role of play in learning and technology. She is the author of 17 books (including coauthor of the bestselling *Becoming Brilliant: What Science Tells Us About Raising Successful Children*) and hundreds of publications and has won numerous awards.

CHAPTER 11

Observing, Planning, Guiding

How an Intentional Teacher Meets Standards Through Play

Patricia McDonald

It is early in the day. Kris, one of my 22 kindergartners, is sharing with me her journal entry and drawing. After our talk, she walks to the carpet to play. She observes a group of children who have discovered that the magnifying glasses we used during this morning's math lesson to observe and describe attributes of two- and three-dimensional shapes can enlarge words found throughout the room. She then joins a group that is building a house out of blocks, carefully balancing different shapes on top of each other. After about 30 minutes, I announce it's time for our morning meeting. The class responds with, "Aww! Can't we keep playing?"

In my kindergarten classroom, I strive to provide an engaging environment where play is the prominent support for and means of learning. But in truth, I find it challenging. Earlier in my career, I used a didactic approach full of worksheets and drills because it was expected. While direct instruction is effective in certain contexts, I also know that play-based learning is essential for young children. Play encompasses knowledge building, problem solving, communicating, and collaborating (NAEYC 2020). Yet throughout my career, I've often felt the slight nudge toward "skills and drills." Even after 23 years as a teacher, I feel the tension between ensuring my students achieve specific benchmarks at certain times throughout the year and offering a more child-centered education that creates opportunities for exploration.

The educational emphasis on standards and high-stakes assessments places tremendous pressure on teachers and children, potentially leading to "adverse impact[s] . . . on young children and on instructional practices" (NAEYC 2020, 19). Considering the long lists of specific objectives that must be accomplished by the end of the year—usually without extended learning time or other additional resources—it is easy to understand why teachers

would be skeptical about devoting their limited class time to child-centered approaches to instruction. Child-directed, playful learning is often more challenging to plan and assess than teacher-directed learning, but if we value healthy child development across all domains and all content areas, we must find a balance in our classrooms (Hassinger-Das, Hirsh-Pasek, & Golinkoff 2017; NAEYC 2020).

The Teacher's Role

Deja and Lizbeth are buying items at the "grocery market," a project the children initiated and constructed after a social studies lesson on community. The children sorted grocery items, made discount signs, and set up a checkout area with bags and play money consisting of pennies and one-dollar bills. Today I see an opportunity to observe how or if the children are applying the math concepts we have learned this year. I walk over to Arun, the cashier, and ask, "How much are the grapes and one banana?" "Well," she replies, "the grapes are five cents, and the bananas are two cents." I hold out a handful of coins and say, "What is the total number of pennies that I need to give you?" Deja says, "Seven pennies. Five and two more equal seven, so you need to count out seven pennies."

During children's play, teachers are researchers, observing children to decide how to extend their learning both in the moment and by planning new play environments. As an educator, it is crucial to actively monitor, assess, and capitalize on opportunities to enhance students' learning (Taylor & Boyer 2020). By strategically expanding play and asking questions that challenge children's thinking, teachers create meaningful learning opportunities to help children draw an understanding between their observations, ideas, and judgments (Strasser & Bresson 2017). A mix of children's self-directed and guided play (in which the teacher has a learning goal that they help children move toward while children have agency to lead the experience) incorporated throughout the day provides learning opportunities as deliberate and logical as in any teacher-directed lesson. Additionally, preparing activities that are appropriate to the development of each child can provide a learning environment in which all children have a chance to learn in an enjoyable and captivating way (Leong & Bodrova 2012; Pyle & Danniels 2017).

> Curious, I watch David and Marco grab a stack of playing cards. They look tentatively at each other, then turn to me, saying, "We're not sure what to play." I show them a card game that allows practice with cooperation and further develops their number sense. I explain the need for a "caller" who distributes the cards and directs the other players when to flip over the top card of their deck. The player holding the card with the highest numerical value wins that round.

> Anna walks over and watches. "Would you like to play?" I ask. She smiles and joins in. After we play another round, I excuse myself from the game; the players all agree to vote on who will take my place as the caller. Anna is chosen, but it isn't long before I observe Marco throwing his cards on the floor, frustrated that Anna is telling him what to do. I remind the group about their vote, and they continue playing.

> Later, when another child joins in, the same problem arises—but the children do not need my help this time. Marco explains that only one person is the caller.

Observing, assessing, and seizing opportunities to enhance students' learning is a crucial responsibility of a teacher. As a guide, educators can encourage play, broaden students' perspectives, and create more opportunities for learning (Taylor & Boyer 2020). During play-based learning, teachers are often subtle participants or gentle guides seeking to enrich or expand the present experience (Zosh et al. 2022). With the card game, I reinforced an important math concept (comparing number values) and supported the children's growing abilities to work with others and regulate their feelings. Thus, setting time aside for play resulted in a teachable moment when David and Marco asked for my help. However, such opportunities do not always occur. As a teacher dedicated to providing significant amounts of playtime every day,

I continually ask myself how can I extend the play experience that I'm watching to connect it to the standards I'm required to teach (Clements & Wright 2022). However, I realize that play in the classroom is often evaluated in connection to educational goals. For example, self-directed play is recommended for social development and child directedness, whereas structured play is specific to teaching skills (Pyle & Danniels 2017). Therefore, recognizing the value of self-directed play for self-regulation and social development while keeping the focus on standards is a continuum that I encounter every day.

 Providing different levels of support to children based on individual strengths and prior knowledge is the most equitable approach because it helps to meet each child's needs.

From Theory to Reality

Some may argue that play is an inappropriate means of achieving standards. However, many teachers have observed that children can meet and exceed standards through playful learning that combines open-ended experiences, child-directed initiatives, and teacher-guided activities (Zosh et al. 2022). However, facilitating a play-based learning approach while incorporating academic expectations is a challenge many teachers confront (Pyle & Danniels 2017). Through experience, I have learned that there are three primary factors I need to address to bring play and standards together: being intentional in crafting experiences, identifying children's developmental needs, and assessing growth.

Intentionally Crafting Experiences

To address specific academic standards, I sometimes introduce a concept with a whole group activity, then establish an environment that supports further exploration during self-directed playtime. I consciously determine the purpose and intentionality of all activities (including play), asking myself, "Do all materials and activities connect to the standard intended to be learned? How do I modify the planned experience to connect to the children's prior knowledge and allow each child to engage?" When organizing activities, it's crucial to consider how I can make them meaningful and inclusive for all children yet connect to the academic content I am responsible for facilitating (Taylor & Boyer 2020).

An example of my effort to use play as a primary means of learning is a lesson in which I introduced the concept of sink or float. We were investigating materials and motion in science, explicitly developing and using models of wood production, which prompted a child-directed discussion about wooden boats and the number of passengers a wood raft would hold. I engaged the children in making boats out of foil as a model and seeing how many dice it took to sink their boats. Density and shape, not size, was introduced as the determining factor of an object floating. After giving a demonstration to the whole group, I made the activity an independent center for the children to explore. I watched as they eagerly tried to make their boats float while adding the dice, leading to revisions of their initial designs. Afterward, I reflected on the experience and noted that while the beginning of the activity was a group demonstration, it motivated the children to explore their questions independently and to investigate and challenge their assumptions.

I am confident that the children enjoyed and learned from this activity—but was this an example of play? If play is open ended, child selected, and voluntary, then play did not happen until after my demonstration. However, my modeling of the playful learning activity sparked the children's curiosity and provided some basic concepts to investigate. By having the time, space, and materials to explore further and experiment independently, the children engaged (albeit unknowingly) with science and engineering standards (i.e., making observations, gathering information, and using tools). They tried out their ideas through a playful experience. As a result, the children acquired new knowledge about developing and designing potential solutions and new language. This allowed me to create more intentional plans for future learning.

Teachers can think about learning experiences not as being *either* play *or* teacher directed but as being on a spectrum of playful learning, from self-directed play to guided play to games (Pyle & Danniels 2017; Zosh et al. 2022). Looking at playful learning experiences in this way allows teachers to consider various activities that meet children's needs and interests, match specific learning goals, and support children's social and

cultural contexts. Although children may need to fully understand the broader ideas they are exploring while playing, play provides experiences that contribute to their present knowledge and abilities that they will rely on when solving problems in the future (NAEYC & NCTM [2002] 2010).

Identifying Developmental Needs

One of the most significant yet challenging facets of teaching kindergarten is accepting that individual development has its own time frame. To honor individual development, teachers do their best to implement culturally, linguistically, and developmentally appropriate activities for each child (NAEYC 2020). Play is beneficial because it allows for more variation than many teacher-directed lessons. It allows children to solidify concepts and understandings that are new to them, provides opportunities to practice the new skills in meaningful ways until they are mastered, and supports them in extending their learning with new applications or more complex ideas. As children vary in their cognitive, linguistic, social, emotional, and physical abilities and needs, a flexible approach to teaching and learning—including sufficient time for self-directed and guided play—is essential. One way I applied this understanding was by modifying my classroom schedule to allow the children to practice their recently acquired puzzle-solving strategies.

> Four children walk over to a puzzle on a table. They try to put the pieces together through random trial and error. Seeing that they have no strategy to solve the puzzle, I initiate a conversation on how to use the different attributes of the puzzle pieces (e.g., shapes of the lines) to connect pieces and how to look for key images to determine the overall picture. Ten minutes later, the timer rings to clean up. "But we didn't finish!" they tell me.

> Realizing the high-quality learning they were engaged in while working on the puzzle (an activity that the children chose), I tell them that they will have more time later in the day to finish. At lunch, I rearrange the schedule to offer more time for intentional choices and flexibility rather than defined and required work. Had I not been able to rearrange the schedule, I was prepared to guide them in problem solving and lead them to find a

solution of leaving the puzzle as is, knowing they could trust that they could come back to it the following day.

Knowing that a developmentally appropriate environment does not mean giving the children complete control of the classroom, I focus on designing active and engaging choices. "An activity that contains teacher-directed elements can be child-centered in nature" (Pyle & Danniels 2017, 286). For example, I incorporate math games (such as board and card games) into our morning meeting and restructured recess to allow more time for outdoor exploration (including science investigations). Occasionally I make available materials such as paint, stamps, and musical instruments for the children to use at their will during self-directed play. Sometimes my observation of the children may lead to a more individualized modification of routines, such as allowing a few minutes of individual quiet time to read or play for the child who prefers not to participate in group work. For a child who appears overwhelmed with choices, I might provide more specific materials based on that child's interests.

Assessing Growth

My instructional approach is based on my knowledge of children's development and effective teaching practices. However, my ongoing observations and understanding of the children's interests, abilities, efforts, and social and cultural contexts determine the direction of learning and specific activities. Assessment includes seeking evidence of children's learning and honestly reflecting on my practice. I regularly ask myself whether I have an effective instructional plan that is responsive to the children's strengths and needs and, if so, what I can expect the children's growth to look like after completing the learning experience I provided.

In kindergarten, teachers use various informal evaluation tools, such as portfolios, running records, and anecdotal notes and narratives, and formal assessments that measure the acquisition and application of skills and concepts (Taylor & Boyer 2020). As I have shifted toward play-based learning and crafted more time for child-directed activities, I have carefully observed children's interests, efforts, and growth. Over time, I have found that observing play and conducting skill-specific assessments provide well-balanced information. However, I must know the

purpose of play and the learning I want the students to acquire before I determine my role in the play environment. This helps me plan experiences that are appropriate, flexible, challenging, and self-guided.

 By maximizing children's choice, promoting wonder and enthusiasm for learning, and leveraging joy, playful learning pedagogies support development across domains and content areas and increase learning relative to more didactic methods.

Reflection

In my experience, there are times when trying to make academic standards meaningful while guiding and extending children's interests and curiosity feels like a walk in the dark. In putting aside the security of worksheets and instead trusting in the guidance provided by the children, I find myself wondering daily, what did the children gain today from being in my class? What opportunities for learning might I have missed? How did I reinforce the connection between intentionality, developmentally appropriate activities, and assessment? Based on my observations, what did the children learn from their play? My answers are almost always more insightful than when I use worksheets for instruction.

Teachers' professional knowledge of child development and individual children's abilities, needs, and experiences directly affects instruction and the creation of an effective play-based learning environment (NAEYC 2020). When teachers connect academic standards to play experiences, they free themselves to support the overall development of each child.

PATRICIA MCDONALD, PhD, a former kindergarten teacher, is an instructional systems specialist for K–5 mathematics. She is dedicated to assisting educators and school leaders with implementing active and engaging learning experiences that promote transferable skills across various subjects. She also advocates for play-based learning to be accessible to all students.

CHAPTER 12

Assessment in Kindergarten
Meeting Children Where They Are

Amy D. Blessing

Over the 20 years I have been a kindergarten teacher, assessment has changed dramatically. When I first began teaching, educators' observations and self-made assessments were honored as appropriate ways to document young children's growth and mastery. My colleagues and I used our own assessments and observations to plan instruction based on what our students needed. We had the flexibility to evaluate children in areas that were appropriate for them. For example, we could delay assessing reading skills if a child did not yet show an understanding of the difference between letters, words, and numbers.

Assessment in today's kindergarten classrooms, unfortunately, looks at times like what we would expect in upper-grade classrooms, with proctors and secure testing materials. Teachers are often not allowed to assess their own students (to protect the integrity of the results), and the results are sometimes used to measure teacher performance (whether or not the assessments have been designed and validated for use in high-stakes decisions).

Timed assessments and scripted directions, which must be read word for word, provide valuable information but offer no flexibility for young learners. Even when children are just beginning to learn English, I am required to assess them in English—according to the script, not to their needs. I have sat with many frustrated children, some near tears, as I asked them to read sight words during their second week of kindergarten. I will never forget the defeat on one child's face as she looked up at me with a quivering chin and said, "But I can't read." Despite how positive and nonchalant I tried to be during that assessment, assuring her that I did not expect her to read the words, the formal assessment experience affected this child's confidence and her excitement for learning.

It would be easy to have a sweeping negative view of assessments in the current climate. Like many teachers, I have felt dread when someone mentioned assessments. But I know that long before this age of high-stakes accountability, intentional teachers were developing and using assessments as appropriate, powerful tools in their toolboxes.

Intentional teachers gather data that are needed to guide instruction, ensuring that all children grow and learn at the right pace. They use assessments to find their students' strengths and to figure out which areas they need to target for early intervention. They use varying methods of observation and assessment to find out what young learners are able to do, so that they can help them progress. In this chapter I discuss varied strategies that are important for all young children, but especially for dual language learners (DLLs).

School and Classroom Background

I teach kindergarten in a rural, high-poverty school in North Carolina that has a diverse student population, including children who speak a language other than English at home and whose parents (and often other family members) are migrant workers, often coming from Mexico. Most of my DLL students live in homes where Spanish is the primary language; some children are learning both Spanish and a dialect of Mixtec at home, and these students communicate in Spanish (and in their emergent English) in the classroom. Many of our migrant families return to the area year after year during spring and early summer. These families travel up and down the East Coast, as well as to areas such as Michigan, to work in agriculture. My experiences as a teacher in this setting have shown me the importance of digging deeper to discover the strengths of my students, to provide opportunities for them to show what they know, beyond scripted or standardized assessments.

For many years I served as a North Carolina demonstration classroom teacher, which meant that my role extended beyond my classroom work with students. My classroom was open to teachers and other educators for professional development in the form of full-day guided observations. Although the official program is no longer up and running, I continue to have an open door to my classroom and have stayed connected to my fellow demonstration teachers as we strive to provide the most appropriate and engaging experiences for our young learners, including how to balance effective assessment practices.

Intentional Assessments Prevent Unintentional Errors

I often begin the school year with children who speak little to no English. These students struggle on our required early literacy assessment—the previously mentioned assessments that I am required to administer in English, word for word, in September—and are automatically labeled *at risk*. My colleagues and I are able to use the data from these assessments to help identify students who need more support and interventions in literacy skills. The danger with relying solely on scripted, inflexible assessments, however, is the labeling and grouping of children with a broad stroke. We might target skills based on these test results without fully realizing what our children need.

It would be easy for me to group all of these children who are "at risk" together in the same skill-based intervention group because they all have the same score on the reading assessment that focuses on book and print concepts. But for me, the mandated assessment is just the beginning. I dig deeper to find out what else I need to know to provide opportunities for growth for each of my students. I have learned valuable information by using my own observations and assessments to find the knowledge and skills the children *do* have. With book and print concept inventories from the works of literacy researcher Marie Clay (1993), along with my own very limited Spanish skills, I try to assess my Spanish-speaking students in their native language as much as possible.

Our school has been fortunate to have an English as a second language (ESL) teacher who speaks Spanish. She serves all of the emergent bilingual children at our K–5 school. I try to assess what I can using my limited Spanish skills and then use the ESL teacher as a resource to dig deeper when needed.

More Nuanced Assessments

Administering my own additional assessments with the children who had scored similarly on the book and print concepts assessment confirmed that a number of these children did not, in fact, know any print concepts. They were unfamiliar with holding a book, turning the pages, and using pictures to enhance meaning. It was evident they'd had very limited early literacy experiences, even in their home language. But I also found out that some of these students who were "at risk" *were* familiar with book and print concepts. My assessments showed that they understood the difference between the front and back of a book, knew the difference between print and pictures, tracked left to right when looking at the text, and looked closely at the pictures on each page. Some even knew that a period at the end of the sentence signifies a stop. Their at-risk scores on the required assessment were not representative of poor early literacy knowledge and skills, but rather, were indicative of their emerging English language skills. They clearly had engaged in many literacy experiences with their families before entering kindergarten. While all of these students had the same results on the mandated assessment, my more nuanced assessments provided valuable information that enabled me to target the children's very different needs.

To ensure that I have all necessary information, I begin each school year with informal checklists assessing children's alphabet and numeral recognition, knowledge of colors and shapes, and rote and object counting abilities. I have found that this is important for all of the children, not just the DLLs. For example, I often have students who speak only English who are not able to count past five or to identify basic colors and shapes. I observe and assess these children frequently in the first weeks and months of kindergarten to see if and to what extent they are making progress. That helps me determine whether their limited knowledge is due to lack of exposure to these concepts—a problem I can address—or whether there are other issues, such as cognitive or developmental delays, that would require additional assessments and supports by specialists.

One pitfall I have learned to watch out for is not giving my DLL students the same attention to their cognitive and developmental growth by solely focusing on their language acquisition. I once again gain valuable information by evaluating which DLLs can identify numbers, shapes, and colors in their first language and which children cannot. That way, I can provide struggling students with the same opportunities for individualized early interventions as their English-only peers, which may include early math interventions or speech articulation interventions. I do not let them slip through the cracks simply because of their limited English.

The ESL teacher, Ms. Worley, and I regularly share observations with each other. Her fluent Spanish skills allow her to find out more about our Spanish-speaking students' strengths and needs in their home language. While she focuses in Spanish and English on building the conceptual knowledge of the DLLs with the most challenges (and on determining whether additional supports are called for), I target English vocabulary with the students who already know basic shapes and colors in their first language.

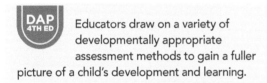
Educators draw on a variety of developmentally appropriate assessment methods to gain a fuller picture of a child's development and learning.

Intentional Assessments Throughout the Day

Doing my own flexible assessments enables me to collect information about students that goes beyond the scripted, mandated assessments. I do observations and keep running records that allow me to look at each student as a whole child, including a child's approaches to learning, language development and communication, cognitive development, emotional and social development, and health and physical development.

What I find most useful is systematically observing children throughout the day in the natural learning environment. This practice, which all intentional teachers use, does not interrupt instruction and is valuable because it provides additional information about children beyond summative or diagnostic data. The challenge comes in recording or documenting what I learn from watching the children so that I can reflect on the information and use it to guide and differentiate instruction. Current technology aids in information gathering. Photos and videos are quick and easy ways to document student learning. Some free software platforms (such as Seesaw, available at https://web.seesaw.me) even empower children to use technology to document their learning. (The book *Digital Tools for Learning, Creating, and Thinking*, by Victoria Fantozzi [2022], has more ideas on ways children can do this.)

Assessing Children During Engaging Play

I have found that my classroom schedule and environment play a large role in my ability to collect data throughout the day. Large blocks of uninterrupted time, when children can play and make choices, set the stage for gathering meaningful information about each of my young learners. When children can choose where they are going to play, they tend to pick areas where they feel safe and experience some confidence. This is a great opportunity to observe their skills and strengths. *North Carolina Guide for the Early Years* states that "preschool and kindergarten children are more likely to perform at their best when engaged in interesting and meaningful classroom projects they choose themselves—such as real reading and writing activities rather than only skills testing" (Public Schools of North Carolina 2009, 79). Anecdotal notes, photos, and videos are useful for documenting children's abilities. They provide additional evidence, especially when children's oral language does not fully showcase their learning (NAEYC 2022). This may arise among both DLLs and monolingual English speakers, such as children with speech and language impairments or autism.

I have had several DLLs who were not able to retell a story in English. This was a concern because they would need to retell a simple story on the state reading assessment. One student, Alonso, stands out in my mind. Ms. Worley and I had been observing him closely for possible developmental delays that might be hidden by his limited English proficiency. Alonso could not orally retell familiar stories that we had read together over and over. It would have been easy to believe that he lacked an understanding of sense of story and that his receptive and productive language skills were lacking—possibly in both Spanish and English. Observing him during play provided me with valuable information that debunked these assumptions.

Alonso loved the block center and, even with limited English, was able to engage with his peers. He had confidence when playing in this center and felt comfortable taking risks. One time when he was in the block center, he built three small structures. When I asked him about the structures, he said they were the pig houses. I realized he was retelling *The Three Little Pigs*, a book we had been reading. I sat and observed Alonso as he used small wolf and pig figurines to act out the story, completely in order, including the beginning, middle, and ending.

Alonso used simple, key repetitive phrases in English from the story (such as "I'll huff and blow house down") and showed an understanding of character and setting. I knew then that his receptive language skills were stronger than I had thought and that, while he was not able to successfully retell a story orally with many details in English, he did in fact understand the story we'd read together and had a concept of story sequence. I updated Alonso's learning target to

"building vocabulary in order to retell simple stories," replacing the assumed learning goal of sequencing stories. Because of my careful observations and record keeping of Alonso's engagement in play that was meaningful to him, I was better able to address his needs.

Another example of choice and play creating great opportunities for information gathering is when students play with their peers. When my DLLs play with peers who are bilingual, they show more confidence and I am then better able to observe their strengths. I recently observed a student who did not speak English playing a counting game with a bilingual peer; both were counting and conversing in Spanish. I listened to and saw their oral and object counting skills while they played. The student who was just beginning to learn English performed much better in this setting than he would have if I had called him over to a table and asked him to count. In the midst of play, he was not as self-aware or worried that he did not yet know how to count in English as he would have been if he were trying to answer my questions.

Asking Probing Questions

Early childhood educators are skilled at asking questions in different ways to find out what young learners know and understand. In many instances I've had to reframe questions asked by another staff member or an administrator so that my 5-year-old students comprehend what is being asked. Often the adult laughs and responds, "See, that's why you're the kindergarten teacher and I'm not!" Teachers must use this same skill when observing their students by intentionally reframing questions to elicit the information they are looking for. There are times when I can simply ask questions and use the children's oral responses as evidence of learning, but there are other times, especially with DLLs, when I must break apart the question or say, "Show me." As I listen to my students explain what they are showing me, I gain valuable insights.

Several resources that promote effective practices in early childhood classrooms have helped me plan and set up environments that lend themselves to assessing and questioning throughout the day. Many research-based and teacher-tested strategies can be found in both NAEYC's position statement (2020) and book (2022) on developmentally appropriate practice. The *North Carolina Play to Learn Center*

Planning Guides and Posters (Public Schools of North Carolina 2023) is a collection of resources for planning center-based classrooms, including information on learning centers for art, block, books and listening, dramatic play, math, science, and writing. The planning guides explicitly describe how children may engage in each center and how intentional teachers can support their learning. They serve as a starting place for teachers to think about what types of skills are addressed and what types of data they could gather at different centers. The posters include standards for all development and learning domains that might be addressed when children are working in the centers. A quick glance at these standards serves as a reminder of how teachers can use centers as assessment tools. The posters also include several questions to ask, prompting teachers to use questioning as a way to gather information and promote learning. To access the planning guides and posters, visit www.dpi.nc.gov/districts-schools/classroom -resources/office-early-learning/kindergarten#Playto LearnCenterPlanningGuidesandPosters-3286.

You can also find examples of questions that extend children's thinking in the *North Carolina Guide for the Early Years* (Public Schools of North Carolina 2009; www.dpi.nc.gov/documents/publications/catalog/ kg106-ncguide-early-years/open). This resource is

Questions to Promote Children's Thinking

Creative Arts

- How are these alike or different?
- Is there a pattern in this?
- What do you think should happen next?
- What would happen if . . . ?

- Which is . . . (e.g., larger or smaller, louder or softer, brighter or darker)?
- What can you tell me about your work?
- How did you feel when you heard/saw that?
- How is this . . . (e.g., shape, sound, movement, phrase) different from the other one?

Block Play

- What other block shape might work there?
- How did you decide to put all those blocks together?
- It looks like you are all out of the long blocks. What else could you use to fill up the same space?

- Tell me about your building.
- How will the firefighters get into your building?
- How will people know which way to drive their cars on the road?
- Which animals will live in each part of your zoo?

Science

- What do you suppose would happen if . . . ?
- Do you have any ideas about how we might begin?
- What will you do next?
- Why do you think that?
- How did you figure that out?
- What changes do you see? What has changed the most?

- How do you know?
- What characteristics do the . . . (e.g., flower, caterpillar) have that make it a . . . (e.g., plant, insect)?
- Can you draw a picture of your findings? Can you add some words?
- Which holds more: the tall, thin jar or the short, fat one?

Adapted from *North Carolina Guide for the Early Years* (Public Schools of North Carolina 2009). Creative arts questions can be found on page 159, block center questions on page 139, and science questions on page 153 of that document.

older and more extensive, with a full chapter dedicated to a different learning center and a list of associated questions. I have adapted the lists of questions to make small charts that detail ways to check for understanding and place them in each center in my classroom (see "Questions to Promote Children's Thinking" on the previous page for a few examples). They serve as reminders not just to me but to my teacher assistant, interns, and volunteers as well. For example, questions to promote children's thinking in the math center include "What other ways can we show that?" "How can we do this differently?" "Tell me how you did that" "Why do you think that?" and "Tell me how you figured that out." Over the years, this shift in thinking has allowed both my teacher assistant and me to focus on the *process* of learning—not just on our students' finished products. In the art center, for example, the teacher assistant and I both make comments such as "You worked really hard on that. How did you come up with that idea?" instead of something more general, such as "That's a beautiful painting." For teachers who are struggling with how to uncover their students' thinking and understanding, all of these resources are great places to start.

AMY BLESSING, MEd, NBCT, is a kindergarten teacher in southeastern North Carolina. She has taught kindergarten for more than 24 years and has worked with statewide professional development initiatives as well as national organizations to effect change for children.

Conclusion

By focusing on flexible, ongoing, intentional assessments, teachers are better able to fully address their students' needs. My colleagues and I are ensuring that all of our young learners have the same opportunities to grow and succeed. My assessments allow me to focus on the children's strengths and dig deeper into their individual needs. This is true with all of my students and is especially true with my DLLs.

I hope that by sharing my experiences, I have motivated you to feel empowered to continue using a variety of formal and informal assessments as powerful tools in your toolbox. Step back when you feel overwhelmed by mandated assessments, particularly those that interrupt instructional time, and take inventory of the countless other ways you dig deeper to identify the strengths of your young students. They deserve nothing less.

CHAPTER 13

Assessing Young Children in the Inclusive Classroom

Using Data to Create Equitable and Joyful Learning Experiences for All

Christan Coogle and Heather Walter

Assessment data is critically important in people's everyday lives as it provides forms of information to help them make decisions—more specifically, data-informed decisions. For example, data such as body temperature can tell someone if they are sick and if they need to seek medical attention. Data kept by road surveyors can indicate whether new signage or traffic signals might be necessary to ensure safety. Similarly, engaging in assessment and examining student outcome data can help kindergarten educators make important decisions about their students.

Understanding children's unique strengths and areas of need is the foundation for instructional planning and for students' success. This is critical for all learners, including learners who have delays and disabilities. All learners have areas in which they have strengths and targeted areas for growth. Often, educators implement strategies without gathering data to find out what a child actually knows or why the child is struggling with a skill, or they continue to do what is not working because they are unsure what else to try. Data helps educators know what a child needs and determine how to plan their instruction to ensure that it is meaningful and relevant to each learner so that they experience joy and success in their learning. In this chapter, we discuss how collecting data and using the information it provides can help you make instructional decisions that support each student.

Inclusive Instruction

Inclusive instruction refers to teaching approaches that address the needs of *all* children, taking into account their individual interests, strengths,

preferences, personalities, approaches to learning, knowledge and skills, abilities, cultures, and family languages. Inclusive learning practices include differentiated instruction (tailoring instruction to meet individual needs), universal design for learning (ensuring access to instruction), and tiered instruction (varying levels of support). A combination of these approaches contributes to an overall inclusive learning environment; equitable assessment practices; and a classroom in which students, families, and educators are valued and perceived as competent and able to succeed.

As you engage in assessment practices, data-informed decision making, and instruction, you have an obligation to consider how to design inclusive instruction for students, including students with disabilities. Multitiered systems of support is one model you can use to ensure that instruction is inclusive to meet the needs of your diverse learners (Carta 2019; Coogle, Storie, & Rahn 2022; DEC 2014, 2021). Within this model, teachers use assessment data, including data obtained through authentic observations of children, to make instructional decisions that are responsive to students' individual needs through the delivery of three potential tiers of instruction. These tiers are used as a foundation for high-quality instruction that every child receives, and a tiered approach helps teachers make decisions to move to the most targeted, intensive, child-specific intervention when appropriate. A multitiered model changes the narrative from "The student is not getting it" to "What can I do in my instruction to ensure they do get it?"

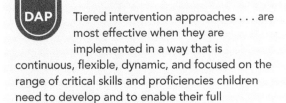

Tiered intervention approaches . . . are most effective when they are implemented in a way that is continuous, flexible, dynamic, and focused on the range of critical skills and proficiencies children need to develop and to enable their full participation in the classroom.

In tier one, all students receive high-quality instruction and, in addition to other supports the students might need, this tier of instruction is what they consistently receive. Tiers two and three can be described as an additional dose of instruction to tier one. In tier one, educators use universal design for learning (UDL) and a school's evidence-based curriculum. UDL enhances access and participation for all learners through various means of representation, engagement, and expression (CAST 2018). **Representation** is related to the ways in which educators present new information. For example, providing information using stories, videos, and through verbal explanations are all different ways information can be represented. **Engagement** is the way in which students practice or engage with content to develop new skills. Students can engage with peers, one on one, or in large groups and through various activities such as scavenger hunts, creating materials, and answering questions. **Expression** is the way in which students demonstrate mastery. Expression can include verbal responding, written expression, or responding through actions. By providing various means of representation and various ways to engage and promote expression, educators ensure that every child has access to and participates meaningfully in the curriculum and interactions in the classroom (DEC & NAEYC 2009).

Not all students, however, respond to tier one instruction, so it is important to collect data to learn which children are or are not yet responding to instruction so you can make some adjustments (see Table 1 for a sample checklist at NAEYC.org/dap-focus-kindergarten). Using a regular data collection schedule and system as you conduct tier one instruction will facilitate this. This might mean collecting data related to literacy using authentic assessments, such as work samples, anecdotal records, and checklists, as well as more formal screening and progress monitoring assessments once every trimester to gain a comprehensive understanding of the whole child and their strengths and needs. (See Table 2 for a

sample anecdotal note format at NAEYC.org/dap-focus-kindergarten.) Collecting data can help you determine whether tier one is effective for each student and whether a student needs extended learning opportunities, continued instruction, or differentiated supports.

Use authentic assessments that seek to identify children's strengths and provide a well-rounded picture of development. If you are required to use an assessment tool that has not been established as reliable or valid for the characteristics of a given child, recognize the limitations of the findings.

Making Data-Based Decisions

First, data can help you decide whether students need an instructional extension. These extensions are necessary when a student has demonstrated mastery of a target skill. When you observe a student demonstrating mastery through an informal and authentic assessment such as an observation, a student work product, and/or something they verbally share, instead of continuing with instruction on that skill, extend your instructional plan to create additional learning opportunities within the scope and sequence of learning as it relates to the mastered skill. For example, if your observations of a child in small group activities as well as through their play consistently suggest a student has mastered a skill such as blending words with the /at/ rime (e.g., *cat, bat, hat, mat, fat, sat*), consider how you can extend the instruction. This might mean moving to another rime family to generalize blending words in other rime families such as /it/ (e.g., *bit, hit, fit, sit*) or /et/ (e.g., *bet, met, set*).

Data that demonstrates progress on a skill, yet is more variable, suggests there is a need for continued instruction on that specific skill. Perhaps you are observing that a student is making some progress toward a skill, but you do not yet observe consistency. Using the data to continue to engage in instructional procedures may result in positive student outcomes. For example, if you've observed a child counting small collections of objects accurately (with cardinality) to

10 but they are not yet consistently counting larger collections, more practice may be needed with this specific skill. Observing some progress suggests that the instruction is effective but that more practice is needed.

Within the multitiered systems of support framework, students who have had ample time to practice and learn a new skill but do not seem to be responding to instruction may need tier two or three supports. Keep in mind that young children's development and learning occurs in spurts and bursts; sometimes they appear to regress until something is mastered. However, if data continues to be variable or a child isn't yet demonstrating progress, reexamine your instructional decisions and decide whether more individualized instruction is needed for the child to master the specific skill. This instruction is above and beyond what the child receives through the core instruction.

Revisiting your instructional plan allows you to determine what you can change to reach a different outcome, considering both the *how* and *what* of instruction. When a student is not yet demonstrating progress, consider *how to intensify instruction*. Intensifying instruction means creating more practice opportunities. We all learn through practice. Think about a new skill you have recently developed or perhaps a new exercise you added to your fitness regime. It is likely that you did not suddenly do this well but rather mastered this achievement through repeated practice. Young children too need multiple opportunities to practice new skills and concepts in meaningful and developmentally appropriate ways.

The *what* of instruction is related to the number of different skills or the complexity of skills that are being taught. As you intensify instruction—provide more practice—you can also decrease the complexity of the skill by using an intentional process to promote a student's mastery. This is often referred to as *scaffolding*. For example, perhaps your authentic assessment data indicates that a child can successfully decompose 4 and 5 into pairs in more than one way but that they are not yet fluent with all of the parts of 5. Instead of moving on to focus on decomposing 6 and 7 into pairs, you can decrease the complexity to promote mastery by focusing on 5.

Instructional Considerations for Students with Disabilities

Students who are identified with a delay or disability have a legal document known as an Individualized Education Program (IEP). This document is a written plan that ensures students receive access to equitable learning experiences in educational settings. Like other data documentation processes, IEPs should be collaborative, reflective, and process oriented. When educators collaborate with other IEP team members, they use their current data to determine the next step in a student's education progression. Data related to long-term goals and short-term objectives for the student allows teams to identify when a goal has been achieved. For example, a social and emotional development milestone for children around the age of 3 and 4 is to be able to transition from activities and environments easily; therefore, a child who is 5 should be working toward successful transitions. If you notice that a child continues to struggle—for example, they often do not want to stop what they are doing when it is time to transition to a new activity—you can first collect data, such as observing and documenting antecedents (what happens before the behavior), behavior (the observable behavior—what does the child do?), and consequences (what happens after the behavior) to understand what is going on and why this may be occurring. Analyzing the data for recurring patterns then allows you to begin to develop goals that can support that individual child's needs. These goals are directly connected to instruction, which is called *embedded learning opportunities*. For example, after collecting and analyzing data on Jana's behavior during transitions, her teachers developed a transition goal for Jana and identified a related embedded learning opportunity:

Sample Goal and Embedded Learning Opportunity to Support Developmental Milestone

Developmental Milestone	Goal	Embedded Learning Opportunity
Social and emotional development: transitions	Jana will transition from circle time to choice time with visual and/or verbal cues within two minutes 90 percent of the time for three consecutive trials.	Providing meaningful opportunities to practice transitions with a visual timer and picture cards

In addition, students with delays or disabilities may need support to ensure access and engagement through accommodations and/or modifications. **Accommodations** are instructional strategies that support how a student learns, such as extended time for completing tasks; visual supports such as picture schedules, manipulatives, or number lines; and instructional breaks. **Modifications** are changes to the curriculum that alter *what* the student learns and allows students to access information at their individual learning level. Examples include using the numerals 1 to 5 when counting as opposed to numerals up to 10 or modifying an independent reading level text with adapted vocabulary and pictures. When you make decisions about appropriate accommodations and/or modifications, base them on data that identifies what a student needs to be successful. This sometimes will not align with grade- or district-level curriculum or assessments. Ask yourself what barriers are preventing access and engagement for a child, and the answer can guide your selection of accommodations

and/or modifications (see Table 3 for a sample of how you can record barriers and solutions for overcoming them at NAEYC.org/dap-focus-kindergarten).

For example, here is what Jana's teachers discovered after implementing the embedded learning opportunity for transitions:

> During center play time, Jana often goes into the block area and pushes over the children's creations, which are quite complex. Her peers become very upset, and Jana reacts by kicking, screaming, and curling into a ball on the floor. The teachers are perplexed because they thought that the data and other anecdotal notes they had analyzed illustrated that Jana has a hard time transitioning, but the embedded learning opportunities they have been providing have not decreased her behavior. The teachers return to their data-based decision-making approaches to identify what is happening and what accommodations or modifications would be appropriate. By recording more data, the teachers notice that Jana has difficulty joining other children's play and realize that the issue may not be about transitioning at all. A lack of knowledge and/or skill at entering play is a barrier preventing Jana from engaging with her peers and is contributing to her behavior. The teachers decide that accommodations rather than modifications would be best to help Jana and begin using modeling, picture cues, and sentence starters to help her successfully approach her peers during play.

Collaborating closely with colleagues and analyzing data for patterns help you ask questions such as "Is this the right embedded learning opportunity to be using?" or "Is there something we are missing, and do we need more or different data to understand more deeply completely?" Asking these questions leads you to reflect on what is necessary and why, and it results in identifying accommodations and modifications using a cyclical data-based decision-making process.

Common Challenges and Solutions

Data collection can be challenging and time consuming for educators, especially when there are few resources such as time, materials, and collaboration (see Table 4 to see sample challenges and resources for addressing at NAEYC.org/dap-focus-kindergarten). However, the benefits outweigh the challenges when done with efficacy and care. Sharing data collection with coteachers, paraeducators, other school-based professionals, and families helps to support a holistic perspective of the child. Planning together, identifying roles, and having the support necessary to collect data, analyze it, and use the findings to drive instruction is critical to high-quality equitable and inclusive classrooms and improved child outcomes. All those working with a child understand their role and have the support necessary to carry it out.

Note how Ms. Byron collaborates with Mr. Walters to support Mario's acquisition of skills through the use of meaningful activities and everyday materials:

> Mario enjoys going to school to play and learn with his friends. He enters the room each day with a big smile on his face and asks if he can draw with a whiteboard and marker. Mario, who has cerebral palsy and uses a wheelchair, requires additional support including a one-on-one aide for health-related services and adaptations for writing and reading. Mario loves learning but is academically and socially below kindergarten level. While Ms. Byron, his teacher, supports all the children using inclusive approaches, she has struggled to find ways that she and Mr. Walters, Mario's aide, can support Mario in the ways he needs.
>
> One day Mario is at the easel, painting a picture with Mr. Walters, who is supporting him hand-over-hand because of his low muscle tone. Noticing that Mario is making dots in a row on the page, Ms. Byron goes over to him and says, "Mario, I see that you have blue dots!" Mario says excitedly, "Yes, a lot of dots—four dots!" Although there are five dots, Ms. Byron realizes that paint might be a motivating medium to use when exploring future counting concepts. She talks with Mr. Walters about pairing painting with supporting Mario in understanding quantities from one to five. During future math activities, Ms. Byron makes sure to incorporate paint and other paint-like materials, such as dot markers and stamp pads, in the counting activities she provides. As she expects, Mario (and some of the other children) choose to work with these new materials each time they are offered. As she does for all of the children, Ms. Byron collects data by taking videos and using a checklist to note how Mario's counting skills develop. As Mario works, Mr. Walters continues to use accommodations (e.g., modified paintbrush and hand-over-hand when pointing to the objects he is counting) to support Mario's physical needs. Ms. Byron also refers to the state-approved modified standards to keep in mind Mario's alternative math goals as she reflects on the data she's collected.

Conclusion

Using a variety of assessment practices for data-based decision making is critical to ensure all students receive appropriate support. It is therefore important to understand the ways in which data might inform instruction. This includes decisions such as extending instruction, providing additional practice, and adapting instruction to ensure all students have access, are engaged, and receive the individualized support necessary to be successful. When instruction aligns with students' needs, they are more engaged and successful, resulting in joyful learning.

CHRISTAN COOGLE, PhD, is an associate professor of special education and early childhood special education at George Mason University and a board-certified behavior analyst. Her focus is on supporting educators to ensure equitable learning environments where both students and educators are successful.

HEATHER WALTER, EdD, is an assistant professor of early childhood special education and special education at George Mason University. Her focus is on personnel preparation, mental health and well-being, and systems-level change to support retention of educators and increased outcomes for children and families.

CHAPTER 14

Adding Play and Hands-On Learning into the Kindergarten Classroom

Balancing Mandated Curricula and Assessments with Developmentally Appropriate Practice

Kacey Edgington and Amy Prosser

Kindergarten teachers work hard to balance mandated curricula and assessments with meeting the developmental needs of their students. The child-centered learning environment that children often experience in preschool seems to compete with the academic standards and requirements of the kindergarten classroom. Fortunately, there are things you can do to make the kindergarten experience more suited to how young children learn and bring play, hands-on learning, and joy into your classroom. You can create an environment that allows space for children to take different paths to achieve common learning goals and provide room for individual interests and needs—while meeting the rigorous standards of the K–12 system.

This chapter identifies some common concerns we hear from teachers around these issues. We discuss easy-to-implement tips and strategies that can empower you to balance mandated curricula and assessments with developmentally appropriate practices—thus meeting the needs of the whole child.

Balancing DAP with Mandated Curricula

In this section we dive into four of the most common challenges teachers encounter when trying to balance adopted curriculum with developmentally appropriate

practices. While it may not be possible to change your mandated curriculum, the learning standards, or the initiatives of your teaching context, there are small things you *can* change in your own practice to improve on the mandated elements. We know the "greatest effects on children's learning come from the expertise of the early childhood educator" (Thunder, Almarode, & Hattie 2022, 8).

Curriculum Challenge 1: Making Challenging Concepts More Accessible to Young Children

Many curricular programs are designed for kindergarten through fifth grade. Consequently, there may be universal themes that publishers attempt to adapt to each grade level. There is almost always some disconnect when developers try to make a concept that is appropriate for fifth grade work in kindergarten. This can result in abstract concepts that do not match the developmental needs of kindergarten students. While teachers want to make sure that students are exposed to high-level content and the related vocabulary to build background knowledge, they also look for ways to adapt lessons to be as comprehensible and meaningful to the children as possible. When a concept is too sophisticated for young children, one way to meet that challenge is to add materials and experiences to make the concept more concrete.

Here are some tips for making challenging concepts more accessible for children:

> Make two-dimensional resources three dimensional by providing manipulatives and real-life experiences. If your curriculum teaches a concept using pictures, text, or a worksheet, think about how you could augment it with manipulatives to scaffold the learning, provide additional practice, and engage young learners. For example, if your class is studying shapes, go on a shape walk around the school or ask students to bring in objects of different shapes, like soda cans and marbles, and create a classroom shape gallery. It may also be best "to let children explore before any instruction or guidance is given" (Zosh et al. 2022, 93). Exploration before direct instruction can help children ask questions naturally, setting the stage for the lesson to follow.

> Look for a guided play opportunity to reinforce learning. For example, one curriculum begins with learning about the government and relates that concept to kindergarten using rules. Of course, this concept is related to classroom rules, but can the group also come up with some rules for the zoo they are building or the cave tours they are leading in the dramatic play area to extend the learning? How can you integrate the concepts into play? High levels of joy are experienced when "teachers actively encourage curiosity" and "children are given agency and the ability to explore topics of interest" (Zosh et al. 2022, 98).

> Identify the supporting skills for a concept and work backward to provide your students scaffolding for the larger ideas. If possible, check the pre-K standards for a starting point. Explain what you want the students to understand to someone outside the field of education, such as a family member or friend. Their questions can help you identify what is most challenging about a topic.

Curriculum Challenge 2: Making Experiences and Materials More Engaging for Young Learners

Some teaching materials just do not engage young children. Endless worksheets and uninteresting writing prompts can make a lesson fall flat and hinder meaningful learning. Here are some tips to increase

children's engagement with a concept through more meaningful materials:

> Recognize that some materials that seem boring to you might be exactly what one of your students needs. Rather than remove an item, add other choices like puppets, videos, read-alouds, or movement activities to bring a concept to life. We can make choice work within our individual teaching styles by offering students choice of "materials, location, collaborators, process, and product" (Thunder, Almarode, & Hattie 2023, 198).

> Consider the children's funds of knowledge and invite families to be a part of the classroom as guest speakers or readers. Connecting a concept with people and events in your students' families or community makes the learning more relevant to them.

> Create interest in the concept with real-world experiences. For example, when studying the weather, supplement read-alouds and videos with a hands-on study of your local weather. If it rains or snows, head outside to observe and experience the weather, encouraging children to ask questions for the class to explore. Conduct a virtual visit with a kindergarten class in another area of the country or world and compare your weather with theirs. Remember that one key to meaningful learning opportunities is understanding that "children can work together to practice communicating their ideas, collaborating to achieve something they would not be able to accomplish on their own, and learn both from sharing their ideas with others and hearing new information from their peers" (Zosh et al. 2022, 96).

DAP 4TH ED Provide opportunities for children to engage in sustained conversations throughout the day in the context of play, problem solving, daily events, and routines.

Curriculum Challenge 3: Effectively Managing Learning Materials

With the many worksheets, flash cards, sound spelling cards, and vocabulary pictures included with an adopted curriculum, the amount of materials can be overwhelming. Think about which materials really support the concepts and understandings you are trying to teach, and which could be better used for emergency substitute plans or last-minute music class cancellations. Here are some ways to manage learning materials:

> If you find a quality resource, make it reusable. Lamination, plastic sheet holders, and file crates can upcycle printed materials originally designed for individual printing into reusable, more environmentally friendly materials.

> Rather than have students write a response to a read-aloud, invite them to create the characters in the loose parts station or retell the story by acting it out.

> Instead of a commercially prepared word wall, have students create personal word walls using words that are important to them and that reflect their interests and personalities. For example, we once saw the word *braids* under the letter *b* with a picture of the child's own braids. This is one example of ways that "teachers can think deeply about the strengths of the communities in which they serve and ask questions to help children generate examples from their lives" (Zosh et al. 2022, 95).

> Identify the most efficient use for the material, and then ask yourself some questions to help clarify the best uses:

  • Would it be best used in a whole group, small group, or independent setting?

  • When looking at the materials for the week, could you choose the passages that best support your unit and eliminate those that are less useful?

  • Can you shorten a lengthy whole group lesson by using part of it for demonstration, another part for partner work, and a third part for individual application?

  • Could students sometimes listen to a read-aloud on an electronic device, thereby freeing you up to work with a small group before bringing the class back together to discuss the work as a closing activity?

Strategies like these can buy back essential chunks of time that can help address the ongoing issue of too much to do, too little time.

Curriculum Challenge 4: Focusing on the Essential Objectives

Sometimes curricular materials include every possible standard or objective that could fit into a particular lesson, making it confusing and disjointed. Other times, the developer unsuccessfully tries to relate upper-grade concepts to kindergarten, resulting in lessons that are vague. Keep in mind that curricular materials are designed for a norm that may not match your students' developmental levels or needs. Try these suggestions to sharpen the focus on critical objectives:

> Look at all the suggested objectives and think about the strengths and needs of your students. Then make informed decisions on what to take out or add to any given unit. If you remove parts that are unrelated to kindergarten standards, enjoy any extra time it buys you by adding more purposeful playtime. If what you took out is still necessary to teach in order to meet your standards, see if it can be added to the end of the unit or integrated into another content area.

> Incorporate the concept into a guided play experience! Intentionally designed play can address multiple standards at the same time. If your unit addresses two genres of writing in two weeks, students can get practice in both genres through their restaurant play by writing recipes for how-to text *and* writing reviews of the restaurant for opinion text.

Balancing DAP with Mandated Assessments

In an effort to improve rigor and remain accountable to stakeholders, many school systems have pushed unrealistic expectations into lower grade levels, sometimes with little regard to the realities of child development. As a result, children are being identified "at risk" at younger ages. While you certainly want to identify delays and disabilities as early as possible, a single assessment should never lead to a label.

Using assessments in ways that do not support enhancing the child's education is not developmentally appropriate practice. Yet, decisions regarding assessment practices are often outside of the control of individual educators. . . .When educators are aware of inappropriate assessment practices, they have a professional ethical responsibility to make their concerns known, to advocate for more appropriate practices, and, within their learning environment, to minimize the adverse impact of inappropriate assessments on young children and on instructional practices (NAEYC 2020, 19)

The following are three common challenges teachers face with assessment, along with suggestions for making the assessment process more developmentally appropriate and using them to improve teaching and learning.

Assessment Challenge 1: Ensuring That Assessments Are Efficient, Responsive, and Purposeful

You may not be able to get around some assessment requirements, but you can take steps to make assessments less intrusive and collect information in additional ways that are more responsive and purposeful.

> Be as efficient as possible with test taking. For example, to avoid an extra transition for an assessment that takes place in the computer lab down the hall, schedule the assessment to start immediately following an already planned transition time, like lunch. Perhaps students can take the test in a whole group or small group setting instead of one at a time.

> Use personalized portfolios to augment information from assessment results and support instruction. Include writing samples, teacher and family observation notes, photographs, and video/audio recordings. Portfolios have the potential to tell an individualized learning narrative across a developmental timeline, helping teachers understand where children are and improve their teaching practices to support further learning.

Assessment Challenge 2: Valuing Teacher Expertise and Individual Variation in Learners

Adding observational assessments can provide a fuller picture of a student's strengths and areas of need. Observational anecdotes are a favorite form of assessment for kindergarten teachers because they reflect the expertise of the teacher and enable children to show their knowledge and skills in different ways (NAEYC 2020). This is particularly important for dual language learners (for an example, see teacher Amy Blessing's "Assessing Children During Engaging Play" on pages 68–69) and for children with delays or disabilities. Observational notes capture a moment in time and share your knowledge of a child with their family and other stakeholders, allowing them to "see" and "hear" what happened. Anecdotes with quotes and specific details make learning visible and can be directly related to academic standards.

Assessment Challenge 3: Understanding the Benefits and Limits of Specific Assessments

State- or district-mandated assessments often come with a manual that provides directions for administering the assessment but lacks an explanation of the purpose behind it. Have a conversation with your administrator or in your professional learning community about the benefits and limitations of an assessment you are using. A better understanding can help you reframe the assessment, find redundancies, and make connections between what you're asked to do and what you know is right for the child. For example, perhaps the timing of an assessment does not match the scope and sequence of your curriculum. Recognizing that the child may not have had direct instruction in that area yet can help you better understand the results of the assessment.

Although you might not be able to avoid long testing periods where students must sit for an extended amount of time, you can intentionally and heavily infuse playful, joyful learning into the schedule both before and after the sessions. Recess can provide a needed brain break and reset the attention span of a young child so they can perform better during subsequent instruction. After an extended time sitting still, these movement opportunities are critical. Short periods of movement improve memory and cardiovascular health.

Conclusion

Undoubtably, curriculum and assessment are key components of the kindergarten experience and provide important guidelines for teachers when planning and implementing learning opportunities for students. Although you cannot eliminate mandated curricula and assessments, you can manipulate the elements within your control and work to mitigate the elements that aren't. Advocate for yourself and your students to retain the joy, engagement, and playful learning in kindergarten. Authentic, developmentally appropriate experiences encourage natural conversations and questions so that we as teachers can determine individual students' interests, strengths, and misconceptions. Focused observation of students engaging in these experiences allow us to document student learning in the context of fun, playful activities, eliminating the need for yet another formal assessment. We hope these tips and strategies will help empower you to find a balance between the mandates and the needs of the children you serve.

KACEY EDGINGTON is the building learning facilitator for the Washoe County School District in northern Nevada. She has a passion for early childhood and has worked alongside kindergarten teachers for the past 10 years.

AMY PROSSER is the pre-K through third grade literacy facilitator for the northern Nevada region. She enjoys the "light bulb moments" and the humor consistently found when working with young children and wishes all kindergarten teachers could always have another adult in the room for eye contact and other support.

PART 4

Teaching to Enhance Each Child's Development and Learning

RECOMMENDATIONS FROM THE DAP POSITION STATEMENT

Developmentally appropriate teaching practices encompass a wide range of skills and strategies that are adapted to the age, development, individual characteristics, and the family and social and cultural contexts of each child served. Through their intentional teaching, educators blend opportunities for each child to exercise choice and agency within the context of a planned environment constructed to support specific learning experiences and meaningful goals.

Outdoors, a boy in my kindergarten class quietly picks up a piece of chalk and begins to draw a straight line across the middle of the play yard. Another child grabs a piece of chalk and draws a wavy line. Soon the ground is streaked with lines of all shapes and sizes. I begin to document with photographs and notations, asking the children to describe their lines.

Our conversations continue in the classroom and turn into an ongoing hands-on activity during choice time. After several days, I notice that most children are making connections between the shapes of the lines and the letters of the alphabet. Building on their emerging knowledge, I read *The Line* and *Lines That Wiggle* to help demonstrate how a line can be turned into anything with just a bit of playfulness and imagination. (Adapted from "Joyful Learning Through Science Inquiry Projects: Snails and Letter Learning," page 94)

Recognizing play as an essential way for children to experience joy and wonder in learning, kindergarten teachers provide opportunities for children to learn and master content and skills through play and playful experiences. At times they use a guided play approach, initiating a playful learning experience with an explicit learning goal, carefully selected materials, and probing questions that respond to children's actions and guide the learning, as illustrated in the opening vignette. This approach is very appropriate for all content areas as it enables children to construct their own knowledge and understand concepts and skills in a deep and meaningful way. There are other times when children initiate and direct their own learning, further solidifying their development of important emotional, social, and cognitive skills (e.g., creativity, perseverance, and conflict resolution).

A direct instruction teaching approach is also a tool for supporting kindergartners' learning. Although these learning experiences often involve little input from the students, you can intentionally make the instruction engaging to pique children's curiosity and ensure that they are active and "minds-on," with opportunities to ask questions, make mistakes, and revise understanding.

Teachers use their knowledge and understanding of child development, their individual students, and students' and families' social and cultural contexts to make intentional decisions about the materials, interactions, and learning experiences likely to be the most effective for the group and each individual child. Like selecting a tool from a toolbox, you draw from a number of effective practices to support diverse learners, depending on the learning goal, specific situation, and characteristics of the child. Your toolbox contains such teaching strategies as **encouraging persistence and effort** ("That wasn't easy, but you stuck with it until you zipped your jacket all the way to the top"); **asking questions that encourage children to explain, justify, reason, reflect, and draw connections** ("Ava and Luis think there are nine dots. Does anyone have a different idea?"); and **scaffolding** to help children achieve independence at a higher level ("Each of the strategies you tried keeps the playdough in a *ball*. What if you shaped the playdough . . . ?"). These are just a few of the strategies teachers employ (see NAEYC.org/dap-focus-kindergarten and Chapter 9 in the fourth edition of *Developmentally Appropriate Practice* for many more strategies and examples).

It's important to have a variety of effective practices at the ready, know each child well, and remain flexible and observant. Carefully assess whether the instructional decisions you make are informed by diverse and inclusive perspectives, fully support each child and family rather than ignoring or devaluing some, and help children recognize and celebrate diversity and the full inclusion of all individuals (NAEYC 2020).

In addition to different teaching strategies, educators incorporate a variety of learning formats throughout the day. While large group settings provide an opportunity for all the children and adults to come together for a shared purpose, small groups are the bulk of the learning formats used in kindergarten. This setting allows you to observe the children carefully and provide individual attention, support, and challenges. Small groups are also the primary grouping means for learning centers and learning stations. In kindergarten, learning centers, or playful learning areas such as art, blocks and manipulatives, dramatic play, reading, math, and writing, offer students a variety of carefully selected materials from which to choose and have a sense of agency over their own learning. Sometimes learning stations are used for children to complete specific tasks, such as literacy and math games and activities.

Strategically and intentionally using multiple teaching strategies and learning formats enables you to respond to the diverse and unique needs, abilities, interests, and characteristics of your kindergarten students, as the chapters in Part 4 illustrate.

READ AND REFLECT

As you read the chapters in this section, consider and evaluate your own classroom practices using these reflection questions.

"Centers in Kindergarten: When Do You Have Time for That?" explains the importance of using learning centers and how to do so with purpose and intentionality. **Consider:** As you read, consider if and how you use learning centers.

"The Fine Art of Scaffolding Kindergarten Learners" provides an in-depth look into how to become more adept at supporting young learners. **Consider:** How can the methods used in this chapter enhance your own art of scaffolding?

"Joyful Learning Through Science Inquiry Projects: Snails and Letter Learning" shares a Reggio Emilia– inspired approach to supporting children's learning of important topics through inquiry and project learning. **Consider:** What strategies provided in this chapter encourage you to provide joyful experiences in your kindergarten classroom?

"There's a Story in My Picture! Connecting Art, Literacy, and Drama Through Storytelling" describes the integrated learning that occurred when children had multiple opportunities to carefully examine their artwork and tell its story. **Consider:** How could you use storytelling as a strategy for integrated learning?

"Teaching Writing with Mentor Texts in Kindergarten" explains how a study of carefully selected texts can lead to powerful learning. **Consider:** How might you use the concepts in this chapter with texts that you typically use in your classroom?

"The Healing Power of Play" articulates the importance of play, particularly for children who have experienced trauma. **Consider:** How does your classroom convey the message that play is a child's universal right? How might you use the strategies in this chapter to increase opportunities for play?

NEXT STEPS

1. Would an observer in your classroom see examples of how play and playful learning are an integral part of the day? Identify a strategy from these chapters that you would like to try. As you incorporate it into your routine, reflect on how the strategy fits with your curriculum and lesson planning. Modify and adjust as needed.

2. Do you tend to lean on large group instruction? If so, how might you increase the use of small groups, including learning centers and stations? Talk with other colleagues about how they incorporate small group opportunities for their students. Then, choose one aspect of the day and identify a way to provide opportunities for children to work in small groups.

3. Scaffolding is a daily teaching practice. Pick a day (or two) and pay particular attention to what you say and do when you are scaffolding children's learning. Identify one or two additional strategies you could incorporate.

References for the chapters in this part can be accessed online at NAEYC.org/dap-focus-kindergarten.

CHAPTER 15

Centers in Kindergarten
When Do You Have Time for That?

Juliana Harris

Blocks, sand, and dramatic play in kindergarten? When asked, many current kindergarten teachers and their administrators view developmental centers as a thing of the past, with typical responses being "There isn't time for that" or "That's what they do in pre-K." The prevailing mindset is that was how kindergarten was done years ago. Today's kindergartens are dominated by intense pressure to have children fluently reading, adding, and subtracting by the time they leave kindergarten. But does it have to be an either/or choice? Can a developmental, constructivist approach be paired with the content included in state standards to meet the developmental needs of children and the expectations of today's accountability system?

Before my present position as principal of an elementary school in rural North Carolina, I served as one of six demonstration kindergarten teachers for the North Carolina Office of Early Learning. From firsthand experience in my classroom and from observations of demonstration teacher colleagues as well as a handful of dedicated teachers I have taught with, I can confidently say that center- or play-based instruction and content standards are not mutually exclusive. In fact, in each of these settings, the two seemingly opposites coexist seamlessly.

A Different Approach

As a demonstration teacher, one of my responsibilities was to host teachers, instructional specialists, and administrators in guided observations of my classroom. Visitors quickly noticed that my classroom was not the typical kindergarten classroom. Children spent very little time sitting at tables quietly completing seatwork. Instead, much of their time was spent working in teacher-led small groups, content-based stations, or in the hour-and-a-half block of time for developmental centers. Children moved about the classroom independently, gathering materials they

needed for a project. There was the constant ebb and flow of busyness and noise as children settled into a task, often one of their choosing. During literacy and math stations, children had the autonomy to select which content-based station activity they wanted to engage in on a given day. They understood the process of learning; eight or more stations might be going on simultaneously, and once finished, the children would independently transition themselves into developmental centers without much more than a hiccup. In our classroom, the children did *a lot* of talking and asking questions, and I spent a lot of time listening, observing, and asking questions that encouraged children to think deeply about their own or others' questions, areas of interest, and yes, content. We built a community of learners—an environment in which we were all respected for the strengths we brought and the growth we were all making, teachers included.

Why are developmental centers so important for young learners, and what can teachers learn about children while they are in centers? Why is choice an important part of the day? Why do children need opportunities to talk to each other? The answers lie in what we have known about play and its role in children's development along with more recent research about executive function and self-regulation. Opportunities for play in developmental centers provide children with time to make sense of their world. In dramatic play, they role-play their interpretation of what it is like to be a particular community helper, for example, exploring a future career endeavor. With puzzles and games, they practice waiting for and taking turns, counting as they move spaces on a game board, or expanding their visual-spatial abilities as they piece together floor puzzles.

With purposeful planning by teachers, every center can provide children with opportunities to further develop more than just social, emotional, and language skills: these centers are a prime opportunity to engage children in content in a manner that invites them to be active participants in the learning process. In every center, teachers who know the curriculum and the children are able to observe children's ownership of skills and what has truly become a part of who they are as a learner. Teachers can also gain significant information about children's abilities to sustain attention to self-selected tasks, their interactions with peers, and their personal interests. Careful questions and comments can scaffold children's thinking to move them forward in all developmental domains. By being observant and intentional, the teacher makes all the difference in the level of play and learning that takes place during this period of the day.

EQUITY Actively promote children's agency. Provide each child with opportunities for rich, engaging play and opportunities to make choices in planning and carrying out activities.

What Is It Called?

I once hosted a team of visitors from a neighboring county who were, like educators in many districts in the state, trying to define what constitutes a high-quality kindergarten program in preparation for the roll-out of the Early Learning Inventory (formerly called the Kindergarten Entry Assessment), which began in North Carolina in the fall of 2015. The question was posed to me, "What do you call your approach to teaching?" The question caused me to pause for a moment, and suddenly, 17 years of training, experiences, and self-reflection flashed through my mind. What is my teaching approach? What has influenced me to make the decisions I have made as a kindergarten teacher to create the type of environment that invites children to thrive—not just cognitively but in all domains of development?

One thing I knew for sure—my approach didn't come packaged in a brightly colored box or in shrink-wrapped plastic. It came from learning about child development as a university student. It came from working with multiple principals who were grounded in the fundamentals of early childhood education and who understood the significance of thinking through how to approach mandates in ways that meet both the

learning and developmental needs of kindergarten children. It came from district and state professional development opportunities that encouraged me to examine my practices and make changes according to research. It came from the developmentally appropriate practice resources from NAEYC. In essence, my approach came from understanding what we have always known about how young children learn and meshing it with current research, mandates, and standards.

According to Graue (2009, 14), "A high-quality program is a hybrid of yesterday's and today's kindergarten." Yesterday's kindergarten focused on the developmental domains of learning, including physical, social, emotional, language, and cognitive development. Today's version focuses on how children learn content and the teacher's role in supporting that learning. In addition, a high-quality program considers and supports children's cultures and individual ways of being and learning (NAEYC 2020).

Is the Pendulum Swinging?

At a training where we were discussing effective practices, a district director said, "It sounds like the pendulum is swinging the other direction." I responded by saying, "I don't think the pendulum is swinging all the way back the other way. Perhaps the pendulum has found its center." By utilizing a hybrid or balanced model of what we have known about children's development, academic content, and what we have learned in more recent years about the science of learning and the importance of considering the cultural contexts of children, families, and educators, we are responding to children's development, instructional needs, and cultural contexts, focusing on where children are at present, what they need, and where they are headed in the future.

Finding Common Ground and Understanding

How do we help administrators and teachers who have become so accustomed to focusing almost exclusively on reading and math begin to understand why a shift in thinking about children's education in a broader context is crucial? Although my understanding has evolved over time with several unique experiences, I feel strongly that others can achieve a similar level of understanding with time and clearly defined, focused, ongoing professional development and supportive administration. My experience in the Power of K, a North Carolina state-level three-year comprehensive kindergarten-focused professional development opportunity, afforded me the chance to reflect on and ultimately improve my practice. Learning through sessions with numerous national early learning experts, meaningful conversations with peers and administrators, visits to other kindergarten classrooms, and access to a multitude of important resources over those three years and beyond are what made the difference for me. I experienced much more than a one-day training session on the newest curricular program. As a cohort of dedicated educators, we became colleagues who worked together to strengthen our overall programs for our own kindergarten classrooms as well as those across our state. We are still connected today as we continue to advocate for programs and practices that are equitable and developmentally appropriate for all kindergarten children.

One example of how professional development supported my work occurred when a reading coach stated after observing in my classroom, "You actually taught reading and literacy-based content *all* morning, not in just one block of specified time." That is the beauty of this approach. Children receive instruction in literacy and math in a relevant, integrated manner all day long, not in isolated blocks of time. The result is happy, eager-to-learn kindergartners who are well prepared for the challenges of first grade by the end of the year.

Conclusion

So often the question is posed, "How do you have time for centers?" Perhaps very soon, the question will be "How do you *not* have time for centers?" Children are more than academic beings. They face many challenges in today's world. If we are only nurturing the academic part of their cognitive development, how are we preparing them for the many challenges of life they will face in their future? Kindergarten sets the stage for at least 12 more years of formal education. We owe

it to children to make time in kindergarten for what is important so that every child is fully educated in every domain of development.

Additional Resources

> *Reading Instruction in Kindergarten: Little to Gain and Much to Lose,* by Nancy Carlsson-Paige, Geralyn Bywater McLaughlin, & Joan Almon (2015). https://allianceforchildhood.org/publications-and-reports

> "Building the Brain's 'Air Traffic Control' System: How Early Experiences Shape the Development of Executive Function," by Center on the Developing Child (2011). http://developingchild.harvard.edu/resources/reports_and_working_papers/working_papers/wp11

> "Crisis in the Kindergarten: Why Children Need to Play in School," by Edward Miller & Joan Almon (2009). https://allianceforchildhood.org/publications-and-reports

JULIANA HARRIS, a former North Carolina demonstration kindergarten teacher, is principal of Hobgood Charter School in Hobgood, North Carolina.

Editors' note

This chapter is adapted, with permission, from *Milestones: A Publication of the North Carolina Association for the Education of Young Children,* Spring 2015, 19–22.

CHAPTER 16

The Fine Art of Scaffolding Kindergarten Learners

Elena Bodrova, Barbara Wilder-Smith, and Deborah Leong

Ms. Rodriguez, a kindergarten teacher, has been studying scaffolding and learning how to leverage it to empower her teaching team to meet the children's diverse needs, provide individualized support that meets each child where they are, and propel their development. How can scaffolding enable her to do this? Let's take a look at her scaffolding in action:

The children in Ms. Rodriguez's kindergarten class are sorting small animal figures and objects into tubs labeled with letters, working on sound-to-symbol correspondence. Typical of a kindergarten classroom, there are children at many different skill levels. There are children who do not yet know all the letters of the alphabet, some who are unsure of the letter-sound relationships, and others who know all of the letters and sounds and are fluent in many. For some children, this is their first school experience, so they are learning the content of the activity and, at the same time, how to interact with peers.

Jaheem raises his hand, and Ms. Rodriguez goes over to him. "Is this a /b/-/b/-/b/, bunny or a /r/-/r/-/r/, rabbit?" Jaheem asks. "That's a great question," she responds. "Both are right, but you have just two tub choices here, a *b* tub and a *t* tub . . . I wonder if that can help you figure it out. What do you think? Talk with Olivia and see if you can figure it out together."

Felicia and Tomas have already finished sorting the objects in the *d* and *t* tubs. Ms. Rodriguez saw that they did not have any difficulty sorting by these two sounds, but she noticed that they never said the letter name in addition to the initial sound. She gives them another set of tubs and says, "Remember to say the letter name before you put it in the tub." She gets an alphabet chart and says, "Let's try this. We can put the alphabet chart here. It will remind you to say both the letter name and sound as you sort." Felicia picks up a picture of a sun and as she moves to put it in the tub with the letter *s*, she glances at the alphabet chart and says, "I remember—it's the letter *s* . . . /s/."

At another table, Amala and Bogdan are struggling with the task. Amala holds up a car and puts it in the *r* tub. Bogdan picks up a rake and puts it in the *c* tub. Ms. Rodriguez notices that neither child is saying the name of the object out loud and wonders if they are not paying attention to and hearing the initial sound. She holds up the car and asks, "What is this?" Amala and Bogdan say, "Car." Ms. Rodriguez says, "What is the first sound you hear in *car*? Say it with me and watch my lips: /c/-/c/-/c/, car." Bogdan and Amala both say it with her. Bogdan gets excited. "*C*!" he exclaims as he puts the car in the *c* tub. "Do you agree that this is where the car goes?" Ms. Rodriguez asks Amala. Amala agrees. Ms. Rodriguez grabs a sticky note and draws two pairs of lips on it, and she puts it on the table in front of them. "These lips are to help you remember to do what we just did together. Pay attention to how your lips move when you say the name of each object out loud. It will help you to figure out the sound and letter it begins with." She hands Amala an object and points to the note, asking, "What does this help you remember to do?" Both children say, "Say it out loud: /c/, cat! Starts with *c*!" Amala puts the picture of a cat in the *c* tub. Ms. Rodriguez steps back and pauses to see what happens when the pair chooses another object. When they say the object's name aloud and identify the correct sound and the correct letter, she moves on.

Across the room, Justin and Vincent are rapidly finishing sorting, making many appropriate letter-sound matches with a few errors. They dump the tub out and begin the sorting again. They start to make intentional errors and correct one another. "No . . . that doesn't begin with *p*. It's a /c/, cat, silly!" "I was trying to trick you!" Justin pretends to make the cat eat the objects on the table. As Ms. Rodriguez and her assistant teacher, Mr. Davis, are working hard, circulating around to provide support, they exchange a raised eyebrow glance at one another as some of the buckets from Justin and Vincent's table topple on the floor with the pieces scattering everywhere. Ms. Rodriguez remembers that they have cycled through all the single initial letter-sound tubs, so she decides that what the boys need is a challenge. She hands Mr. Davis a new bag with objects to sort that start with blends /bl/ and /br/ and three new tubs labeled *bl, br,* and *b.* Mr. Davis explains that some words start with two-letter blends. He demonstrates what a blend is by having the boys listen carefully as he pronounces the sounds. Justin and Vincent are immediately intrigued by figuring out the two sounds the object names start with. Mr. Davis stays with them until they sort a few objects correctly and then moves on to another group.

Ahmed is a new student who joined the class recently, moving to the United States from Turkey. Ms. Rodriguez pairs him with Meili, who easily sorted the objects she had by initial sounds. The teacher is putting Meili and Ahmed together even though they are at different skill levels because her goal is for Ahmed to be exposed to English vocabulary as well as learn initial sounds. Ms. Rodriguez spills out the contents of four tubs, objects that begin with *t, d, s,* and *m.* Then she tells Meili, "I'm going to change the game a bit for you two today. I am going to hide two of the tubs, and your job will be to say the name of each object, figure out if it belongs in the *t* tub, the *s* tub, or whether it doesn't belong in either of these. Put the ones that don't belong in a pile here to the side. Ahmed can teach you how to say the names in Turkish, and you can teach him how to say the names in English. Then, you'll use the English names to guide where you place the objects as you both listen for their initial sounds and say them out loud."

When kindergarten teachers think about scaffolding, they probably picture something like Ms. Rodriguez's classroom: children with many different background experiences and levels of development; children learning foundational literacy and math concepts in addition to learning to follow school rules and classroom routines; children who are just beginning to learn about themselves as learners. Providing appropriate assistance to every child and gradually reducing that support as each child's mastery grows—a critical component of putting developmentally appropriate practice into action in a kindergarten classroom—may easily overwhelm even an experienced teacher.

In this chapter, we focus on how to scaffold children's learning in today's kindergarten classrooms. First, we define scaffolding in relation to student learning. Next, we discuss the hallmarks of effective scaffolding.

Finally, we suggest ways to organize your scaffolding so that children not only master the content but also learn how to learn. We hope these ideas will empower and equip you to engage in the fine art of scaffolding.

What Is Scaffolding?

The term *scaffolding* describes the type of assistance offered to a student by a teacher or a peer to support the student's learning. This assistance comes in many forms: hints, cues, questions, modeling, eliciting students' use of strategies, drawing their attention to critical dimensions or concepts, and/or pointing out and fixing errors. Scaffolding is temporary: it is provided while a new concept or skill is being mastered and then removed once the student has mastered this new skill or concept and is able to use it independently.

The idea of scaffolding first appeared in psychological and educational literature in the 1970s (Bruner 1975; Cazden 1979; Wood, Bruner, & Ross 1976) to describe processes of teaching and learning in the child's zone of proximal development (ZPD). Over the past half-century, the term *scaffolding* has become very popular and is currently used to describe many situations where teaching and learning take place. However, the broad use of this term has separated it from its real meaning, leaving many teachers without the understandings they need to really put it to good use in their work with children. Reconnecting the concepts of scaffolding and ZPD not only helps to clear these misconceptions but also allows teachers to identify which skills and abilities to target each time they interact with a child.

Zone of Proximal Development

The concept of ZPD was first introduced by Lev Vygotsky (1978). He proposed that what a child knows can be thought of in terms of a zone defined by what the child can do independently and what the child can do with assistance.

A child's ZPD changes over time: the skills that required a lot of assistance yesterday will require less assistance tomorrow and will eventually become something the child can do independently (Vygotsky 1978). The transition from assisted performance

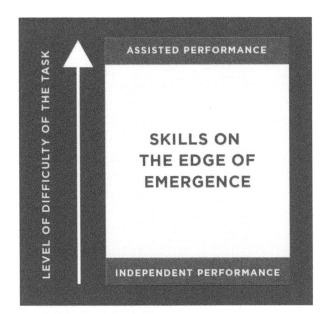

The zone of proximal development (ZPD).

to independent performance largely depends on what kind of assistance is provided and how it is provided (see the figure). This is why it is essential to understand the relationship between ZPD and scaffolding.

Scaffolding the Skills Within a Child's ZPD

Effective scaffolding focuses on the skills that are "just right"—the skills that lie within a child's ZPD. These are the skills the child can perform with the right kind of assistance but cannot yet perform independently when no assistance is provided.

There are skills that lie outside of the ZPD that children cannot learn at this point in time, no matter how much assistance is provided. For example, a multiplication table might assist students as they practice multiplication but will not help students who are still learning what addition and subtraction are. Teachers who try to scaffold a skill that is beyond a child's ZPD will know they are aiming too high because the child may get frustrated or ignore their scaffolding. The other telltale sign: when the teacher withdraws the assistance, the child's performance suffers.

There are also skills that were within a child's ZPD in the past but are now fully mastered. Scaffolding these skills squanders the opportunity to target the skill that currently is in a child's ZPD. Aiming too low or failing

to scaffold the next skill within reach does not provide a child with the opportunity to independently practice a newly learned skill or concept and does not allow the teacher to start scaffolding the child's mastery of a new, more advanced skill or concept. It's like keeping training wheels on a child's bicycle for too long.

Using Dynamic Assessment to Target the Right Skills

How do you know if you are aiming scaffolding at the skill or ability that is "just right" in a child's ZPD and scaffolding effectively? Usually, it can be done by first assessing a child's current level of independent performance and then trying out different kinds of scaffolds to see which one enables the child to perform at a higher level. This method of identifying the child's ZPD and the scaffolds that work within it is called *dynamic assessment* (Tzuriel 2000).

If the child already can successfully complete a task, it is time to challenge this child to a more advanced one. If the child cannot manage the current task independently, see what they can accomplish with just a little help. If this does not work, increase the amount of help.

Here are some other things to watch for when doing dynamic assessment:

> Do children use the support you provide, or do they ignore it?

> Are children able to quickly move from being assisted to being independent?

> When children do not show progress after multiple scaffolding interactions over a short time, take time to reflect: Does this child typically need more time to gain independence in skills like this? Would a different approach to scaffolding be helpful?

Knowing individual children well is critical. This knowledge enables you to adjust scaffolds based on children's funds of knowledge (Moll et al. 1992), address individual motivation, and provide the social and emotional support needed as children learn how to learn. You will continually learn through your one-on-one dynamic assessments with children and can apply your cumulative experience to plan scaffolding for other children needing the same learning support. This accumulated experience over time enables you to identify the most helpful scaffolds for each of the skills you are supporting.

 Build on children's strengths and interests to affirm their identities and help them gain new skills, understanding, and vocabulary as you scaffold their learning. Provide supports as needed while you communicate—both verbally and nonverbally—your authentic confidence in each child's ability to achieve these goals.

Key Features of Effective Scaffolding

Interactions Are Short and Focused on *One* Thing

Targeting one skill at a time is key. Kindergartners have limited working memory capacity, so keep your hints and prompts focused. For example, for a beginning writer, you may choose to scaffold leaving spaces between the words; the use of a capital letter at the beginning of the sentence; *or* the child's attempts to write a particular word using invented spelling—but not all three things at the same time. You also want to be able to provide scaffolding for as many children as possible; keeping these interactions short and focused on one thing with each child is key to having the time and flexibility to do this.

Scaffolding Is Provided "Just in Time"

Teachers artfully scaffolding kindergarten learners recognize that they need to *wait and observe* to see if the child can use the skills and strategies that were scaffolded in the past. It may take the child some time to come up with the correct answer as they try different strategies. Jumping into scaffolding too quickly can impede a child's ability to learn. Children who frequently receive scaffolding before they've had time to struggle with the task on their own may lose task

persistence—they can stop trying to learn on their own, give up if they get to a learning challenge, and look to a teacher to provide support.

Scaffolding is most valuable when it is provided when a child is *engaged in a learning activity*. Scaffolding that takes place after a child has completed an activity means *missing a key window of opportunity*. Children who don't receive scaffolding while they are actively learning and practicing may internalize an incorrect way to perform a task, requiring greater support to disrupt something incorrect that has become habitual.

Scaffolding Is Interactive and Responsive

Effective scaffolding is a two-way street: the teacher actively provides support, and the child actively engages in receiving it. Even the best scaffolding fails if the child is distracted or is not paying attention to what the teacher is saying and doing. When providing scaffolding, constantly monitor the child's level of engagement. It is common for young children not to be able to concentrate for a long time—all the more reason to keep your scaffolding *short and targeted!*

Responsive scaffolding means that the teacher responds to the child's reaction to scaffolding, providing more scaffolding when a child struggles and gradually decreasing the scaffolding as the child gains more independence. The key word here is *gradually*: scaffolding that is removed too abruptly when the new skill is not yet established can result in errors and frustration. This incremental removal of scaffolding is sometimes called *fading* (Collin, Brown, & Newman 1989) or *gradual release of responsibility* (Pearson, McVee, & Shanahan 2019).

Responsive scaffolding involves probing a child's thinking by asking thoughtful, open-ended questions, observing, and adjusting your support. Scaffolding is thus a nuanced dance between the learner and the teacher. For scaffolding to be responsive, teachers need to be open to different ways a child might demonstrate their knowledge or mastery of a skill. Children may show they know something by, for example, correcting or modeling the skill to a peer, not just by answering a teacher's direct question.

Individualizing Scaffolding

Here are some general suggestions for individualizing scaffolding for children who have delays or disabilities:

> Whether you are designing new scaffolds or adapting existing scaffolds, it is critical that the child using these scaffolds continues to engage in the same activity as their classmates and does not feel singled out by being given a different activity. Children adapt to needing materials or other supports that differ from their peers' as long as they continue to participate in the same activity. Creating an inclusive community of learners is essential for each child's academic achievement and social and emotional development.

> Engage the specialist who is working with the child in developing scaffolds that can be incorporated into an activity to support a specific child's needs, such as auditory processing, processing speed, or language disabilities. As much as possible, the same scaffolds, whether visual aids or techniques, should be used both in a child's work with the special education teacher and in the classroom.

> Dynamic assessment is essential to developing scaffolds for learners with delays or disabilities as it allows teachers to try out scaffolding techniques and observe whether they make a difference for that child. Teachers have to judge whether the scaffolds help the child or whether their use would alter the activity too much for the child or for the group of children in the activity.

> Specialized visual aids may be needed to help individual children with the substeps in an activity or to prompt specific actions. Such aids are important because they allow the child to keep learning alongside their peers. For example, you might supply a pictorial version of a strategy for solving a problem or engaging in the activity, prompting a child to remember what they did, ask a friend, or use the alphabet chart.

> Accommodations such as adaptive technology can be incorporated into a scaffold to support a child's performance and allow them to continue to participate in a learning activity. It is important to teach peers how to interact with a child who is using adaptive technology; for example, you might remind a peer to allow time for the child to use their device to respond to the peer.

> A child's particular disability could make the peer scaffolding suggestions described in the chapter difficult. Consider acting along with the child with the delay or disability as a partner with the peer. You can model the response for the child, who repeats your actions, or coach the child on how to respond. You might also teach the child's peer how to interact with the child effectively.

Not Only Teachers Provide Scaffolding

There is a tremendous opportunity for scaffolding that cannot possibly be met by teachers in a classroom in which many children need support at the same time. Kindergarten teachers who actively facilitate peer scaffolding and who leverage specifically designed instructional materials can amplify the scaffolding of every child's learning. Peer scaffolding and the use of instructional materials solve the short-term problem of providing just-in-time support and lay the groundwork for teaching children how to learn (Bodrova & Leong 2024).

Peer Scaffolding

Ramona, who recently joined Ms. Rodriguez's classroom, is in a learning center with a group of children dramatizing "The Three Little Pigs." Ms. Rodriguez says to the children, "You are so good at helping one another remember what to say and do and what happens first and next. Today Ramona is joining, and she hasn't heard the story—what could you do to help her join the play with you?" Children are quick with ideas. "I'll get the book and show Ramona the pictures of what's going to happen next before we play it." "Ramona can play the Big Bad Wolf with me—we'll have two wolves! We'll whisper together about what to do before we do it . . . so get ready, friends, there will be two wolves blowing your houses down!"

Engaging in peer scaffolding is beneficial for both participants. When they help a peer, children strengthen their own understanding as they explain or model the steps to do a task. For peer scaffolding to be effective, teachers pay attention to two things: the activity where peer scaffolding happens and the interactions that occur during the peer scaffolding (Leong, Bodrova, & Wilder-Smith 2023).

Peer scaffolding can happen in various activities. Sometimes, all it takes is for the teacher to prompt children to help their peers—something Ms. Rodriguez is skilled at. For other activities, it may take some extra planning and coaching children on how to help their peers.

During the sorting activity at the beginning of this chapter, Ms. Rodriguez enlisted the power of peer scaffolding:

> Ms. Rodriguez notices that Rishi hesitates over which tub to place a toy cow in: the *c* tub or the *p* tub. Natasha tries to help him by pointing to the tub with the letter *c* on it. Ms. Rodriguez intervenes by saying, "Natasha, you're trying to be really helpful to Rishi! We can help each other not by telling the answer, but by helping our friends learn how to find the answer themselves. So what you can do is to remind Rishi that the *c* tub has objects that start with /c/ sound and the *p* tub has objects that start with a /p/ sound. Natasha, can you show Rishi which tubs are which?"

It is important that children take turns scaffolding each other and that teachers take an active role in facilitating this. Sometimes, teachers pair children in such a way that a more advanced student always scaffolds a less advanced peer. These partnerships do not utilize the entire potential of peer scaffolding in terms of strengthening the academic and social skills of all children, building an equitable classroom culture, or boosting both partners' self-esteem. Use scaffolding opportunities to elevate each child's unique strengths and talents. By engaging in peer scaffolding, children become aware of their partner's strengths, how their partner learns, and, as a result, how learning happens for themselves.

Scaffolding Through Strategically Embedded Classroom Materials

Materials like pictorial reminders of strategies to use or steps to follow can also be used to scaffold children's learning (McNeill et al. 2006). One advantage of such materials is that they do not require the teacher to be physically present after the beginning stages of an activity. In essence, when children use these materials, they are self-scaffolding. For example, children struggling with forming specific letters can be taught to use letter formation cards that illustrate the correct strokes done in the correct order. Remember, for this scaffolding to be effective, children should focus on learning how to form *one* letter at a time. Having an entire alphabet marked with dots, numbers, and arrows will be overwhelming and thus counterproductive!

As is the case with any scaffolding, make sure the materials are designed and used to meet the students' needs and developmental levels. As these needs change, the materials should change as well. While some materials may be helpful for the entire class, others may benefit only certain students. As children use these materials, they become aware of what helps them to remember or pay attention, taking the first step in learning how they learn. The photograph below shows two children taking turns counting and checking the correctness of the answer. Cards with pictures of a hand and a checkmark help the children remember their roles. When children no longer need the scaffolding, celebrate their learning!

In kindergarten, academic skills are not the only ones that benefit from scaffolding: social and emotional skills can use some scaffolding as well, and some materials may help with this. For example, patiently waiting for one's turn—an expectation for many large group activities—does not come easily to many kindergartners, as their self-regulation skills are still developing. This skill can be scaffolded by handing a specific object—a talking stick or a toy microphone—to the child whose turn it is to talk and then passing it to the next speaker. To help a child listen all the way through a story instead of blurting out comments, the teacher gives him a stuffed bear and asks him to "help the bear"

listen without interrupting. As children's skills grow, the need for scaffolding decreases, and pretty soon, kindergartners will be able to take turns without holding on to the talking stick and listen to a story without help from a stuffed bear!

Conclusion

Scaffolding is an essential teaching strategy, the essence of developmentally appropriate practice, and crucial to child learning. It is the way teachers differentiate support for individual development within a community of learners and provide intellectual equity in learning opportunities. Scaffolding is a strategy for fostering learning so children can make the information their own and become true coconstructors of their knowledge. Scaffolding is more than a formula or set of steps; it is an art requiring teachers to be in tune with how each child thinks, understands, and develops. To become a master at scaffolding, teachers use their own deep expertise and knowledge of each child to create the learning experience that allows each child to thrive.

ELENA BODROVA, PhD, is a cofounder of Tools of the Mind and has cowritten books and articles with Dr. Leong on Vygotskian theory, early literacy, play, child assessment, and child development.

BARBARA WILDER-SMITH, EdM, is the executive director and a codeveloper of Tools of the Mind. She has more than 35 years of experience in early childhood, including teaching, coaching, training, and research.

DEBORAH J. LEONG, PhD, is president and cofounder of Tools of the Mind and professor emerita at the Metropolitan State University of Denver. She has cowritten books and articles with Dr. Bodrova on Vygotskian theory, early literacy, play, child assessment, and child development.

CHAPTER 17

Joyful Learning Through Science Inquiry Projects
Snails and Letter Learning

Melissa Fine

There is no place quite like a joyful kindergarten classroom. It is a place where wonder is seen on children's faces and heard in the tremor of their voices; a place where love and curiosity emanate from authentic artwork lining the walls; a place where children's identities and ideas are honored and respected; a place where children can be themselves no matter who they are or from where they originate.

The design and framework of a joyful kindergarten classroom requires care, intention, and trust in children and families. As a kindergarten teacher, I yearned to create such a classroom where children's voices and ideas were always in the forefront. Along my journey, I learned to take many of my cues from Reggio Emilia, in which observing, listening, and nurturing are essential to the teaching and learning process.

In this chapter, I highlight two inquiries that demonstrate the joy and spark of learning when the tenets of the Reggio Emilia approach come alive in a kindergarten classroom. The stories of both these experiences originated from observation of children in a state of scientific wonder as they explored something new in their environment. Children's observation led to questions, theories, and new understandings that stemmed across content areas.

In this chapter, I invite you to reimagine your role as educator in the classroom—to include the roles of learner and facilitator alongside curious children. I furthermore invite you to consider how to implement excellent practices more effectively and intentionally into your work, such as thoughtfully integrating content areas, strategically observing children, listening to their ideas and conversations, nurturing and validating their contributions, and allowing their inquiries to take root and blossom.

In the first inquiry, "A Jungle Gym for Snails," the children involved were deeply invested in a scientific exploration of the snails and their home in our classroom. This new habitat, which they coined the snail "jungle gym," was born of their own conversations and explorations. As I followed and documented the exchanges, I aimed to validate the children's ideas and encourage collaborative learning. Although the inquiry originated in the science center, the children's curiosity and interests catapulted learning across content areas such as literacy and mathematics.

The second inquiry, "A Journey from Lines to Letters," highlights a yearlong investigation into letter knowledge that stemmed from an observation of children creating their own lines with chalk in the play yard. I differentiated learning activities to meet the interests and needs of the children to ensure that meaning making remained at the forefront. Throughout the inquiry, children were given multiple opportunities to also engage in scientific practices such as observing, experimenting, creating and sharing their learning with others.

A Jungle Gym for Snails

The energy in the science center is palpable today during choice time. Six children have elected to clean out the snail tank, a popular weekly activity. I listen to the children's dialogue as they decide how to design the tank this week.

Annie: Look, over there—the snails are going round and round in circles on the branch.

Sophie: They like to climb.

Jessie: Let's give them a little jungle gym.

Melissa (me): A jungle gym?

Jessie: A jungle gym for snails.

The children want to design a two-sided gym for the snails. One side will have soft leaves and soil and the other will house climbing equipment such as twigs, branches, and rocks. The children sort through the materials in the nature center and consider how each may be instrumental to the jungle gym.

Mason: We could make a slide for them out of dead sticks.

Annie: And leaves at the bottom of the slide. If the snails go down a branch they will fall and hurt themselves.

Sophie: We could put leaves and plants on one side and shells and sticks on the other side.

Annie: One side is for snails to play. One side for snails to eat.

I offer the children paper and writing tools to create detailed drawings of their design plans. After more discussion, the children begin the construction. They proudly share their progress with the rest of the class at the end of choice time.

Young children enter the kindergarten classroom brimming with curiosity and wonder. They express big ideas with their bodies and active imaginations. However, kindergarten teachers battle academic pressures and more demanding academic expectations formerly reserved for primary grades. These pressures make it all too easy to mute or dismiss the child's voice, spirit, and joy in the classroom. The Reggio Emilia approach, in contrast, encourages teachers to step back and consider their image of the children in the classroom environment, their own role as facilitator in learning experiences, and the curriculum. Here are some suggestions for encouraging exploration in your classroom:

> **Consider the learning community and environment.** Create an aesthetic environment that reflects the children's interests and identities. Think of your classroom as a living laboratory filled with strategically placed materials that invite exploration.

> **Consider your role.** Act as an observer and researcher listening to and documenting the conversations between children during play so you can plan activities that match the areas where

children exhibit excitement and wonder. Join in the conversations at times to pose questions which extend a child's line of thinking or inspire more ideas.

> **Consider the curriculum.** Children are motivated to explore and learn in a classroom where the environment, projects, and activities have been carefully designed to reflect their ideas and interests and integrate content areas.

DAP Recognizing the value of the academic disciplines, an interdisciplinary approach that considers multiple areas together is typically more meaningful than teaching content areas separately.

A Journey from Lines to Letters

During the following investigation into letter knowledge, I was teaching in a public school in Manhattan, New York, where I was given time and space to infuse inquiry into the curriculum. My class was diverse, consisting of children of families from European, Latin American, and Asian countries as well as the United States. Several children were dual language learners (DLLs).

My kindergarten class is enjoying the crisp autumn air as they play outside. A boy quietly picks up a piece of chalk and begins to draw a straight line across the middle of the play yard. When his line reaches the wall, he changes course, crawling and ducking through balls and jump ropes to extend the line around the perimeter of the yard. Another child, observing his friend's actions, grabs a piece of chalk and draws a wavy line next to the straight one. Soon the ground is streaked with lines of all shapes and sizes. A chorus of scuffling footsteps and giggles permeates the air as children begin to follow the lines cast before them. Acting as scientists, some children are observing the changes in the environment, while others are actively experimenting with creating new lines with the colored chalk. Children appear to be happy, bouncing gleefully from line to line as their lines are tested and explored by others.

I begin to document with photographs and notations, asking the children to describe and name their lines based on their attributes. They offer complex names—*zigzag, loop-dee-loop, roller coaster, squiggly slide.* The children also comment on the appearance of the lines: whether or not they are wavy, pointy, or a little of both.

Our conversations about lines and curves continue in the classroom and turn into an ongoing hands-on science exploration during morning and afternoon choice time. We create an "interactive line" center and fill it with materials the children can manipulate—flexible sticks, pipe cleaners, aluminum foil, tape, and string. "Can you make a line?" I ask each child as they visit the center.

After several days of open exploration, I notice that most children are making connections between the shapes of the lines and the letters of the alphabet:

"This line curves like the letter *c*."

"This one looks like the letter *o*. It's a circle."

"I made the *A*, *u*, and *d* in my name, Audrey."

Building on their emerging knowledge, I read *The Line*, by Paula Bossio, and *Lines That Wiggle*, by Candace Whitman and illustrated by Steve Wilson. These books help me demonstrate how a line can be turned into anything with just a bit of playfulness and experimentation.

It is important for children to learn the distinct features of letters and the types of lines and curves with which they are composed (McKay & Teale 2015; Piasta et al. 2022). Research suggests that the development of strong alphabet knowledge in kindergarten is a critical skill and predictor of future reading success (Piasta et al. 2022; Stahl 2014): the stronger children's knowledge, the less likelihood that reading difficulties will occur in later years (Gerde et al. 2019; Piasta et al. 2022; Stahl 2014).

Our initial focus on the attributes of lines paved the way for multicomponent instruction, which included activities to promote letter recognition, letter formation, and the alphabetic principle. Throughout our investigation, I emphasized meaning making. In other words, it was important to me to connect the learning happening in the classroom with children's personal lives. I encouraged children to consider the letters in their own names and the names of their friends and family and looked for teachable moments to highlight these connections. When meaning making is part of instruction, children are more likely to learn and recall information because they feel connected to the content (Aldridge, Kilgo, & Kirkland 2020; McKay & Teale 2015).

From Lines to Letters to Names

My kindergartners' enthusiasm segued into an alphabet study. The range of alphabet knowledge ranged from just learning how to hold a pencil and draw scribbles to identifying and forming letters. I intentionally added alphabet picture books and cardboard letter cutouts to our line center to help bridge connections between lines and letters. I also incorporated other materials to increase fine motor exploration, such as playdough and flexible sticks. These materials were helpful for everyone and gave all learners a sense of accomplishment as they could construct a line or a letter in this tactile and nonjudgmental environment.

Research indicates that children learn the letters and sounds in their names and their families' and friends' names much earlier and quicker than letters they use less frequently (Aldridge, Kilgo, & Kirkland 2020; Piasta et al. 2022; Stahl 2014). During morning meeting I would pull a name from our name jar and invite the child selected to sit next to me as we went through our name routine steps. This included identifying the name of each letter, which I wrote on the whiteboard. We pointed out other words or names in the class that began with the same first letter as the child's name. When we were done, I posted the child's name so that others could see and use it.

Children engaged with lines and letters during our literacy centers. In one group, children sorted letters into categories using their own descriptions about a letter's attributes, such as *diagonal, straight, curved, skinny,* or *round.* Another group explored lines and letters using tactile materials like shaving cream, sand, or rice. Yet another constructed a class alphabet mural and placed loose parts like buttons, sticks, pom-poms, and small recyclable materials along the outlines of the letters.

The beautiful animal illustrations in Eric Carle's *ABC* inspired us to create our own class alphabet animal book. The children were excited to read it together in our class library, and we made photocopies of our book to share with families.

A Print-Rich Environment

In addition to the letters in our names, we examined letter shapes, sounds, and names in the environmental print in our classroom, such as labels and charts of song lyrics. Creating a print-rich environment gives children frequent opportunities to interact with print, including the alphabet, in meaningful ways for authentic purposes (Piasta et al. 2022). Upon arrival each day, the children responded to a question of the day through drawing or writing. At the start of our line inquiry, one of the questions prompted children to draw a line of any style as their response. Children constructed and hung their own signs for classroom centers using invented spelling, and we referred to those signs on an ongoing basis. We also found and recorded examples of environmental print in the school's hallways, like "Exit," "Bathroom," and "Caution."

Making the Alphabet Approachable for All Learners

I designed the line inquiry and alphabet study to be open ended and approachable so that all children could participate. Justin, who was still emerging in fine motor skills and alphabet knowledge at the start of kindergarten, benefited from bending and sculpting lines and letters with flexible sticks and by forming the letters of his name in a tray of shaving cream.

The DLLs who had limited letter-sound correspondence practice benefited from activities that made the abstract alphabet feel more personalized. Leslie, who spoke Spanish at home and some English in the classroom, looked closely at magazine pictures to find ones that corresponded with each letter of her name, and then pasted those in a book. If she could not find a picture, she drew her own. Visually representing her thinking and learning was an important component of her literacy progress.

Derek, who was able to identify all letters and sounds when he started kindergarten, blossomed during activities that gave his alphabet knowledge purpose and authenticity. He proudly sounded out the letters *m*, *a*, *t*, and *h* before stamping them onto a sign. He enjoyed engaging in detective letter hunts inside the school building.

With these differentiated activities, the children were able to explore the alphabet at their own pace. Individualized activities and projects made a significant impact on their engagement and joy in early literacy and scientific concepts.

Keys to Planning an Inquiry into Letters

> Observe and listen to children at play. Zoom in on their interests and areas of curiosity to find an entry point into showcasing letters.

> Provide stimulating and open-ended materials for active, multimodal letter exploration. Stock the art center with pipe cleaners, clay or playdough, yarn, colorful tape, ribbons, or various sizes and shapes of textured paper.

> Encourage children to ask questions and explain their thinking.

> Scaffold and differentiate learning activities. For instance, children who need more fine motor strengthening may benefit from lacing alphabet cards; those who want more tactile input may enjoy sculpting lines and circles in shaving cream or rubbing their fingers along a sandpaper letter card.

> Document the learning journey through pictures, videos, captions, transcriptions, conversations, and work samples.

> Share children's explorations and discoveries with families. Pictures and videos of children in action can easily be emailed or shared through an educational app.

> Celebrate each child's ideas and contributions.

Assessment Is Key

Frequent formal and informal assessment is key to meeting children's strengths, interests, and needs and in scaffolding their emergent literacy development. Careful data collection and analysis affect both individual and small group activities as teachers use their findings to create intentional and differentiated instruction (DeStefano 2019; Kaye & Lose 2018).

I frequently assessed children's letter knowledge and understanding of the alphabetic principle to create the activities and groupings of children during my literacy centers. I found it important to regularly check in with children individually and to keep track of their progress. My data collection and review consisted of informal observations and anecdotal notes, student work samples, and more formal assessments, like letter identification and sound correspondence assessments. At the beginning of the school year, I individually assessed children on their letter knowledge and understanding of the alphabetic principle, carefully noting patterns in the data to inform my small group differentiation and planning. I repeated these formal assessments before the end of each marking period to provide updated information to share with families and continue using for small group planning.

To facilitate taking anecdotal notes throughout the day, I carried a clipboard as I rotated through the classroom, observing and checking in with children during work and center times. The clipboard contained a grid filled with a box for each child. This came in handy if I noticed a child demonstrating certain skills during other parts of the day, such as a child who was quick to point out words that began with the same letter as their friend's name that we had talked about during meeting time.

DAP Educators embed assessment-related activities in the curriculum and in daily routines to facilitate authentic assessment and to make assessment an integral part of professional practice.

Children's portfolios lined a bookshelf near the entrance of our classroom. These contained pictures of children at play and date-stamped drawing and writing samples that showcased children's progress with letter knowledge and phonemic awareness.

Children were welcome to examine their portfolios and add new artifacts to them on an ongoing basis. The portfolios provided powerful documentation to share with families. The portfolios helped to document the children's learning and discovery throughout the lines to letters inquiry. They also served as a reminder that children's curiosity and wonder about line experimentation gave way to a fruitful inquiry connecting science and literacy.

Conclusion

In an interview for *American Journal of Play*, Lella Gandini (2011, 7) commented that "nothing in the school should happen without joy." In the midst of mounting pressures on early childhood teachers, it is essential that joyful learning continue to thrive in kindergarten classrooms. It is my hope that this chapter offers educators inspiration to cherish and protect children's voices and curiosity. Bestowing children with the tools needed for exploration will set the stage for robust, nurturing early learning that connects and integrates learning experiences.

MELISSA FINE, MA, has worked as an early childhood educator for more than 10 years, including 6 years teaching kindergarten. She supports teachers, program leaders, and children in universal 3K and pre-K programs as an instructional coordinator for the Division of Early Childhood Education in Queens, New York.

CHAPTER 18

"There's a Story in My Picture!"
Connecting Art, Literacy, and Drama Through Storytelling

Bonnie Ripstein

"There's a story in my picture!" exclaims 5-year-old Andrew as he shows me the drawing he has been working on. Anxious to document his comments, I quickly grab my recorder and ask him to tell me his story. After I transcribe his words, we share his picture and story, "The Mystical Tree," with the class.

The Mystical Tree, by Andrew

Once upon a time, there was a little mystical tree and the sun always shined on it when there was sunlight. There was a family called the Leonard's and they had a dog and they lived near the tree. So, the mystical tree had a crystal inside it and if anybody touched it or took it, the whole world would go away. Nobody ever touched it because the mystical tree is guarding it. The mystical tree never ever let anybody touch it, only see it, because that's the way it is. And the tree is old, about 150 years.

This was the first time I had seen Andrew excited about sharing his work. He was a creative artist and loved storytelling, but Andrew rarely revealed these strengths to his classmates because he struggled with literacy, as Russian was his first language. Now, three months into the school year, he was opening up—and we were all benefiting from his creative spark.

I had been teaching both preschool and kindergarten classes at the Henry Barnard Laboratory School located on the campus of Rhode Island College for 14 years. The school partnered with the college's education department to provide its preschool through fifth grade students with experienced faculty who also served as instructors at the college. As faculty members, we had the chance to explore different approaches to teaching, and I had chosen to research and explore the Reggio Emilia approach.

As a Reggio follower, one of my goals was to integrate more visual arts into the curriculum. Reggio fosters children's intellectual development through a systematic focus on symbolic representation, including words, movement, drawing, painting, building, sculpture, shadow play, collage, dramatic play, and music (Edwards, Gandini, & Forman 1993). Loris Malaguzzi, founder of the Reggio Emilia approach, once said, "Our task, regarding creativity, is to help children climb their own mountains, as high as possible. No one can do more. Creativity seems to emerge from multiple experiences . . ." (Edwards, Gandini, & Forman 1998, 76–77). With these thoughts in mind, I began the school year with a

Monday, Washing-Day (Lundi, jour de lessive), 1972, courtesy of Miyuki Tanobe.

study of a painting by Miyuki Tanobe titled *Monday, Washing-Day* (*Lundi, jour de lessive*, 1972), because of its representation of children using a variety of colors, lines, and shapes.

As children look at works of art, they use their imaginations and prior knowledge to determine what is happening, why, and how they would feel if they were in the scene (Mulcahey 2009). When I first introduced *Monday, Washing-Day* to the children, I asked "What do you see?" The children focused on the painting's colors, shapes, and objects.

> **Ellen:** I saw a baby and little lines on her socks.
>
> **Harriet:** I saw some flowers on her umbrella.
>
> **Singh:** I saw underwear and socks.
>
> **Roberto:** I noticed blue, orange, and white.
>
> **Colleen:** The artist had bubbles. He put swirls of colors in them.
>
> **Grant:** I see kind of like squiggly lines.
>
> **Harriet:** He kind of did this. (*Paints in the air with her finger.*) Kind of scribbly.

Over the next several months, as I periodically asked the children to reconsider the painting, they began to engage in more critical thinking—interpreting the feelings represented and the story being told by the artist. We spent approximately 10 to 15 minutes a week reviewing the painting. I began each discussion with a question to promote higher-level thinking. After starting with asking "What do you see?" I moved in subsequent sessions to "What do you notice?" "How does the painting make you feel?" and "What might be happening *outside* of the painting?" Each session began with a review of and reflection on what had been previously discussed.

> **Oren:** Rainstorm is coming, dark clouds and no puddles. Maybe these are bad guys that put the clothes outside before it's going to rain. This sky is dark, no sun.
>
> **Alexandria:** Maybe it was night and it rained and they got dirty and had to wash those clothes.
>
> **Grant:** (*Looks at the boy in a purple shirt behind the fence.*) He sees a flatbed truck, but the flatbed truck has a big box on it. It's nighttime and that is showing the light.

> **Harriet:** It's raining at night and that's why it's bright. Maybe the people are wearing bright colors to make it look like the sun.
>
> **Colleen:** It rained, it is dark, and there's an umbrella. But it is a picnic, and the people are happy.
>
> **Madina:** Happy. It might have rained after they were outside and they're having fun in the rain.

As the school year progressed, I began to see the children's growing abilities to transfer their thinking about painting to other aspects of their day. When I read stories to them, they would stop me on each page with questions regarding the illustrations and how they related to the story line. The children's desire to tell stories about their artwork increased, and their drawings and paintings began including more details. I was excited to see the children expressing their ideas and emotions through oral language and artwork. I also knew that they were building a strong foundation for first grade and beyond. In the early years, creating drawings and talking about them provides a natural transition to writing (Horn & Giacobbe 2007). Adding children's words to their artwork extends the process of learning (Grady 2022).

"My Picture Has a Story Too!"

Andrew's story generated excitement about storytelling through art. After hearing his story ("The Mystical Tree"), many children informed me that their paintings and drawings could tell stories too. Kindergartners have so much to say, but they often struggle to get all of their words down on paper. The basic conventions of writing, as well as their fine motor development, prevent them from documenting all of their thoughts. Kindergartners tend to reduce their ideas to one or two sentences, often leaving out important details because the words are "too hard to write."

Building on our discussions of *Monday, Washing-Day*, in which we uncovered several possible stories behind the image, I challenged the children to create their own artwork and then find the story. I recorded each child's story using a video camera. As Vivian Gussin Paley, early childhood educator and researcher, noted in reference to the tape recorder she used when having conversations with children, "it has become an essential tool for capturing the sudden insight, misunderstood concept, the puzzling juxtaposition of words and ideas" (Cooper 2019). The video was uploaded to a computer and then played back (in a one-to-one session with me) for the child to review or edit. I then typed the story and once more reviewed it with the child for final approval. Once the children's stories and transcriptions were complete, they were shared with their peers using a document projector on a classroom screen.

Their finished products demonstrated their varying levels of understanding of the aspects of storytelling. Some children's work exhibited early knowledge of a beginning, middle, and ending, as well as the use of conflict and (perhaps to a lesser extent) resolution. For instance, Colleen's story, "Piece of Gold," packs all these elements into a brief drama. "Swinging on the Sun," by Bruno, has more details but shows that Bruno is still developing his ability to craft a coherent and complete story.

Others described details in their drawings but had not yet mastered storytelling. Roberto's story "The Treasure Box," for example, is not merely a description—he introduces the conflict of not being able to climb a box— but he seems to be wrapped up in the minutia and does not craft a beginning, middle, and end.

Piece of Gold, by Colleen

The unicorn wanted to have a piece of gold. The leprechaun always came up with a bunch of tricks. One time he pretended he was on vacation but really hid behind a tree. The unicorn tried to take a piece of gold and the leprechaun took his tail.

Swinging on the Sun, by Bruno

There is a swing set on the sun and a meteor is crashing down on the earth. The person on the swing is saying "Run!" to the person on the ground. The person runs quickly and gets away, but the swing shakes and that person falls into the ocean. He swims back to the swing because the other people on the sun pushed a lever so the swing goes really low to the ocean. He swims to the swing and they push the lever and he goes back up.

The Treasure Box, by Roberto

There's a treasure box and the treasure box was shining. Someone wanted to climb the treasure box, but it was too bright, and they fell down. There's another way to get down from the treasure box. Then you should go down here, no lines. It was from the old days, from the pirates and they dug a tunnel. Then you go and follow the path and go swimming with the fishes. If you are going down on the outside path and turn and roll down, you could fall into the shark swamp.

Bringing Their Stories to Life

Paley (1981) designed a storytelling curriculum that encouraged language development and social interactions. It was based on young children's need to act out their thoughts to further their understanding of the world around them. "The holistic nature of the storytelling curriculum is evident in the learning it promotes in almost all areas of development, from using language to express and shape intention to making friends" (Cooper 2005, 230). Inspired by Paley, and looking to further the children's understanding of storytelling, I challenged the children to act out the stories in their paintings. Some of the stories ended abruptly and lacked a true ending. I felt that if the children brought their stories to life, they may become more aware of story structure, with a beginning, middle, and ending. As young children often struggle with presentation skills, I also felt that providing them with a more personalized purpose would give them more confidence. Therefore, the writers became directors, choosing classmates to portray animals, people, and objects. They selected items from around the classroom to use as props.

As each child's turn came, their excitement was evident in their body language and facial expressions. For the children who struggled with writing, language, or social skills, it was their time to shine. Young children have wonderful ideas and thoughts in their heads, but when asked to put those thoughts down on paper, they become focused on the skills required to form the letters and words rather than on the content of their writing. Having the freedom to simply tell their stories provided more opportunities for creativity and detail. The children who struggled with language and/or social skills were provided with support and encouragement throughout the project. Being chosen by their peers as actors gave them the confidence to play their part and to make their own choices later.

EQUITY Provide supports as needed while you communicate—both verbally and nonverbally—your authentic confidence in each child's ability to achieve these goals. . . . [Consider] the messages children take from your verbal and nonverbal cues about themselves and other children.

The joyful atmosphere that surrounded the room was infectious. It didn't matter if the children's stories were not completely coherent or lacked structure; by supporting their development of the stories and providing them with the opportunity to share them with their peers in a new way, I gave their words significance. Many children read their stories as their peers performed in front of the remaining audience. Others asked me to read for them, with some choosing to perform in their own stories. I recorded their dramatics and then played the videos back to the entire class on the "big screen" the following day.

After we watched the videos, I asked the authors and their peers if they had any questions about the stories. The visual reflection and peer review helped the children see what was missing or needed to change so their stories would be clearer to everyone. They began to question each other about the stories, leading authors to add more details to their work. Here are a few examples:

> Colleen included not only more characters but also a new ending. As the story was acted out, she realized that the unicorn and leprechaun didn't solve their problems—one lost a tail, the other the gold. Her revisions demonstrated an understanding of problems and solutions. As she explained, "I would put more trees around and a whole group of leprechauns. And more unicorns would come, and they would all fight over the gold. In the end, a girl comes along and tells them to share the gold—and they do."

> For Bruno, his classmates' questions challenged his thinking, but he remained focused on details rather than on the story structure. The only revision Bruno made was adding a rocket to get to the sun. Many children asked him why there were people swinging on the sun, but he simply replied, "Just because they are." When questioned about the crashing meteor problem, he said it was solved because the person on the swing saved the one on earth.

> After acting out his story, Roberto realized that it didn't have an ending—the boy was stuck in the swamp. To give his story clearer problems and solutions, as well as a beginning, middle, and ending, Roberto said, "I would change the fishes to piranhas and the sharks to sea monsters. The boy tries to get out of the swamp, and he tosses a rock at the sea monster and climbs out. He tries one more time to get the treasure, but he slips and goes back home without any treasure."

Connecting Art, Literacy, and Drama

As I reflected on this project, I was amazed at how the introduction of a single fine art reproduction (and the activities that emerged as a result) fostered the children's developmental growth across many domains. I was particularly pleased to see the connections made between art, literacy, and drama. Through the exploration of *Monday, Washing-Day*, the children's observation skills and critical thinking improved. Their paintings and drawings began to demonstrate an understanding of the use of color, shape, and line to represent meaning. Their oral explanations of their paintings' stories gave significance to the children's work and allowed them to express their full ideas without having to worry about the conventions of getting their thoughts on paper. The children's dramatization of their stories brought their ideas to life and provided a stage for reflection, an introduction to peer review, and a meaningful opportunity for improving their stories. Directing, performing, and revising also promoted social confidence. Ultimately, a seemingly simple spark—Andrew's desire to tell his story—resulted in a combination of art, expression, and discussion that allowed all the children to be successful in multiple ways.

BONNIE RIPSTEIN, MEd, is a retired kindergarten teacher from the Henry Barnard Laboratory School previously on the campus of Rhode Island College in Providence. She serves as an adjunct professor in the Early Childhood Education Department at Rhode Island College.

CHAPTER 19

Teaching Writing with Mentor Texts in Kindergarten

Katie Schrodt, Erin FitzPatrick, Bonnie A. Barksdale, Brandi Nunnery, and Michelle Medlin Hasty

The kindergarten class opens *The Relatives Came* and locates the last page. Ms. Nunnery reads, "And when they were finally home in Virginia, they crawled into their silent, soft beds and dreamed about the next summer." Evelyn's hand quickly shoots up as she exclaims, "Booyah! Cynthia Rylant used 'finally' to show the story was ending."

Evelyn's enthusiastic reaction is a sign that she feels she is working through and understanding text shoulder-to-shoulder with her teacher and with the author, Cynthia Rylant. She is celebrating Ms. Rylant's ending as a fellow author.

Since her students are fairly adept at noticing words and phrases used at the ending of several books, Ms. Nunnery takes the opportunity to extend the learning to this same passage. "Yes, Cynthia Rylant showed us that the story was ending by using the word 'finally,' but what other words does she use on this page to paint a picture of this final scene?" Children generate "crawled into their silent, soft beds" and "next summer."

Ms. Nunnery decides to use the idea of "next summer" to model the use of certain words and phrases to signal the end of a story. As a literacy coach, she has been helping the class write their own books during the past few months; now she revises the final page of her book about a summer trip to say, "And when I was finally home in Nashville, I laid my head on my pillow and dreamed of my next trip to New York." While still on the rug, the kindergartners select one of their own books from personal folders and work to revise its ending.

In this opening vignette, the children were deeply engaged with a book that exemplified a particular writing move—ending a story. As such, it served as a mentor text for the class. Mentor texts are pieces of literature that offer inspiration and guidance for children to try out new strategies, genres, and craft moves in their own writing. They are models of great writing in any form or genre, including both narrative and informational styles, and can influence children's writing from kindergarten through grade 8 (Graham, Harris, & Santangelo 2015). In this chapter, we explore what is known about using mentor texts in the early childhood classroom and provide suggestions for how to effectively choose and use them in kindergarten instruction. Finally, we present examples from two kindergarten classrooms to illustrate mentor texts and children's writing development in action.

Learning from Master Writers

Providing children with good models of written text consistently demonstrates positive effects on their writing quality (Graham, Harris, & Santangelo 2015). Collecting and sharing strong mentor texts is akin to "gathering a multitude of teachers into your classroom" (Heard 2013, 4) as children encounter and reencounter the writing moves made by professional authors, then ask themselves how those moves might serve their own writing (Culham 2014): "How does Mo Willems use dialogue and speech bubbles to make his characters come to life?," "Can I write about my relatives, just like Cynthia Rylant?" Good mentor texts inspire children to try out new writing techniques (descriptive language), writing conventions (dialogue), text genres (narrative), and writing craft moves (print manipulation) as they establish their own identities and skills as writers (Cleaveland 2016). The masters share the tools that apprentice writers then use to construct their own works.

Author Study: Framing Mentor Text Instruction and Materials

One of the first steps in guiding children toward authorship is to conduct author studies. Graves and Murray have both emphasized the importance of teaching children to write as "real writers" do (Graves 1983; Murray 1985, 1989). An author study sets the stage to look deeply into the life and work of an author with the intention of learning from them. Writers have thoughts, ideas, and passions for writing about topics they love or know a lot about. The author study shows the real people, their writing craft, and the themes within their books, creating a relatable concept of authorship (Snyders 2014). Through this, children can see themselves as authors and "take on" the writing moves of the authors they study.

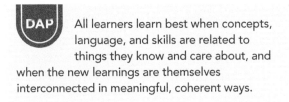 All learners learn best when concepts, language, and skills are related to things they know and care about, and when the new learnings are themselves interconnected in meaningful, coherent ways.

Take the following steps to conduct an author study:

> Consider a diverse group of authors.

> Choose an author with multiple texts and, ideally, a digital presence.

> Gather a set of books written by the author and read them to yourself, paying particular attention to how they can generate reflective, follow-up questions.

> Study the author's digital presence with the class (including the author's biography and photos).

For example, emerging writers can study popular children's book author Mo Willems. Willems's website (www.pigeonpresents.com) shares a host of information about his work, including his writing and illustration processes. There, children can learn about each character Willems has created and generate ideas for creatively responding to his texts through art and writing. The website provides photos, biographical information, and a list of Willems's books. Anyone can email him with questions and comments. Beginning with a study of Willems will help young children understand the concept of authorship as they grasp the idea that a real person wrote the stories they love to read in class or at home. This concept of authorship lays a foundation of thinking that they too can be authors. Then, after studying Willems's life with the class, you can begin the work of studying his writing with them.

Selecting Powerful Mentor Texts

After examining an author's background and work, introduce the specific books you want to use as mentor texts. The most effective mentor texts offer teachers and developing writers ideas for writing about diverse characters, settings, and topics while sparking their creativity. As Kissel (2017, 92) writes, "Strong writers are well-read readers. Strong writing teachers are well-read readers of children's literature." Teachers should constantly be on the lookout for texts with interesting craft moves, such as the use of sensory images, figurative language, and examples of strong voice that engage readers with uniqueness and ingenuity. Children's book award lists are a good place to begin looking for high-quality texts, including the Pura Belpré Award, Coretta Scott King Book Awards, Charlotte Huck Award, and the Schneider Family Book Award. Look for books in which all children can "see themselves, their families, and their communities reflected" and also "learn about peoples, places, arts, sciences, and so on that they would otherwise not encounter" (NAEYC 2020, 25).

Mentor text selection should also be driven by a teacher's intended learning outcomes. For example, if you want children to use more action verbs in their writing, look for books with dynamic dialogue and descriptions, pointing out those features during read-alouds and writing activities. It is critical to consider the children's interests, prior knowledge, and needs, building on "ideas and experiences that have meaning in the children's lives and are likely to interest them" (NAEYC 2020, 27). Choose books with diverse authorship and in the children's home languages where possible.

A potential drawback to mentor texts is the time-consuming nature of selecting and using them. It can be tempting to grab a book and use it in superficial ways, encouraging children to simply imitate an author's craft without understanding *why* the author used it (Laminack 2017). By contrast, the processes of studying a body of work from an author and returning to their books again and again enhance the connection between the master and the apprentice, creating a true writing mentorship. Choosing, reading, and analyzing the craft of a mentor text for a lesson could take anywhere from 30 minutes to an hour and a half. (See "Considerations for Selecting Powerful Mentor Texts" on the following page.)

Mentor Texts in the Classroom

Instruction with mentor texts should follow a gradual release of responsibility instructional framework (Duke & Pearson 2002; Pearson & Gallagher 1983; Vygotsky 1978). Here, the teacher moves from explicit instruction ("I do") to guided instruction that can include intentional interaction among peers ("We do") to independent student work ("You do"). However, before being employed as an instructional tool, teachers should introduce mentor texts through read-alouds so that children can first listen to, enjoy, and understand the book as a whole (Laminack 2017). During subsequent readings, the children can begin the process of "reading like a writer"—noticing powerful craft, naming it, seeing it modeled by their teacher, and trying it out in their own writing. (Visit NAEYC.org/dap-focus-kindergarten to view steps that guide this process in "Read Like a Writer; Write Like a Writer.") Helping children read like a writer activates the power of reading-writing reciprocity during literacy instruction and activities. When students can return to the text and view it through a writer's lens, they can fully immerse themselves in both meaning *and* craft. They can then use this deeper understanding and capability in their own writing.

The gradual release of responsibility instructional framework assumes sufficient time and support exist to shift the cognitive work of writing from teacher to children. (A chart on how to gradually release responsibility during an author study, accessible at NAEYC.org/dap-focus-kindergarten, displays how this process can be divided across multiple days.) Teachers should pay careful attention to children's current knowledge and skills and the amount of time necessary for each component. In general, teacher-directed mini-lessons should last no more than 15 minutes in a kindergarten classroom. Intentionally allow time and space for approximately 20 minutes of independent or small group writing time after the mini-lesson.

A Study of Mentor Texts in Two Classrooms

For this chapter, we showcase two kindergarten classrooms where the teachers used quality picture books as mentor texts to help young writers envision the authors they might become. In my work with Acorn Elementary School (pseudonym) before becoming a professor, I (Katie Schrodt, first author) was guiding my kindergarten class through a study of narrative writing. At another school but working along with me, Ms. Wenz's class was focused on narrative as well as how-to writing. Each time we used a mentor text, Ms. Wenz and I documented it on an author gallery wall. The cover of each book was copied and, in the style of Vasquez (2004), anchored on the wall to keep an audit trail of the characters and ideas learned from each book. The kindergartners could reference this trail while writing, considering which skills the authors used that they might adopt as their own. When children applied a taught strategy in their writing, Ms. Wenz and I encouraged them to put their work on the wall for their classmates to see. Not only were they sharing, but they were also celebrating the new skills in their writing.

The impact of the mentor texts in these kindergarten classrooms stretched to all facets of the writing process—from finding writing ideas and identifying surface-level features (fonts and thought bubbles) to examining and using more substantive writing skills (theme and voice). Following are examples learned from mentor texts, along with reproductions of some of the children's writing.

Finding Writing Ideas

Writing is a difficult process, especially when facing the blank page (Schrodt et al. 2019). The picture book *The Relatives Came* sparked writing ideas for one reluctant writer, Cory. Typically hesitant when starting a new story, Cory knew exactly what he was going to write about after hearing Rylant's joyful story of relatives gathering together. With powerful simplicity, he independently wrote, "I have my cousins at my house," then drew each one of them. Later, while seated in the class author's chair, he elaborated on his illustration, pointing to each cousin represented and sharing their names and the games they played during their visit.

Considerations for Selecting Powerful Mentor Texts

Katie Wood Ray and Matt Glover (2008) titled their popular writing book *Already Ready*. This sentiment should drive the decision making of teachers as they decide whether their students are ready to take on writing. They are "already ready!" Remember that talking, drawing, and labeling are all developmentally appropriate for young writers. For mentor text resources, check out *The Ultimate Read-Aloud Resource: Making Every Moment Intentional and Instructional With Best Friend Books,* by Lester Laminack (2019), and *Mentor Texts: Teaching Writing Through Children's Literature, K–6,* by Lynne Dorfman and Rose Cappelli (2017).

	Reflective Thinking	**Potential Book Choices**
Consider the reader	■ Based on what I know about them, will the children in my class enjoy this book? ■ Do I enjoy reading this text as a teacher? ■ Does this book represent the cultures, interests, and experiences of the children in my classroom?	■ *Jabari Jumps*, by Gaia Cornwall (small moment ideas, descriptive writing) ■ *Don't Let the Pigeon Drive the Bus!*, by Mo Willems (persuasive writing, movement, dialogue)
Consider the book	■ What genre are children writing in right now? ■ Does this book show a range and variety of features within a particular genre of writing? ■ Can this book be used for multiple purposes; can we return to it again and again? ■ Can I find other texts by this author? ■ Have I selected a range of diverse authors and characters? ■ Does the author have a strong digital footprint? ■ Do I have access to this text? (Digital resources such as the library app Libby can help teachers and students access books for free). If not, do I have a connection to someone who does?	■ *Dreamers*, by Yuyi Morales (illustrations, font changes, translanguaging) ■ *Each Kindness*, by Jacqueline Woodson, illus. by E.B. Lewis (descriptive language, narrative writing) ■ *Owen*, by Kevin Henkes (repeating lines, dialogue) ■ *My Papi Has a Motorcycle*, by Isabel Quintero, illus. by Zeke Peña (vivid language, translanguaging, speech bubbles, narrative) ■ *Saturday*, by Oge Mora (sequencing, onomatopoeia, small moments)
Consider the overarching author or topic of study and the skills of focus	■ What skills or aspect of writing do I want children working on as writers? Writing ideas? Voice? Leads? Dialogue? Structure? ■ Does this book represent good examples of those writing skills? ■ How does this connect to skills and knowledge already acquired by children? ■ How might this set the stage for future learning?	■ *The Relatives Came*, by Cynthia Rylant, illus. by Stephen Gammell (ideas) ■ *Chester*, by Mélanie Watt (voice) ■ *Bigmama's*, by Donald Crews (leads) ■ *Pluto Gets the Call*, by Adam Rex, illus. by Laurie Keller (dialogue, speech bubbles) ■ *If You Give a Mouse a Cookie*, by Laura Numeroff, illus. by Felicia Bond (structure)

Surface-Level Features

Surface-level features include changes in font (typeface, weight, and color) and dialogue that is embedded in illustrations rather than within the narrative text. Examples of each follow:

> **Font:** The book *Scaredy Squirrel* (by Mélanie Watt) contains many details within the words and layouts on each page. Watt uses font changes as a writing craft to emphasize the range of emotions Scaredy Squirrel is feeling and to encourage reading in an excited voice. For example, when Scaredy Squirrel warns the reader of the dangers of the unknown, Watt writes the word *warning* in all caps, bolded, and with exclamation points. My class read, noticed, and named the writing craft of Watt. Prior to leaving the rug for writing time, I said, "Today and every day you can write bold letters like Mélanie Watt in your writing."

> **Speech and thought bubbles:** The picture book *Ralph Tells a Story* (by Abby Hanlon) uses speech and thought bubbles throughout the text as the character Ralph struggles to find his voice as a writer. "Abby Hanlon uses speech bubbles to help bring her characters to life by making them talk," I told the children. "When you are drawing your picture today, you might want to make your characters talk with speech bubbles."

Theme

After Ms. Wenz read *The Lorax* (by Dr. Seuss), Corbin was inspired by the book's environmental theme to write a book titled "How to Keep Trees Alive." Corbin was clearly inspired by Seuss's whimsical book, using bright colors for his trees in a way similar to Seuss's Truffula trees.

Voice

Mo Willems was the focus of an in-depth author study in my (Katie's) kindergarten class. The students read many of the books in the *Elephant and Piggie* series and in the *Pigeon* book series. Willems is famous for his use of speech bubbles and dialogue: Elephant and Piggie banter back and forth, and the books' illustrations convey their movement and conversation. Willems also creates memorable and lovable book characters that show up continuously across his series.

After studying Willems and his writing craft moves, 5-year-old Drake was inspired to combine the ideas from Willems's books into one piece of writing. He illustrated it in the style of Willems, carefully making Pigeon's wing move to his "new hat," and he used Willem's signature dialogue banter in his writing. As Drake was writing, he rehearsed his lines orally as he wrote them down. I commented, "I hear you going back and forth with your characters, making them talk!"

Celebrating Children as Authors Now

Many young writers believe that "one day" they will be able to write, citing "first grade" or "when I am 8 years old," rather than believing they are writers right now (Schrodt et al. 2019). Writing shoulder-to-shoulder with a mentor can bolster children's confidence, empowering them to take writing risks, try out new writing moves, and eventually integrate those moves into their own writer's voice and texts.

KATIE SCHRODT, PhD, is an associate professor in the Department of Elementary and Special Education at Middle Tennessee State University. She teaches graduate and undergraduate courses in literacy. Her research interests include early reading and writing motivation.

ERIN FITZPATRICK, PhD, is an associate professor in the Department of Special Education and Child Development at the University of North Carolina at Charlotte. She teaches graduate and undergraduate literacy courses. Her research interests include elementary writing and practice-based professional development.

BONNIE A. BARKSDALE, PhD, is an assistant professor in the College of Education at Middle Tennessee State University. She works in the Elementary Education Department with preservice teachers in the area of literacy in the undergraduate and master's programs. Dr. Barksdale has worked in various literacy roles in public schools in Texas and Illinois.

BRANDI NUNNERY, EdS, is an assistant principal with Metropolitan Nashville Public Schools and an educational consultant with American Alliance for Innovative Systems in Nashville, Tennessee. For more than 20 years, she has worked with teachers to bring authentic writing experiences to the classroom using mentor texts within the writer's workshop framework.

MICHELLE MEDLIN HASTY, PhD, is an associate professor in the College of Education at Lipscomb University in Nashville. She serves as the lead faculty for instructional coaching and works with preservice and in-service teachers.

The Healing Power of Play

Laura J. Colker and Sarah Erdman

The importance of play in children's learning and resilience is well documented (Mardell et al. 2023; Whitebread et al. 2009; Yogman et al. 2018; Zigler, Singer, & Bishop-Josef 2004; Zosh et al. 2022). Through their interactions with materials and peers, children practice and hone social skills such as collaborating and negotiating conflicts. At the same time, it is a medium for gaining critical skills like executive function, language, and math reasoning. It even helps children become better people and citizens, supporting their developing skills at following directions, compromising, and persevering. As they accomplish all these things, children develop confidence and competence.

Benefits of Play When There Is Trauma

While play is beneficial to all children, it has a crucial role in supporting healing for children who have experienced trauma. Play and the reduction of stress are closely linked (Yogman et al. 2018). As the amount of play increases, levels of the stress hormone cortisol go down and norepinephrine is activated, increasing the brain's ability to rewire itself to be more compatible with coping and resilience. Sorrels (2015, 203–4) cites several benefits of play that are particularly important for children who have faced trauma:

1. Play facilitates brain organization and healthy development. During play, brain cells create critical brain architecture. Specifically, play allows the prefrontal cortex—the brain's executive center for regulating emotions, planning, and solving problems—to grow and work faster.

2. Play disarms fears. Having control of their play, including what and whom they play with, helps children develop a sense of security.

3. Play offers opportunities for important and purposeful behavior. As children use play to try out roles such as being a teacher, a veterinarian, or a florist, they build real-life skills like planning, organizing, navigating different opinions and ideas, and celebrating successes.

4. Play allows children to regain their voice. During play children can express their fears, hopes, dreams, and needs in a safe place. Play validates children and allows them to be their authentic selves, even when they do this through their imagination.

5. Play reduces shame and helps children regain a sense of competence. Many children with a background of abuse or neglect blame themselves for their circumstances, creating feelings of shame and low self-esteem. Through play, children gain competence as they solve problems and learn skills. Confidence and pride may be new sensations for children who have experienced trauma.

6. Play gives children an avenue for emotion expression. A child who is fearful might find comfort in pounding on clay or covering themselves in a parachute outdoors. On a more joyous day, a child might jump wildly to music or create a story about an optimistic gopher.

Although play provides many benefits to children who have experienced trauma, these children also need ongoing understanding and support in all areas of their lives.

The Impact of Trauma on Play and Schooling

Trauma can affect how children play and learn. Consider the following examples:

> Everyday events may trigger a child and cause them to become fearful, aggressive, or seemingly shut down: Watching Sebine follow a recipe card for making a lettuce roll-up, Antonio thinks about all the times he has been hungry at home

lately and gets upset. He goes over to the snack table and pushes the tableware onto the floor, surprising everyone.

> Children's ability to connect socially with others may be impacted by trauma: During outdoor play, Saroj, whose family recently began experiencing homelessness, stands alone on the playground watching the other children. When his teacher comes over to encourage him to join in, he buries his face in her side.

> Children with a trauma history often have difficulty navigating conflicts with peers: Dion, who was emotionally abused in the past, is playing a board game with Marcius. When Marcius earns an extra turn, Dion, who was expecting to go next, grabs the dice from Marcius and angrily announces it's his turn. A confused Marcius tries to explain the rules to Dion, who refuses to listen.

> Trauma may make it difficult for children to concentrate and complete tasks: Working in the literacy center, normally one of her favorites, Mattie, whose father is very ill, is distracted and stares blankly out the window. She ignores the assignment in front of her.

> Trauma may cause children to show extreme concern for others: Lilly, who has a history of physical abuse, stores all of the puppets under the puppet stage, refusing to let anyone else play with them or move them elsewhere. "They have to hide so no one will be able to hurt them."

Using Different Types of Play to Address Trauma's Negative Effects

Play is not just a vehicle for observing the effects of trauma; more importantly, it is a tool for lessening those effects. Taking a strengths-based approach, educators can support kindergartners' play, using it to encourage and promote healing as well as bring pleasure. Self-directed play and guided play together can be described as playful learning (Zosh et al. 2022); both are associated with healing.

Self-Directed Play

When children engage in self-directed play, they are in charge of what, with whom, where, and for how long they play. Three major characteristics of self-directed play help define it (Sorrels 2015, 202–3):

1. It is chosen by the child. This means that Elena may spend a significant amount of time listening to audiobooks in the literacy station before deciding to join two other children in making a volcano in the science center.

2. The child is motivated by the pleasure of the activity. If Pedro enjoys painting a section of a mural outdoors, he could happily spend the entire choice time engaged in this activity.

3. Children make the rules of play. When setting up a dice game in the math center, the children decide together that they will each get to roll two times instead of one. They also pick a silly noise to make if they roll a one or a six.

When teachers provide opportunities for sustained time in self-directed play, children with a trauma background can gain the following capabilities that aid in their recovery (Mardell et al. 2023; NPR 2015):

> Sense of trust

> Emotional regulation

> Ability to make choices about their lives

> Empathy

> Diminished tendencies toward violence

Guided Play

Guided play involves the intentional adding of specific learning goals to children's play. It gives children choice in their play and teachers the opportunity to monitor for progress toward the curriculum's learning standards and objectives. Guided play is not telling the children how or what to play, but rather acting as a guide or coach during their explorations. "By infusing play with purposeful learning goals, educators empower children to learn in a playful, joyful context" (Zosh et al. 2022, 84).

Supporting the Play of Children with Trauma History in Learning Centers

Learning Center	Actions and Questions
Blocks	The block area is an ideal venue for children to re-create traumas they have experienced. For example, an incident involving a plane that crashed into a home in their city can begin to be processed when a child builds a house out of blocks and then flies a large block "airplane" into it, crashing the structure over and over again. To help a child process the traumatic event, you might pose questions such as: ■ What can you do to make the people in the house safe? ■ What could we do to prevent another accident like this?
Math	Open-ended toys like magnetic blocks and loose parts such as buttons and keys offer children with trauma backgrounds the opportunity to impose order and control on their world. Extend children's play by asking questions like the following: ■ How did you pick which item(s) to play with? ■ What made you want to group the items like this?
Literacy	Choose books, read-aloud texts, and storytelling topics specifically designed to help children exposed to trauma deal with their feelings and heal. Children can use these materials without feeling singled out. Books such as *The Day My Daddy Lost His Temper* (by Carl Santana McCleary, illus. by Naomi Santana), *Once I Was Very Very Scared* (by Chandra Ghosh Ippen, illus. by Erich Ippen Jr [also *Una vez tuve mucho mucho miedo*]), and *Visiting Day* (by Jacqueline Woodson, illus. by James E. Ransome) are especially helpful for children who have experienced abuse, been severely frightened, and have an incarcerated relative, respectively. Add materials for children to write, listen to recorded stories, or publish their own books. To guide children's use of books, ask such questions as: ■ What do you think [the main character] is feeling? ■ Who is there to help them?
Art and Music	Dark colors, for instance, may reflect a dark mood. Music can help children who have experienced trauma self-regulate. Group art and music experiences increase endorphins and oxytocin in the brain, relieving stress and anxiety. They also promote a sense of belonging that many children with trauma histories yearn for. Some helpful questions to ask children include: ■ Why did you choose those colors to draw with/instrument to play with? ■ What is the best part about doing a project together like painting a mural or marching while we play our instruments?
Outdoors	Bringing beneficial indoor activities outdoors offers children exposed to trauma more opportunities to engage in these healing activities. In addition, children are able to work through stress and unwanted feelings through gross motor activities like climbing and throwing or kicking balls. Educators can enhance these experiences by asking questions or making comments like these: ■ I know you are upset right now. Try throwing a ball at a target and see if that helps you feel better. ■ How do you feel when you make the swing go high in the air?

Learning Center	Actions and Questions
Science	Caring for plants and classroom pets is especially valuable for children who have experienced trauma. These activities offer children a chance to safely develop nurturing feelings that are helpful in forging relationships with educators and peers. Educators expand on children's feelings of attachment by asking such questions as: ■ How do you feel when you feed our classroom pet and/or care for plants? ■ In what ways is caring for pets and plants like having friends?

Guided play may be as simple as suggesting children write up "health reports" about the status of the stuffed bears whose health they are assessing using stethoscopes, scales, and magnifying glasses (Blessing 2022). It may involve more guidance and scaffolding on the teacher's part. Suppose, for example, you are observing 5-year-old Shaniqua in the block area, where she frequently chooses to play alone. She hands you two triangles put together and announces that it is a sandwich cut into pieces for you. You can use this as an opportunity to teach her about the mathematical concept of equivalence and math vocabulary words like *half* and *whole*. You tell Shaniqua that her block sandwich looks mighty tasty but that you like your sandwiches whole, not cut in half. Perhaps Shaniqua then hands you the blocks held tightly together announcing that you now have a whole sandwich. Draw her attention to the two triangle halves and ask if she could get you a sandwich that hasn't been cut at all. Through your prompts, you lead Shaniqua to hand you a rectangular unit block that is the same size and shape as the two triangles held together. You can then place the rectangular block against the two triangle blocks held together and ask Shaniqua to compare their sizes and shapes for equivalency.

If needed you can scaffold her learning, fastening the two triangle blocks together with rubber bands and then holding them against various unit blocks until she finds a matching shape. Your thoughtful questioning and probing will enhance Shaniqua's understanding of age-appropriate concepts without derailing her play. Following this guided play experience—including your exuberant "eating" of the sandwich shared with you!—Shaniqua can return to self-directed block play. In the meantime, she will have gained new skills and a sense of accomplishment.

Guided play is an especially useful approach for children who have experienced trauma. It meets them where they are and supports the work they are doing in ways that are comfortable for them.

The chart "Supporting the Play of Children with Trauma History in Learning Centers," above, offers ideas for using self-directed and guided play in your learning centers.

Supporting Playful Learning for Children Who Are Distressed

It can be disconcerting for an educator to watch what might seem distressing themes in a child's play, such as "dead dog" play after a pet dies, but it is their way of working through the experience. You can use this as an opportunity to watch what children are doing and to clear up any misconceptions you see in their play.

You don't need to intervene if the play seems to be helpful. However, if children are getting more upset or scared, consider what supports you might offer. See if you can redirect the play or add context. If a child is playing "car crash" and seems upset, ask if someone is calling 911 and bringing in emergency vehicles to help. If that doesn't work, you may need to change the setting. Say, "Wow, this seems to really be upsetting you. Let's talk about it." This lets them know that what they are feeling is okay and that you are there to help them deal with it.

Children may also draw, write, or dictate a story to you about how they are feeling. Open-ended inquiries like "I wonder what is happening in your picture?" followed by a pause to give a child a chance to respond will let

them express themselves. If the trauma is not reflected in their art or writing, that doesn't mean they don't have feelings about it. It may just mean they are not ready to deal with it now or that they are expressing their feelings in a different way.

If the intensity of the play continues, if a child becomes fixated on events during play, or if you have any other causes for concern, talk with the child's family and perhaps consult your school's guidance counselor, social worker, or family liaison. If these specialists are not available in the school, you might contact an outside professional for advice with the family's permission.

Providing Children Enough Time to Become Fully Engaged in Their Play

All children need long stretches of uninterrupted play to become fully involved in what they are doing. Those with a trauma background may need to calm down and self-regulate before they can even begin playing in a way that leads to learning. Educators need to take this into consideration when planning projects and structuring the day.

EQUITY Differentiating support in a strengths-based way is the most equitable approach because it helps to meet each child's needs.

Suppose that the children are conducting a study on birds native to your area. Together you create a web of what they want to explore: bird habitats, nest type, what the birds eat, and so on. These ideas are organized into questions the children can investigate.

Jordan, who has been withdrawn since his mother was hospitalized with cancer, has accepted Kendrick's invitation to work together on studying bird habitats. They scour the loose parts bin for materials like popsicle sticks, pipe cleaners, and glue and begin construction. You notice their interest and enlist a parent volunteer to get some sturdier materials and come in to help them. Over the next week, the boys plan the birdhouse, checking pieces for size with rulers. The volunteer comes back to guide the process as they attach the pieces together. Then the boys work independently on sanding, painting, and decorating the structure. Upon completion, the boys present their birdhouse to the class at group time and answer questions. With your assistance, the boys hang their homemade birdhouse from a tree.

The next day, Jordan draws a picture of the birdhouse on the computer and emails it to his mom. He thinks it will cheer her up to see how he is helping the birds at school. Periodically over the next few months, Kendrick and a less withdrawn Jordan check on the birdhouse and discuss new designs or improvements they want to make it even better for their bird friends. They ask the school librarian for more books on woodworking and construction.

By allowing children extended time to work on projects of their choice, both independently and under your guidance, you give play the time it needs to work.

Using Play to Offer Children Joy and Hope

While play helps children affected by trauma move toward healing and is a vehicle for learning skills for all children, remember that there is a light side to play. So share a laugh with a child as a Hula-Hoop twirls off their body. Encourage children to enthusiastically sing a song with new words they have made up or the goofy rhymes they have created. And share a child's delight and pride as you together make a frame to showcase their artwork on the wall. All kindergartners, including those with trauma backgrounds, are children first. And every child needs to savor the joys of play.

LAURA J. COLKER, EdD, is an author, lecturer, and early childhood education coach with more than 45 years of experience. She has written or produced more than 150 books, articles, videos, and podcasts for educators, administrators, families, and children.

SARAH ERDMAN is an early childhood educator and museum professional with more than 15 years of experience in the field. She is an author as well as a lead teacher and assistant director at a play-based preschool/kindergarten.

PART 5

Planning and Implementing an Engaging Curriculum to Achieve Meaningful Goals

RECOMMENDATIONS FROM THE DAP POSITION STATEMENT

Based on their knowledge of what is meaningful and engaging to each child, educators design the learning environment and its activities to promote subject area knowledge across all content areas as well as across all domains of development. Educators use their knowledge of learning progressions for different subjects, their understanding of common conceptions and misconceptions at different points on the progressions, and their pedagogical knowledge about each subject area to develop learning activities that offer challenging but achievable goals for children that are also meaningful and engaging.

In the kindergarten children's rural community, spring storms have been strong. Ms. Williams reads *Thunder Cake*, by Patricia Polacco. After the story, Ms. Williams asks, "What do you do to help your family get ready for a storm?" Brennon says, "I make sure my dog is in the house." Kaleigh, who lives on a farm, says, "I help tie the gates open." Ms. Williams says, "Those are important ways to help." She continues, "Each of you will write a story and draw a picture about helping your family. Then you can share your stories with each other."

Next, Ms. Williams draws a graphic organizer with the word *storms* in the center. She asks, "What do you wonder about storms?" The children have many ideas: "Why does the wind blow so hard during the rain?," "Do animals know when a storm is coming?," and "How much rain falls?" Ms. Williams writes the children's questions. To discover the answers, they decide to record the rainy days on a chart, measure rainfall in a bucket, interview their families, and find other books about storms. (Adapted from Masterson 2022, 244)

This excerpt shows how educators can create plans that help children reach "desired goals that are important for . . .development and learning" (NAEYC 2020, 25). Curriculum planning is an important part of how educators make sure they address key concepts and skills using strategies that maximize children's engagement and progress.

Some of the most important decisions you make as a kindergarten teacher occur around selecting what *and* how to teach important content and skills, using your school's curriculum as a guide. "At its foundation, developmentally appropriate curriculum requires careful and thoughtful planning of meaningful, engaging, and play-based activities, materials, and environments that stimulate children's holistic growth and learning" (Meier 2023, 103). Educators' intentional decisions about what and how to teach are carefully made in consideration of students, state and local mandates, developmental milestones and learning trajectories, and their own knowledge of and experiences with teaching young children. Ms. Williams's selection of storms as a topic for the children to study was not arbitrary. She used her knowledge of her state standards and the context in which she and the children live to launch the study about weather and climate.

When you plan a unit of study, the first step is to identify clear learning goals for the children. This is often done using a graphic organizer, with learning goals springing from the topic in the center. Ms. Williams might use the children's interest in measuring rainfall to write this integrated learning goal: "The children will use nonstandard measurement to describe and compare the weather (such as rainfall) and explain their observations and make predictions using words such as 'more than,' 'less than,' 'same,' and 'different' as well as numbers."

With the learning goals as the focus, curriculum planning then involves identifying developmentally appropriate activities and experiences that will help the children move toward achieving each specific goal. For the goal of measuring rainfall, Ms. Williams could implement one lesson in which the children brainstorm ways to collect and measure the rainwater; in subsequent activities, they could test some of these methods, record their findings, and discuss the need for any modifications. Each of these activities is tightly connected to the learning goal.

It's hard not to begin by identifying all the "fun" activities first. While you want your kindergartners to have engaging learning opportunities, it's important to use the learning goals to guide your planning. Otherwise, you'll end up with a string of activities that are not tightly connected—and children's learning will likely stay at a surface level, hindering them from using and applying the concepts later on.

It is also important to consider the needs of the individual children in your classroom. While everyone will have access to learn about the selected topic, you'll need to adapt materials and vary how information is presented so that *all* children make progress toward competence in the standards.

While you may or may not have flexibility in what you teach, consider where you can add hands-on learning and play opportunities to support learning goals. Be focused, incorporate what you know about young children and learning progressions, and make the best decisions you can within the parameters that you have. "An effective curriculum is never static: it is continually changing as educators seek to make meaningful connections in children's learning experiences" (Meier 2023, 103).

READ AND REFLECT

As you read the chapters in this section, consider and evaluate your own classroom practices using these reflection questions.

"Engaging and Enriching: The Key to Developmentally Appropriate Academic Rigor" addresses various strategies for ensuring that the developmentally appropriate experiences planned for kindergarten children are also rigorous and address learning goals. **Consider:** What strategies might you consider including or enhancing to ensure that your kindergarten curriculum is both developmentally appropriate and rigorous?

"Incorporating Play-Based Learning into the Kindergarten Classroom" describes an approach to making mandated curriculum and materials more accessible to kindergarten students while addressing state standards. **Consider:** What changes could you make to ensure that curriculum implementation is appropriate for your students while still meeting local and state requirements?

"Finding Joy in Kindergarten Mathematics" acknowledges that many early childhood teachers have a phobia of mathematics and shares the author's story of overcoming her own math phobia as a teacher. **Consider:** What mindset do you have about mathematics? How might your fears or lack of confidence affect your students?

"Joyful and Equitable Literacy: The Intersection of Access and Opportunity" offers ways to ensure that joy and equity are linked in your language and literacy curriculum. **Consider:** What strategies might you use to plan and implement literacy lessons that both focus on skill development *and* are joyful and meaningful to children?

"Adapting the Curriculum to Incorporate Student Inquiry Through Teachable Moments" gives an inside look at how a kindergarten teacher used student interest to launch an integrated unit of study. **Consider:** How might you use children's interests to guide your curriculum planning?

NEXT STEPS

1. Select one lesson or activity that you often use that could be made more accessible to all your students. Use the concepts and strategies presented in the chapters to enhance the lesson, ensuring that all children have an increased likelihood of achieving the learning goals it was designed to accomplish.

2. With your colleagues, choose an existing unit of study to refine, using these chapters to help you clarify your learning goals so that they are clear and specific. Modify learning experiences so they are meaningful, engaging, equitable, and directly linked to the learning goals.

3. Make a list of topics that would be of interest to the children, using your state standards as a guide. With your colleagues, choose one topic and develop a new unit of study for it, meeting regularly to work on it together. Implement the unit and make notes about what worked and how it could be improved.

4. Consider how your curriculum planning reflects what you have learned about children through assessments, observation, and documentation.

References for the chapters in this part can be accessed online at NAEYC.org/dap-focus-kindergarten.

CHAPTER 21

Engaging and Enriching
The Key to Developmentally Appropriate Academic Rigor

Shannon Riley-Ayers and Alexandra Figueras-Daniel

In a time of accountability, push down, and high-stakes assessments, many early childhood educators feel pressured to focus on academic rigor—often with instructional practices that are not developmentally appropriate. A misconception among some educators, administrators, parents, and policymakers is that a narrow definition of academic rigor—one that emphasizes worksheets and other highly teacher-directed activities—is especially necessary for children growing up in underresourced communities. Research shows that a more beneficial approach is to offer an even richer, more well-rounded education in which children have meaningful, frequent opportunities to be self-directed scholars (Adair 2014; Sisson 2023). With the right supports, young children flourish when given opportunities to engage in investigations that integrate content. In addition, it is important to immerse children in an educational environment that maximizes use of academic English to build knowledge about the world (Snow 2017). Developing academic vocabulary is *critical*. In later grades, decoding problems are relatively rare, but comprehension problems—driven by lack of vocabulary and background knowledge—are rampant (Snow & Matthews 2016). In early childhood, complex oral language skills, such as grammar usage, an extensive definitional vocabulary, and good listening comprehension, have strong relationships with later reading ability, including decoding and reading comprehension (NELP 2008).

While we understand the urgency and good intentions that propel some educators toward overemphasizing teacher-directed learning, we also grasp the importance of child-directed activities to maximize development. Rigor and developmentally appropriate practice are both essential to early childhood education; done well, they are mutually reinforcing (Brown, Feger, & Mowry 2015). We make

this claim based on long-standing and current (see, for example, NAEYC 2020) research and practice as well as the research and practice evidence from the project we discuss here. In this chapter, we describe the transformation of 17 kindergarten classrooms from places of didactic, whole group instruction with few opportunities for social interaction, playful learning experiences, or rich dialogue to rigorous *and* developmentally appropriate student-centered learning environments. We closely examine the changes through the eyes of one partner teacher, and we present formal and informal classroom observation data to document these changes. Throughout, we focus on practices that support children's language and knowledge growth, using vignettes and reflections to provide meaningful examples of how to build on children's activities and interests.

A Partnership Based in Professionalism

Developmentally appropriate academic rigor for all students was the goal of our work with kindergarten teachers in one urban district in New Jersey. At the time of our work, the city that the district serves was 72 percent Hispanic, with 81 percent of families reporting Spanish as their home language. One hundred percent of students in the school district qualifies for free or reduced-price lunch (ACNJ 2016).

The school district receives state preschool aid dollars as part of legislation in New Jersey that mandates that all 3- and 4-year-olds living in the state's lowest income districts have access to full-day, high-quality preschool programs. Although thorough evaluations (Barnett et al. 2013; Barnett & Jung 2021) have demonstrated that these preschool programs are effective, the district's state-mandated standardized reading and math test results remain worrisome. While attendance in high-quality preschool shows great value, it is necessary to focus on teaching and learning quality in subsequent grades to build on gains made in preschool (Stipek et al. 2017; Unterman & Weiland 2020).

As active participants in this work, we engaged directly with practitioners throughout the school system to shift the mindset and practices to blend the required academic rigor with a more developmentally appropriate approach. As former early childhood teachers, we drew on our experiences and expertise to guide both administrators and teachers through a transformation that demonstrated research results of increased teaching quality.

Aiming to support teachers and empower them to use their professional decision making in the classroom, we partnered with administrative staff (building and central office) to boost administrators' understanding of effective teaching practices and to initiate policy revisions, including providing teachers the professional discretion to change their practices.

The teachers, full of desire to succeed, at first wanted a script or a step-by-step recipe. One teacher explained, "We've piloted programs before where we were told exactly what to do and say. I think that's why our mindset is just 'tell us what to do and how to do it.'" The core of our approach, in contrast, is guiding and facilitating change through a process of self-reflection, not offering specific scripts. This intervention would support the teachers' pedagogical approaches and understanding of teaching and learning.

Research has found that teachers' use of two instructional strategies—using sophisticated vocabulary and giving sustained attention while talking with children during self-initiated play—in preschool and kindergarten is related to fourth grade reading comprehension and decoding skills (Dickinson & Porche 2011). However, teachers cannot practice either of these instructional strategies if there is not sufficient time to spend with children in student-selected and student-directed centers. Our work with the teachers focused on helping them to broaden children's background knowledge with language and to follow children's leads in creating learning activities that were both rigorous and developmentally appropriate.

Broadening Background Knowledge with Language

During center time, Paola (a dual language learner) approaches Ms. Hall, the teacher, with a playdough pie and proudly says, "Look! I made a cake! It's blueberry." Ms. Hall responds, "Oh, I think you made a pie!" Paola exclaims, "Yes!"

This appears to be the end of the exchange, so Dr. Figueras-Daniel, the coach, interjects, "Look at this design you put on the top! It reminds me of warm blueberry pie. My mom used to make this for me in the summer, when I was a little girl like you." Paola smiles.

Dr. Figueras-Daniel continues, "Have you ever had a piece of pie?" Paola shakes her head.

Dr. Figueras-Daniel asks, "Do you know what this design is called on top of your pie?"

Paola answers, with a smile, "Lines."

Dr. Figueras-Daniel responds, "Yes, and those lines make a lattice. See how each line overlaps the other?" Paola nods, and Dr. Figueras-Daniel continues, "This is the crust of the pie. The crust is made of sweet dough that keeps the fruit filling inside. When you bake it, it gets crunchy or crusty."

Paola says, "I make more pie."

Dr. Figueras-Daniel and Ms. Hall follow Paola back to the playdough table and work alongside her, rolling the playdough flat and cutting it into strips. Dr. Figueras-Daniel uses Paola's interest to continue teaching vocabulary, building background knowledge, and modeling language: "When you use the dough as a lattice top, like you did, it makes a cover. Sometimes, pie crusts cover the whole pie, but then you can't see the filling. That's what's on the inside."

The vignette illustrates the importance of extended conversations to build on what children already know, and it shows that meaningful interactions can support students' oral language development. Most significantly, the vignette demonstrates that a teacher must tailor her instruction to address the needs of each child in the classroom. For Paola, a dual language learner (DLL), the coach asked more close-ended questions. This showed that she understood Paola's language abilities in English. She then scaffolded Paola's learning by modeling language and intentionally describing unfamiliar words with concrete, descriptive meanings. As the classroom teacher and coach continued to interact with Paola, other children joined in the discussion about baking.

On a subsequent day, Ms. Hall planned small group time to include reading *The Apple Pie Tree* (by Zoe Hall, illus. by Shari Halpern). She brought in the ingredients and tools necessary to make pie dough and used the recipe at the end of the book to make a pie with the children.

The teacher and coach worked with the children to intentionally integrate domains (here, math) by measuring ingredients and naming utensils, such as rolling pins, measuring spoons, and measuring cups. Ms. Hall mapped her actions to words: "See, I am using the smallest measuring spoon to add a tiny bit of baking powder," and "Now I need to roll the dough out to make it flat. I'll need to use the utensil that rolls—the rolling pin." As the group created the lattice work on their own in small groups, Ms. Hall talked about other objects that have a lattice design on them, such as fences. The children enjoyed describing the types of fences they see on their walks to school.

Ms. Hall effectively built on students' interest in a topic and further engaged them to introduce novel vocabulary and to learn about the nuanced uses of words such as *lattice*. This type of interaction increases students' background knowledge, an important contributor to word learning, reading fluency, and reading comprehension in later grades, when texts are more complex (Neuman, Kaefer, & Pinkham 2014; Priebe, Keenan, & Miller 2012; Smith et al. 2021). Although pie baking was not represented in the district curriculum, it was evident in these interactions and lessons that learning standards related to oral language development and mathematics (including measurement) were being targeted.

Pairing teacher-child interactions (like Dr. Figueras-Daniel's engagement with Paola around her playdough pie) with reading-related nonfiction and fiction texts (like Ms. Hall's selection of *The Apple Pie Tree*) is necessary for building children's content knowledge. It is especially important for DLLs and others who may have fewer opportunities to engage with academic English at home. Using student interest to guide interactions and learning allows students to feel valued as members of the classroom community,

and there is well-documented evidence that play sparks learning opportunities (Nesbitt et al. 2023; Schlesinger et al. 2020).

Paola's experience exemplifies our premise that giving children the freedom to pursue their interests through play and then building on their ideas is developmentally appropriate for kindergarten and can lead to academically rigorous learning. Using children's interests and creations to introduce new vocabulary and complex language enables teachers to provide students with a more meaningful and engaging learning experience.

While Paola did not yet have the vocabulary in English to elaborate on her pie creation, the adults recognized this and quickly engaged in an interaction that provided a rich array of vocabulary. Doing this is particularly important for DLLs; structured talk about academically relevant content (rather than rote memorization of word lists) is crucial (Gillanders, Castro, & Franco 2014; Kane et al. 2023). This discussion-based learning around a topic of interest to children allows them to build knowledge and vocabulary across subject areas, rather than in isolation. To be highly effective, teachers need to model and intentionally teach words' meanings while providing students with multiple opportunities to use the words in context (Pollard-Durodola et al. 2022; Takanishi & Le Menestrel 2017). This simply cannot be done in rote exercises such as those that use flash cards or worksheets.

Developmentally Appropriate Academic Rigor

Ms. Hall plans to study buildings and structures with her students. To gauge students' interests, she begins with an idea web. The students share many ideas, and Juan, a usually reserved DLL, suggests igloos. He expresses interest in constructing a model igloo in the classroom, one large enough to use as a hideout for reading books with his classmates. Ms. Hall seems uncertain about this—her aim was for the students to learn about skyscrapers. Their urban school is housed in an old six-story art deco bank building with a rooftop playground that offers interesting views of other buildings in the city and a blurry but definite view of the Manhattan skyline. But the students agree that they want to learn about igloos, so Ms. Hall moves in that direction.

After reading a few books about igloos to the children, Ms. Hall uses writer's workshop time for the students to draw and write plans for the igloo they will build. She circulates, commenting on their work and engaging in conversation about the drawings. "Can you tell me about your drawing?" she asks Yousef, who has drawn a spiral-shaped design. Yousef explains that his drawing is what the igloo looks like "on top." Ms. Hall responds, "I see! This is the igloo from above, like how the birds would see it!" Yousef nods excitedly. Ms. Hall says, "We call this a *bird's-eye view* because of that. When you see things from above, we say it's a bird's-eye view. It definitely looks different from what Juan drew, which is the igloo as we would see it if we were standing in front of it."

The children begin building the igloo with empty gallon jugs. Ms. Hall infuses academic rigor with math and science concepts, such as using a compass to make the initial circle and discussing the number of jugs that might be needed. However, while gluing jugs to form the second and third rows, the children notice that the structure looks like a cylinder—not a dome. In a whole group discussion, Ms. Hall engages the children in solving this problem.

Damian begins almost inaudibly, saying "big to small" while motioning with his hands. Ms. Hall says encouragingly, "Tell us what you mean by 'biggest to smallest.'" Damian motions the dome shape with his hands. "How can we make our igloo get smaller at the top?" asks Ms. Hall, looking at a student holding a small whiteboard. "Maybe if we draw it, we can figure out how to do this." Mateo yells, "It's a circle!" Camila exclaims, "It's a rainbow!" Smiling, Ms. Hall says, "Yes, it's shaped like a rainbow on the outside. Does anyone remember what that shape is called?" After pausing to give the children time to think, she says, "We read a book that had an arc."

Ms. Hall describes the book and the reference to an arc. She uses her hands to show flat versus round to give children a concrete understanding of the new vocabulary. The children exclaim, "It's round!" Ms. Hall says, "Yes! It is round. It is half of a sphere—like if we cut a ball in half. We will have to keep thinking to figure out how to make our igloo take this shape. Do you think we can continue to plan our igloo in the centers?" Damian says that he is going to read a book about it in the library center.

Ms. Hall provided children with opportunities to engage in contextually rich, meaningful conversations that were sustained over several exchanges. Important to note are the multiple opportunities for students to think critically by directing their own inquiry, with guidance from the teacher. The classroom environment played a role as it allowed the students the autonomy to seek materials, tools, paper, pencils, books, and collaboration with peers to carry out their work. The igloo construction was clearly not a "station" with contrived activity sheets for students to follow; rather, it encouraged talking, writing, exploration, and problem solving directed by the students. After construction, the presence of the igloo also provided plenty of natural opportunities for Ms. Hall and the children to use the vocabulary (like *arc*).

DAP Through their intentional teaching, educators blend opportunities for each child to exercise choice and agency within the context of a planned environment constructed to support specific learning experiences and meaningful goals.

The intentional interactions Ms. Hall had with the children contributed to the rigor of the study of igloos without disrupting the children's self-directed learning and exploration. The use of effective questioning techniques enables students to consider various answers and outcomes. Infusing questions that have more than one right answer and encouraging investigation develops in learners the capacity to problem solve and persist. The language and skills Ms. Hall intentionally modeled and the peer collaboration she fostered enhanced the academic learning experience; the children's growing content knowledge, problem solving, persistence, initiative, and creativity were all mutually reinforcing.

The integration of content areas (math, science, language arts, visual arts, and so on) into the igloo project provided opportunities to engage in meaningful, academically rigorous, student-directed work. This was a shift in practice from the typical lessons these kindergartners had experienced in the past. As in classrooms across the country, the teachers in this school had previously taught subjects according to the schedule and only during those times. In contrast, the igloo project demanded an intersection of content areas and skills that could not be matched by a worksheet or a narrow lesson on one skill or in one subject area.

It is crucial to note that while these types of interactions are at times spontaneous and follow the students' lead, all are intentional. Ms. Hall planned activities linked to students' interests and provided opportunities for deeper exploration during center time. At all times, the teacher remains the engineer, infusing key skills, enhancing vocabulary, and linking to learning standards, yet students have the opportunity to independently guide their learning—very often through play. Ms. Hall's ability to shift from her plan to study skyscrapers to using igloos as the means of learning exemplified the role of teacher moving fluidly from leader to guide yet remaining an intentional instructor with specific learning goals (Zosh et al. 2022).

After the igloo project concluded, Ms. Hall reflected on it with the coach. Ms. Hall emphasized the students' interest in asking questions and exploring concepts and the resulting increase in their vocabulary: "The students have more vocabulary, more questioning. Now if I say a word, at least five or six will ask, 'What does that mean?' They want to know more." She considered the students' roles as active contributors to their learning and her role in providing meaningful, rigorous, appropriate opportunities for them:

> The classroom has a better atmosphere because students are more involved in deciding the learning paths in the classroom, and I ask them their opinions more often. I engage in meaningful conversations with the children about content. Before, I was asking questions with one right answer to test them, but now I am asking more *why* and *what do you think* questions, which has increased the talk in the class exponentially!

 Work to embed fair and equitable approaches in all aspects of early childhood program delivery, including standards, assessments, curriculum, and personnel practices.

Conclusion

Many kindergarten teachers (often unwillingly and sometimes unknowingly) succumb to a counterproductive, unrealistic vision of kindergarten that includes test-focused skill development, inappropriate expectations, and misguided teaching practices. It's time for teachers, administrators, families, and policymakers to reject that vison—especially for our learners from underresourced communities and our DLLs. Effective kindergarten classrooms have balanced—developmentally appropriate and academically rigorous—programs in place. Departing from a didactic teaching style that provides minimal opportunities for choice, exploration, self-discovery, or rich conversation is crucial for supporting all children and for offering the enriched learning experiences that are most likely to close the achievement gap. What can lead to academically rigorous learning is a well-rounded curriculum that puts students at the center, giving them the freedom to learn through play and focusing on academic language and content and on approaches to learning (e.g., persistence, collaboration, problem solving). As a field, we must swing the pendulum back toward teachers having the professional discretion to pursue academic rigor in a developmentally appropriate manner.

SHANNON RILEY-AYERS, PhD, is currently director of the Custom Solutions Division at Lakeshore Learning Materials, where she works on special projects and partnerships. Dr. Riley-Ayers was formerly an associate research professor at the National Institute for Early Education Research (NIEER) at Rutgers University, where this research was conducted.

ALEXANDRA FIGUERAS-DANIEL, PhD, is an assistant research professor and bilingual early childhood education policy specialist at NIEER. Her work includes numerous studies on improving outcomes for young children, P–3 alignment, and work on policy and best practices for supporting DLLs.

Authors' note

The work reported here was funded by the Henry and Marilyn Taub Foundation. Views expressed here are the authors' and do not necessarily reflect the views of the foundation.

CHAPTER 22

Incorporating Play-Based Learning into the Kindergarten Classroom

Margi Bhansali, Alli Bizon, and Erean Mei

"So what do we know about the ocean?" I (Alli) ask my group of kindergartners from the West Side of Chicago. We are about to learn about marine life in the district-mandated literacy curriculum, and I want to gauge my students' background knowledge. "I dunno. I've never been to the ocean . . . not even the lake," Tyler says, referring to Lake Michigan, located just a few miles from our school. The other children nod in agreement. My school serves 95 percent low-income families, and this is not the first time the content we are studying has had little connection to the children's prior experiences and knowledge. It is clear to me at this moment that what my students need is to get a sense of the deep blue sea through hands-on exploration. What better way to do this than through play?

The research is clear that young children learn best when they have agency and can construct their learning of new concepts through joyful investigation (see, e.g., NAEYC 2020). As classroom teachers and former Teach Plus fellows (see "Advocating for Play in Kindergarten Classrooms Across Illinois" on page 124), we have seen both the great benefits and challenges of implementing play-based learning—an approach to teaching and learning that uses play as an instructional tool—with kindergarten students. We have found two forms of play, in particular, to be effective instructional tools to support children's learning and eager participation: guided play and student-initiated play.

Guided play is "intentional teacher-directed play with activities set up by the teacher that support whole class and small group lessons and are aligned to learning standards" (Teach Plus 2022, 1). Through guided play, teachers introduce concepts that students may not have experience with, provide more targeted learning experiences, and encourage deeper thinking in an academic skill. Crucially, students can make choices during guided play experiences. In guided play, which may involve predesigned games, students apply their knowledge in a hands-on experience and engage in open-ended conversation with their peers, explain their thinking, bring up questions, support their ideas, and make some choices in how they engage in the activity.

Student-initiated play refers to "open-ended, child-selected opportunities for children to build, pretend, create, move, and explore" (Teach Plus 2022, 1). (NAEYC refers to this as *self-directed play*.) In student-initiated play, students choose tasks and activities on their own; teachers create the environment, observe, and ask thoughtful questions to extend children's play and thinking. Teachers may join in the play, but students retain full control over their play experience. (See "'Look-Fors' When Implementing Play-Based Learning" on pages 128–129 for a list of student and teacher roles typically seen in guided play and student-initiated play.)

Authors' note

The terms and definitions we use for guided play and student-initiated play in this chapter are taken from the definition of play-based learning in our Teach Plus work, which is based, in turn, on the work of several researchers in play and learning (see Teach Plus 2022). These terms and definitions differ slightly from those NAEYC uses (see NAEYC 2020 and Zosh et al. 2022).

While play of all types is important for children's development, student-initiated play does not always lead to academic learning (Weisberg et al. 2016). Play-based instruction that facilitates the achievement of learning goals consists of these crucial components: being intentional, focusing on the goal you want students to achieve, choosing appropriate supports, providing opportunities for student choice, and planning how to assess students' learning.

In this chapter we explore using both guided and student-initiated play and offer steps you can take to make your learning experiences more play based.

Advocating for Play in Kindergarten Classrooms Across Illinois

This chapter is based on research we carried out as a part of the Teach Plus Illinois Early Childhood Educator Policy Fellowship. Teach Plus, a national organization, empowers excellent, experienced, and diverse teachers to take leadership over key policy and practice issues that advance equity, opportunity, and student success.

As part of a statewide observation tool, Illinois requires that kindergarten teachers observe students during play-based learning experiences. In an effort to understand how play-based learning was being implemented in kindergartens in the state, we spoke with stakeholders from four districts. These districts have taken steps to incorporate play-based learning in their kindergarten classrooms. The complete findings and recommendations were published in a brief titled "Implementing Play-Based Learning Across Illinois Kindergarten Classrooms: Recommendations from Teach Plus Early Childhood Fellows" (Bhansali et al. 2022).

Participants noted that play implementation varied across and within schools and that lack of funding for materials, space, and other resources to create a play-based environment was a barrier. Yet every educator we spoke to saw the positive impacts of play in many domains and content areas, particularly in students' social and emotional skills. All of the leaders and educators said that interaction between students is better when they are allowed to play. One principal said that first grade teachers noticed that students who had attended a kindergarten classroom that used play-based instruction have fewer negative behaviors, more conflict management skills, and fewer redirections during group work. Play in the classroom also led to better oral language and vocabulary skills, and higher reading and math achievement in subsequent grades.

Play-Based Learning Example: Marine Life

As I (Alli) began to plan how to support my students' understanding of marine life, I examined our school's mandated literacy curriculum and noted how many of the suggested learning activities left little opportunity for developmentally appropriate play practices. Instead, the curriculum guide indicated that students should build concepts of nonfiction text features through teacher-directed conversations, with minimal assistance other than anchor charts. The books provided by the publisher were engaging and rigorous, but they still required additional scaffolding for those with little background knowledge about a particular subject.

To make the content more accessible, I developed a learning environment that brought the ocean to my students. I reviewed the required texts, considered the Common Core State Standards in English language arts (ELA) on composing informative texts, and developed specific learning objectives for the needs and interests of my particular students. I wondered, "How can my students come up with questions about these underwater creatures if they had never had the opportunity to see, hear, or touch the water of these creatures' home?" To support the children's learning, I planned opportunities for guided play and related materials for the children to explore and play with based on their imaginations and what we were learning together.

To begin building the children's knowledge of the ocean, we watched videos of a variety of fish and marine mammals swimming in the ocean, and children drew pictures on their clipboards of what they observed. The children had a lot of questions, which we recorded on a scroll of large paper. Their inquiries pushed us into the next learning activity. One such question, "Where's the jellyfish's mouth?," launched a collective play-based investigation that lasted several weeks.

With related props and artifacts, students began to swim their way into the learning. A few days later, I observed Taliyah and Jackie looking at the ocean books I had added to the dance area. With classical music playing in the background, Jackie picked up the scarves and twirled them around her body. "Look, look at my long arms," she said as Taliyah pointed to the jellyfish in the book. I picked up several scarves and joined in. "My tentacles are floating in the ocean," I said, reinforcing the vocabulary related to our learning goals by embedding the language into our play. I also placed photographs of various marine life in the art center. As we studied the colors and shapes in the pictures, I provided more language, both academic and content vocabulary, to connect to the children's illustrations: "Oh, I see you added those long lines for the jellyfish, just like the tentacles in these photographs."

 Play is often viewed as being at odds with the demands of formal schooling, especially for children growing up in underresourced communities. But the highly didactic curriculum found in many kindergartens is unlikely to be engaging or meaningful for children or to build the broad knowledge and vocabulary needed for reading comprehension. Playful learning, skillfully supported by early childhood educators, builds academic language, deepens conceptual development, and supports reflective and intentional approaches to learning.

We used what we learned about the parts of the jellyfish's body to build models using clear plastic bags, yarn, tissue paper, and art scraps. Comparing our learning to diagrams in our text, we shared the pen to label the parts before hanging them from the ceiling. When Kennedy wondered, "What are the oral arms for?" and "How do they eat?," we designed our own oral arms (long tentacles that carry food to a jellyfish's mouth) out of cardboard lined with packing tape. Then we ran around collecting giant pom-poms representing the plankton that got in the way!

INCLUDING ALL CHILDREN

Considering Access and Engagement in Guided Play Experiences
by Christan Coogle and Heather Walter

A powerful benefit of play-based learning in kindergarten is that it provides many means of entry so that children of all abilities can access and participate in learning experiences. Achieving this requires intentionality from educators. As you read through the marine life example in this chapter and its connections to learning objectives and standards, consider the following two questions

First, can all students access and engage in the play scenarios? For example, the class watched videos of fish and marine mammals. Later, some of the children danced with scarves as they acted

out moving like jellyfish do, and then the class drew their own representations of jellyfish and built models of the animals. Would a student with a visual impairment be able to access and engage in these experiences? While they would gain some information from the audio part of the videos, they might have difficulty really grasping what a jellyfish looks like and how it moves, which would affect their engagement in the dance play and model building.

Second, what supports could you provide to overcome these barriers? Materials that have other types of sensory input are vital—such as materials that have various textures and perhaps sounds—to provide the student opportunities to access and engage with the play environment. For example, to provide another means of representation of a jellyfish, the teacher might have children take turns moving by their peers with their scarves as they simulate a jellyfish so others can feel the jellyfish "moving by." The teacher might provide a variety of materials to create a jellyfish, such as larger or textured paper and different writing materials.

As another example, some students experience challenges with finishing one activity and moving to another, and thus might not successfully access and engage in some of the marine activities without supports. They might benefit from transition supports such as reminders (e.g., "Five minutes"), visual schedules (showing what will happen before and after the play), or a tangible item (such as a scarf that encourages children to act like the jellyfish they are learning about) to move into the next activity. This allows children to accomplish a transition, connect it to the content, and move while it also addresses many developmental domains.

In addition to access and engagement, think about how you could use guided play to embed opportunities to work on a child's Individualized Education Program (IEP) goals. For example, for a student who has an IEP goal related to letter-sound identification, you might make labels for the parts of the jellyfish and point out the letters and letter sounds on the labels that the child is working on. This simple strategy could support and enhance all of the children's understanding of letter-sound relationships as well as a variety of other literacy skills.

Planning for Guided Play: A Step-by-Step Guide

Kindergarten teachers must teach the curriculum and lessons the school has selected, as Alli did with the marine life curriculum. However, we believe that all curriculum and lessons can be adapted to a play-based learning approach to help students develop their knowledge in a meaningful and joyful way through developmentally appropriate practices. Here we share steps you can take to adapt a lesson to a more play-based learning approach.

1. Analyze the Standard and Assessment Practices Associated with the Lesson

Before beginning a lesson, think about what students are being asked to learn. Identify the overall standard. If there are formal or informal assessment practices associated with the lesson or standard, think about the key objectives and takeaways. Are they procedural or conceptual? To identify *procedural* knowledge, think about the skills students need to complete a task. What must students be able to do? How will they show you the skill? *Conceptual* refers to the factual knowledge and comprehension of the ideas necessary to complete a skill. What must the students know and why?

Here is an example of what analyzing the lesson standard and assessment looks like, using the marine life lesson discussed previously. We'll begin by identifying both the standard and the suggested formal assessment associated with this lesson.

Lesson: Marine life

ELA standard: CCSS.RI.K.9. *With prompting and support, identify basic similarities in and differences between two texts on the same topic (e.g., in illustrations, descriptions, or procedures).*

Assessment: Students will take a paper-based multiple choice formal assessment for this lesson. They will be expected to answer four questions based on two articles about jellyfish and octopuses and note the similarities and differences between the two sea creatures.

With the standard and assessment identified, we can begin to analyze both the procedural and conceptual skills and knowledge students will need to be successful (a chart showing some of these is shown on page 127). We can also identify more authentic ways of assessing student learning to be more developmentally appropriate for kindergartners.

2. Look at the Lesson for Big Ideas

Once you know what students are being asked to learn, transform the lesson and accompanying worksheets into playful experiences that address the same content in more meaningful and engaging ways. For example, create a game. Provide materials and appropriate manipulatives (e.g., cut apart a portion of the worksheet to create game pieces). Have students act out the lesson. Identify related resources such as children's books, community resources, and virtual experiences.

For example, I transformed this marine life lesson into engaging active learning experiences: students viewed videos paired with a drawing opportunity, role-played with props, and drew inspiration from ocean books in the dancing area and from photographs in the art center. Academic language was taught through organic conversation with students, based on their observations of text, videos, drawings, and later the jellyfish they created.

After you have transformed the worksheet for the lesson into a playful learning opportunity, create checks for understanding that keep you on track for supporting the underlying learning standard during activity. Think about the questions you will ask students before, during, and after the experience. What answers or actions will display their understanding? Think about how you will end the lesson. What will you do or say to solidify the key takeaway of the lesson?

In this lesson, many of the questions I asked to check for understanding focused on what students saw in the videos, the texts, and the jellyfish diagram. Students displayed their understanding through creating their own models of jellyfish and comparing them to diagrams in their text and by writing informative books about the sea animals.

Procedural and Conceptual Understandings

Procedural (the How)	Conceptual Understandings (the What/Why)
Students will be able to . . .	**Students must know . . .**
■ Compare two texts on the same topic.	■ When we compare, we find things that are similar or the same. ■ I can find similar people, places, things, and ideas.
■ Identify similarities in the words.	■ I can think about what is the same about the words in both texts. ■ I can think about what I learn from the words. ■ I can listen for people, places, things, and ideas in the words.
■ Contrast two texts on the same topic.	■ When we contrast, we find things that are different. ■ I can tell what is different about the people, places, things, and ideas. ■ Sometimes people have different experiences.
■ Identify differences in the words.	■ I can think about what is different about the words in both texts. ■ I can think about words that I only hear about in one text.

■ Identify differences in the pictures.
  ■ Identify different people, places, things.
  ■ Identify different shapes, colors, and qualities in the pictures.
	■ I can think about what the difference is between the pictures in both texts.
	■ Pictures can show the same things in different ways.

3. Identify Gaps in Students' Understanding and Differentiations

Think about the space between what students already know and what they need to know to be ready for a particular lesson or experience. Consider the implications this will have for your lesson. What possible student misconceptions may occur during the activity, and how can you address them?

For example, in the marine life lesson, students may not understand that they can compare and contrast different topics, such as animals and locations.

You could address this by having students look at their first text and find just one picture, place, or idea to focus on and then see if that one idea is in their second text.

Data Collection Practices

Collecting data is imperative to a successful play-based learning experience. Given that the provided assessment for this content is a paper-based multiple choice format assessment comparing an octopus and jellyfish, consider instead how you will collect observational data and measure students' progress toward the learning goal(s) through your observations of their play. Identify a strategy that will allow for making quick in-the-moment notes. For example, you might use a checklist to quickly identify the major skills demonstrated and write notes in a comment section. This tool will drive your future selection of play experiences and questions to deepen students' understanding.

4. Create a Checklist of Materials

Identify the materials you will need to implement the lesson effectively. Whenever possible, choose open-ended materials that can be reused in future activities.

5. Implementing the Lesson

In a guided play experience, you invite students to engage in a more targeted learning experience. Consider whether the lesson would be best carried out in a small or large group. Think about what you will do and what the students will do (see "'Look-Fors' When Implementing Play-Based Learning"). Although a guided play experience is intentionally planned by the teacher, it also provides students with choices about how they will engage in the activity or carry it out. In the jellyfish model activity, for example, students were free to choose the materials they would use to make their models and how they would do it based on their interpretation of the diagram.

What will make the lesson a playful learning experience is plenty of opportunities for students to engage actively with materials that spark curiosity and to explore through their choice of role playing, art, dance, independent reading in groups, or on their own in different spaces, all of which results in organic conversation. The activity should include the freedom to try something a different way, make mistakes, and try again—and above all, there should be a sense of enjoyment.

6. Reflecting on the Lesson

Analyze your observational data to gain a better understanding of students' ability to apply the concept covered in different contexts, explain it in their own words, and solve problems that require its use. Use what you learn to inform future activities— what can you do differently or additionally to guide students to meet related learning goals and objectives

over time and address gaps in their understanding of the concept? Being successful in creating and implementing play-based experiences requires intentionality and a focus on end goals for students. In addition, it requires you to be mindful in how you will provide opportunities for students to make choices within the experience.

"Look-Fors" When Implementing Play-Based Learning

What does a kindergarten classroom look like when play-based learning is flourishing? Below are some things you are likely to see teachers and students doing during guided play and student-initiated play experiences. Keep in mind that there is considerable overlap between these two lists; both types of play provide opportunities for children's choices and agency and teachers' involvement, but a defining difference between guided and student-initiated play is the centrality of specific learning goals to the former.

During Guided Play or Whole and Small Group Lessons

Teachers are

› Creating and providing materials for play-based experiences that embed the learning standard

› Clearly stating learning objectives for activities and providing clear instructions before beginning an activity

› Supporting instruction through the inclusion of materials that allow for meaningful, active application of the skill being learned

› Encouraging students to use analysis and reasoning skills during experiences by asking open-ended questions

› Modeling curiosity and engaging students in conversation with open-ended questions and advanced vocabulary (Why . . . ? How . . . ? What could happen next . . .?) and providing ample time to pause for students to process

› Scaffolding and differentiating students' learning

› Assessing children's understanding through observations and anecdotal notes

Students are

> Engaging in a hands-on experiences using manipulatives, objects from everyday life, or other materials that support active, contextualized learning

> Having conversations and engaging in back-and-forth exchanges that require expanded verbal responses, both with peers and teachers

> Explaining their thinking

During Student-Initiated Play

Teachers are

> Ensuring the classroom environment supports active learning by including clearly defined play areas, materials that address learning standards, and opportunities to connect play with current curricular topics

> Using self-talk and parallel talk, advanced language, and open-ended questions to expand the complexity of students' play and to encourage them to explain their thinking while playing

> Providing support to resolve peer conflicts as they arise during play

> Creating opportunities to engage in sensory and social and emotional activities

> Encouraging students to persist in the completion of their selected activity

> Offering support to children to enter into play scenarios with peers

> Observing how children interact with materials and making notes on how to modify materials to expand learning based on student interests and needs

> Helping children plan their play

> Assessing students on demonstrated skills within the context of play

Students are

> Choosing materials and activities based on personal interest

> Engaging in an activity or with preferred materials for an uninterrupted, extended period of time

> Engaging in conversation with their peers and teacher about what they are doing (making predictions; brainstorming; experimenting; and explaining what is happening, how they figured it out, or what they could try next)

> Interacting, negotiating, and cooperating with peers in small groups or pairs

> Building upon play schemes over time (day after day, week after week), expanding their original ideas and using prior knowledge to deepen their understanding

Adapted, by permission, from M. Bhansali, M. Hillegass, & E. Mei, "Guidelines for Play in Kindergarten: What You Should Look for in Your School as You Implement Play-Based Learning" (Teach Plus, 2022), 1–2. https://teachplus.org/wp-content/uploads/2022/11/Teach-Plus-IL_Kindergarten-play-Doc3.pdf

Conclusion

Academic learning is a fundamental component of play-based learning as teachers both explicitly teach and embed concepts into students' exploration. The example presented in this chapter shows the possibilities for supporting and enhancing children's play by emphasizing vocabulary and other key concepts while still following the required kindergarten curriculum.

MARGI BHANSALI, MA, is a National Board Certified teacher who teaches prekindergarten at Beard Elementary in Chicago. Her op-eds have been published in the *Chicago Tribune, Chicago Unheard,* and on What's the Plus, among others.

ALLI BIZON, MAT, a National Board Certified teacher, teaches grades 1–3 at Suder Montessori Magnet School in Chicago. She was a 2021 Golden Apple Award for Excellence in Teaching finalist.

EREAN MEI, MEd, is a kindergarten teacher at KIPP Academy Chicago Primary. With more than 12 years' experience, she specializes in trauma-informed practices, comprehensive early childhood growth and development knowledge, classroom management, and data-driven instruction.

CHAPTER 23

Finding Joy in Kindergarten Mathematics

Lauren Solarski

"I hate math" is something I used to say all the time. Ask a roomful of early childhood teachers, "Does anyone here struggle with math?," and many will immediately raise their hands. But imagine if we asked, "Do you struggle with reading?" No hands would go up. Why do we consider these two subjects differently? More important, as educators, how do our attitudes toward mathematics affect our students?

Research with young learners indicates that a positive attitude about math matters just as much as IQ because it enhances memory and allows children to engage in problem solving (Chen et al. 2018). Children are sensitive to the attitudes and indirect messages teachers and other adults express about math (Aguirre, Mayfield-Ingram, & Martin 2013). For example, female teachers who exhibit high math anxiety pass on their anxiety to their female students (Dowker, Sarkar, & Looi 2016). Long term, this can have serious consequences. Despite no evidence of gender-related differences in ability to do math, women are underrepresented in advanced mathematics courses and STEM fields.

Children are also harmed by stereotypes about who can and cannot do math in relation to their racial and ethnic identities. The myth that Asian American children are better at math can result in teachers neglecting to provide necessary supports. Likewise, implicit biases can cause teachers to have dangerous deficit-views about children with minoritized identities including Black, Latino/a, and Indigenous (Aguirre, Mayfield-Ingram, & Martin 2013). As educators, we must reflect on our own—and our students'—intersecting identities in relation to math learning.

Why does this matter so much? Research also shows that early math skills are crucial to overall academic achievement. Children's math abilities in kindergarten are strong predictors of later school success—even more than literacy, attention, and social and emotional skills (Claessens & Engel 2013). To ensure that all students are provided a fair start, teachers must possess robust math content knowledge, use effective teaching strategies to engage children in developing their mathematical understanding, and feel positively about the subject (Solarski 2021). Teachers' aversions to or insecurities about math can disservice children for a lifetime.

How can early childhood professionals find joy in math so they can pass on that joy to children? I offer some practical ideas learned throughout my own journey from hating to loving math.

Begin Within

How do you feel about math? What experiences in your schooling have shaped these feelings? A teacher once told me, with tears in her eyes, "When I was in school, girls were not allowed to take math classes. We had to take sewing instead." Another shared, "When I first moved to the United States and was not confident in speaking English, math became my best subject. I was very proud of that. But now, with the new ways of teaching math, I feel confused and I have a difficult time admitting it and asking for help."

Here's an exercise to try: Think of your best math-related memory. Where were you? What age were you? What happened, and how did you feel? Now think about your worst math-related memory. How have these experiences contributed to the way you feel about math today? Share your stories with colleagues, and listen for clues about barriers to participation in math lessons and moments that provided meaningful access to learning. How might these apply to you? How might they apply to your students?

Most of my formative math experiences are clouded with feelings of anxiety and frustration. I do, however, have a proud math-related moment that occurred in third grade. As a result of intense studying, I was the first student in my class to pass all of our multiplication Mad Minutes quizzes for fact families 1–12. But in fourth grade, when the calculations became more complex, my memorization skills no longer held up, and I received my first-ever F on a homework assignment. Ashamed, I tore the paper into tiny bits, flushed them down the toilet, and concluded I was just not a math person.

Many of the influential women in my life also disliked math but enjoyed writing. This led me to assume that math was a "boy thing" and therefore not for me. From that point on, I struggled with numbers, formulas, and shapes, always terrified of making one fateful mistake that would lead to an incorrect answer. In contrast, I excelled in my English classes because I felt comfortable learning through conversation and creativity. I also benefited from the routine of writing rough drafts, which reduced pressure and increased my motivation to improve, as I knew I could go back and make changes later. These methods were absent from my math classes; as a result, I never grasped the concepts behind math procedures until I was an adult learner.

For this new learning to occur, I needed to change my beliefs and recognize that *everyone* is capable of learning math, regardless of age, gender, ability, interests, culture, or home language. I missed out as a child because of unintended exclusionary messages and math teaching methods that were a poor fit for me as an anxious student. I did not realize this until I was a kindergarten teacher, and then I became determined to ensure that all of the children in my classroom had genuine opportunities to learn math. Instead of avoiding math-related workshops, I began to seek them out; I owed it to my students.

 Early childhood educators must also be aware that they themselves—and their programs as a whole—bring their own experiences and contexts, in both the narrower and broader definitions, to their decision making. Educators need to understand the implications of these contexts.

Increasing Your Knowledge

The surest way to find—and to pass on—joy in math is to deepen your understanding of mathematics. While teaching kindergarten, I participated in professional development provided by Erikson Institute's Early Math Collaborative. It was my chance to learn the math content I had missed in my own schooling and to study videos of teaching and student thinking (available at https://earlymath.erikson.edu). With my new knowledge and the confidence that came with it, I was able to draw attention to mathematical situations that arose during play in my classroom, model more mathematical language, and adjust the curriculum to better fit my students' interests. One particular memory stands out.

Five-year-old Elliott had difficulty sitting with the rest of the class during whole group time. He would wander off to stare at a fan or find light switches to flicker. A scrap of paper could entertain him for an hour. He was full of brilliant questions. But he had difficulty making friends—his curiosity was often too much for other children. Elliott had been tested for autism twice, with both assessments being inconclusive.

My new mathematics understanding inspired me to adjust the curriculum. Math was slated to be taught during a whole group lesson followed by worksheets in which children could practice applying their new math knowledge. Instead of using the worksheets, I led small groups while the rest of the children played with math manipulatives. During this time, Elliott often chose to play with Linking Cubes. I would glance up now and then to see him deeply focused.

On Fridays, I joined the children in math play, jotting notes about their activities and asking questions to provoke their mathematical thinking. Elliott was busy making "spinners." He would take six Linking Cubes and arrange five in a plus sign, with the sixth on the bottom as a base. I decided to join him and construct a spinner of my own. Unfortunately, mine would not spin. Looking at Elliott's example, I realized I needed to leave the peg on the sixth cube pointing down for the spinner to rest on. I tried again to twirl my spinner, this time successful and amazed at Elliott's creativity. My top twirled rapidly, the red and blue cubes blending together to appear as a purple circle, and Elliott squealed with delight.

Over the course of a month, other children noticed Elliott's top making and made spinners along with him. This evolved into a gleeful game in which several players would spin their tops at the same time to see which one could remain on the table the longest without being bumped off by the others. The tops became more and more elaborate, and all the while the children unknowingly studied addition, force, motion, balance, and more.

When symmetry arose as a topic in our curriculum, I replaced the provided butterfly worksheets with a lesson about Elliott's tops. From then on, everyone wanted to be Elliott's friend, and everyone had a deeper understanding of the math concepts that were demonstrated naturally during their spinner play.

Play with Your Colleagues

Another way to find the joy in mathematics is to engage in play with other educators. In my role as a coach and professional development facilitator, I witness laughter as well as productive struggle when we launch workshops with adult learning activities. During a recent session focused on sets and sorting, 20 teachers gathered in the front of the room, each wearing only one shoe. Their other shoes were being silently sorted into three groups by one of the participants. We played What's My Rule?, focusing on the shoe attributes that defined each set. With smiles and curiosity, the teachers studied each set closely and began to share ideas based on color, shape, and style.

> "Is it sandals, gym shoes, and flats?" one teacher wondered. "I thought that too, but this one isn't a sandal," another said, pointing out a black ballet flat with a decorative buckle across the front. "Maybe it has to do with the heel height?" a different teacher suggested, inspecting the bottoms of a few shoes. Others joined in to see if the shoes in the group had similar heels. "Oh, I see! It's buckles here, laces there, and no closures over there!" exclaimed another participant.

Activities like this are fun for adults and translate directly to early childhood classrooms; children love using their own shoes! Other activities are much more advanced, including my favorite, Shepherd's Counting, which challenges participants to make sense of a historic sheep-counting system that has number names such as *yan, tan,* and *tethera* (Hynes-Berry & Itzkowich 2009). As teachers decode, explain, and create symbols for the unusual numbers, they appreciate the complexity of our system and how tricky it can be for a young child.

Playful experiences like this remind teachers what it feels like to be a young learner. They also allow us to exercise the Common Core standard for mathematical practice, "Make sense of problems and persevere in solving them," so that we can nurture it in our students (NGA Center & CCSSO 2023).

These adult activities embody a math culture in which everyone participates, mistakes are expected, and there are multiple ways to approach a problem. This is similar to writing multiple rough drafts in English class, because it emphasizes the process—where learning takes place—not just the final product.

Enjoy the Math in Stories

Most of us *love* stories. It's easy to find the joy in a book and spread that joy to our students. So why not find the math in good books too? A favorite among my kindergartners was Ellen Stoll Walsh's *Mouse Count.* After the children became familiar with the story, we acted it out together. One child would play the hungry snake; 10 other children were cast as sleepy mice; and the remainder of the class acted as the audience, helping to keep track as the snake added mice to the jar. A piece of cloth in the center of our circle served as the jar, intentionally sized so that the little mice could feel the space getting tighter as the snake added *more,* then notice the change to *less* as the mice eventually escaped, a few at a time. I drew attention to mathematical ideas by modeling language such as "Look! Now there are *more* mice in the jar" and asking questions such as "What do you notice about the jar now?"

In the fall, we focused on *more* and *less*, then moved to *plus one* and *minus one*, then to different ways to compose and decompose 10. In the math center, I added props I'd found at a dollar store: a sock for the child who was the snake to wear on one hand, 10 smooth gray rocks for mice, and a clear plastic jar just the right size to highlight the changes in number of mice. The children greatly enjoyed the continuing play of this math-rich story.

Stories are powerful because they put math in meaningful contexts. I have taught many students who could count to 100 or recite addition and subtraction facts but lacked the necessary understanding behind the procedures. While manipulatives usually help if they encourage children to focus on math concepts (Willingham 2017), acting out a story can be even more impactful because it allows children to visualize and experience the way quantities relate and change. Plus, stories bring joy as they are shared again and again. Books can likewise promote positive math identities when they feature diverse children such as in the delightful Storytelling Math series (Charlesbridge 2023).

Engage Children in Math Games

What games did you love to play as a child? I have many happy memories of playing the card game Who Has More? (a.k.a. War) with my grandfather.

Repeated opportunities to determine which quantity is larger help children strengthen their number sense, and the game context motivates them to play countless times.

This game can be modified in many ways, which is important because children need to be exposed to multiple representations of numbers. Many teachers use cards with variations, including numeric symbols, dots, ten-frames, and fingers to represent the quantities (available at https://earlymath.erikson.edu/playing-card-games). With younger children, we use only cards featuring 1–5 to develop a deep foundation. As students advance, the game can be played with 1–10 and then with two or three cards so children practice combining quantities to determine who has the most. This is just one example of the many common games that are mathematically powerful and can become even more so when enhanced by a teacher with strong math content knowledge.

In addition to being fun and motivating, games increase access, cooperation, practice, and learning for all children. Playing games together prompts discussions—and sometimes even passionate disagreements—where mathematical precision matters. At the same time, games are low risk. If you lose, you can just start again. Games allow for differentiation, with students with more advanced skills guiding their peers. They also provide structure, making participation easier for all, and especially dual language learners. And they can be sent home, so children can continue playing and learning with their families. Some schools even host game nights and invite parents to teach math-related games from their childhoods as an opportunity to promote family learning and share cultural traditions.

Games also provide an opportunity for authentic assessment. One year I taught a very shy student, Aaliyah. If I pulled her aside to administer an interview-based assessment, she was hesitate or would not answer at all. But when I quietly observed her playing a card game with her best friend, Naomi, I realized Aaliyah knew more than she demonstrated to me when we were alone.

Conclusion

Just as we seek to educate the whole child, we must consider the whole teacher. Like academics in kindergarten, growing our content knowledge about math is crucial. Like social and emotional skills in kindergarten, our own attitudes, beliefs, and confidence about math are equally important. So, here's a challenge: The next time you're out to brunch and someone jokes about being unable to calculate the tip, or the next time you're in the teachers' lounge with a colleague who is laughing off how bad they are at math, take a step toward ending this negative cultural practice. Help others find the joy in math as you work to find it in yourself and cultivate it in your students. I hope that soon you will join me in proclaiming, "I love math!"

LAUREN SOLARSKI, PhD, is an early childhood educator, researcher, and consultant based in Chicago.

Online Resources for Math-Learning Joy

Browse the websites below and follow these organizations on social media for a daily dose of inspiration.

> Erikson Institute Early Math Collaborative—Lesson ideas, newsletter, videos, summer institute, and more. Twitter: @eriksonmath. https://earlymath.erikson.edu

> NAEYC Early Math Interest Forum—Virtual meet-ups, webinars, book discussions, and in-person conference gatherings. Twitter: @NAEYCEarlyMath. NAEYC.org/get-involved/communities/science-math-technology

> YouCubed at Stanford University—"Open, Creative Mathematics." Twitter: @joboaler. www.youcubed.org

> Young Mathematicians—"Math Games for Fun and School." Twitter: @EarlyMathEDC. https://youngmathematicians.edc.org

CHAPTER 24

Joyful and Equitable Literacy
The Intersection of Access and Opportunity

Ryan Lee-James and Stacey Wallen

Joy should be the ultimate goal of teaching and learning (Muhammad 2023). Joy is not just for students. If the COVID-19 pandemic taught us anything, it's that teacher joy matters. Think back to your best day as an educator. Why do these days stand out? What emotions surface? We would bet that joy rises to the top of your mind. Being an educator in and of itself is joyful for so many reasons. We are joyful when we develop and execute a lesson masterfully. We are joyful when students are learning and applying their learning in context. Above all, we are joyful when we witness students' joy. As educators, we must pursue joy for ourselves *and* for our students.

Joy is essential for the development of literacy. When students experience joy in their learning, the path to acquiring and storing new information is more effective and efficient. The opposite is true when learning is stressful (Willis 2007). Children also show delight when they see themselves and their cultures reflected in what they are learning and reading and writing about. When teachers affirm and celebrate the complexity of children's identities through words and actions, students experience joy. Students are joyful not only when they and their families are included but also when they understand that our community is better when they are present.

In her book *Unearthing Joy,* Dr. Gholdy Muhammad (2023) explains how joy and equity in education are inextricably linked:

> For humanity to experience joy, we must be conscious of what needs to be interrupted, changed, shifted and advanced . . . it is the key to interrupting all that has not served children or educators well. Schools are reflections of society; so as long as there is hurt, pain and harm in society, we will see them come into our schools, which makes joy even more important. (86)

In the United States, where only 33 percent of fourth-graders read proficiently (NCES 2022), Dr. Muhammad's words are critical for understanding why joy and equity must be at the center of instruction.

The following are foundational understandings of equitable and joyful education:

> Every child is considered kindergarten ready. A strengths-based approach is taken—seeing, recognizing, and internalizing that every child has exactly what they need when they arrive at school.

> Leaders and educators recognize and internalize that every child can achieve. They are unwilling to accept failure as an option for any student.

> Leaders and educators prioritize curiosity and critical inquiry as a part of academics.

> Leaders and educators prioritize connection over compliance and reject policies and practices that hyper-regulate students and families.

> Leaders and educators are critically conscious.

> Leaders and educators hold themselves to the highest standards of learning as evidenced by ongoing professional development in content and pedagogy.

> Instructional practices, assessment methods, and curricular materials used by schools are culturally and linguistically responsive and preserving.

> Students' languages and experiences are intentionally leveraged and bridged to support their acquisition of new skills and content.

This chapter offers points to consider as you seek to prioritize joy and equity in teaching and learning with your kindergartners, particularly in literacy instruction.

A Critical Year for Language and Literacy

During kindergarten, marked development and growth in cognition, language, literacy, and *learning how to learn* takes place. Educators are focused on cultivating and building critical skills—emergent literacy, oral language, executive function (e.g., self-regulation, working memory, flexibility, and attention), and numeracy—that provide the foundation for later learning. As science has illuminated more about the impact of trauma on the structure and function of the brain, however, educators have realized that a whole-child approach, rooted in social and emotional learning and trauma-informed practices, benefits children's development. Overall, children thrive when teachers intentionally recognize and implement practices that center children's emotional and mental well-being through safe and responsive relationships (O'Conner et al. 2017).

Because of the critical nature of kindergarten, teachers focus heavily on children's skill development and mastery of standards. And for good reason. They know that if children advance from kindergarten behind in grade-level content, it can become almost impossible for them to catch up. How many times have you said or heard colleagues say things like "My students weren't kindergarten ready. I have to catch them up!"? This sentiment is especially pervasive after the COVID-19 pandemic and the widespread conversation about learning loss and its disproportionate impact on certain communities (Engzell, Frey, & Verhagan 2021). The most well-meaning teachers and leaders have felt or said these things out loud. Unfortunately, the current educational and political context doesn't lend itself to prioritizing joy and equity in classrooms. However, it doesn't have to be an either-or choice. As speech-language pathologists, we propose a framework from the field of communication sciences and disorders to be considered as a path to equitable and joyful literacy teaching and learning in kindergarten classrooms.

A Framework for Integrating Joy and Equity into Instruction

The American Speech-Language-Hearing Association (ASHA) requires an evidence-based practice (EBP) process to guide clinical decision making for individuals with speech, language, swallowing, and hearing disorders. This framework can be used by general education kindergarten teachers (and beyond) to implement developmentally appropriate practices. Educators utilizing this framework should consider three components when making teaching decisions to lead to high-quality learning (ASHA, n.d.):

1. Family perspectives: The unique set of personal and cultural circumstances, values, priorities, and expectations identified by your students and families

2. Professional expertise and experience: The knowledge, judgment, and critical reasoning acquired through your educational training and professional experience

3. External and internal evidence: The best available information gathered from scientific literature (external evidence) and from student data and observations (internal evidence)

In the following section, we've adapted the language of EBP to fit the school context.

Embed Family and Student Perspectives into Lesson Planning for Equity and Joy

Students and families have valuable information to share with you that can influence everything from unit themes to field trips to turn-and-talk topics to read-aloud selections and more. By collecting this information, you will be well positioned to leverage students' cultures, identities, languages, and perspectives to meet learning objectives by building on their existing knowledge to bridge learning of new content and skills.

We recommend three ways to learn about the personal and cultural perspectives, identities, educational values, priorities, and expectations of the families and children you serve (Hyter & Salas-Provance 2023):

1. **Practice cultural humility.** This allows you to recognize what you don't know about a group of people, understand the implicit biases that have the potential to impact your decision making, and identify ways to work toward being more aware and culturally responsive. Practicing cultural humility involves developing cultural self-awareness, gaining cultural knowledge, understanding and redressing power imbalances, and holding systems accountable (Project READY, n.d.). Prioritize cultural humility as a first step for embedding family and student perspectives and as a pathway for building and sustaining relationships with families.

2. **Administer a survey to families.** Ask about their values, cultural practices, home languages, celebrations (and their meanings), and perspectives and experiences with literacy (e.g., In your household, do adults read for pleasure [social media counts]? How is storytelling encouraged and enjoyed? What kinds of activities do you enjoy? How would you like to see your child's culture reflected in the classroom?). Getting this information directly from as many families as possible is critical to being able to implement joyful, equitable literacy practices in your classroom. Provide the survey in different forms (paper copy, phone, in-person, etc.) so families can access it in the way that works best for them. Plan for a translator and/or an interpreter if necessary so all families can access the survey. As you examine the data, you will notice themes you can weave into instruction. For example, a unit on holidays provides an opportunity to study multiple cultural celebrations and make cross-cultural connections through various read-aloud texts. Including intentional questioning, incidental vocabulary teaching, and extension activities throughout the unit that are based on families' experiences will deepen knowledge and inspire students' creativity. (For one example of a family survey, see https://learn.coxcampus.org/resource/family-culture-and-language-survey-fillable.)

3. **Ask children directly about their thoughts and what brings them joy.** Kindergartners are often excited and open about sharing their likes, dislikes, opinions, ideas, and feelings. As an example, during morning or closing meeting, you can ask children open-ended questions to gather their feedback about a particular extension activity. The questions should be focused on their likes, dislikes, and interests and scaffolded appropriately for children who need support to express themselves orally. (This is also a great opportunity for students to practice oral language.) Questions might include these:

> Did you enjoy the activity? Why or why not?

> What was your favorite part about the activity?

> What ideas do you have for making the activity better/more fun for next time? What other activities would you like to do?

> What did you learn? What do you want to learn more about?

It is likely that you're implementing these three strategies to a certain degree already. Being even more intentional in how you address them will lead to a more joyful and inclusive classroom environment. Share the "why" behind these practices with families, colleagues, and leadership to encourage implementation system-wide.

Educator Expertise for Equity and Joy

The knowledge, skills, and expertise you acquired during your preservice education, training, and professional tenure are invaluable assets you bring with you each day to the teaching and learning process. Generally, an increase in professional experience translates to an accumulation of knowledge, skills, and expertise that can be used to inform practice. Regardless of how many years of experience you possess, it is important to remain committed to updating, challenging, refining, and adding to your professional knowledge. Equity, and joy by implication, for students depends on your expertise.

In addition to meeting the expectations of your professional credential, we offer a few simple recommendations:

> Participate in formal professional knowledge and practice learning communities. Engaging in peer-to-peer learning, in a safe space, is a great way

to stay current in knowledge and practice. Social media can be an effective vehicle for professional learning communities.

> Create opportunities to practice newly learned skills and be intentional about shadowing and observing your peers who are skilled in practices and techniques that you would benefit from learning.

> Request instructional coaching support from leadership and have a mechanism for capturing feedback in real time to be able to reflect and act on feedback immediately.

 Engage in continuous, collaborative learning to inform your practice. . . . Recognize that the professional knowledge base is constantly evolving and that dialogue and attention to differences are part of the development of new shared knowledge.

External and Internal Evidence for Equity and Joy

Instructional practices and routines must be informed by both external and internal evidence. External evidence is a synthesis of the best available scientific information in a content area. Internal evidence is student data and observations you gather using methods and assessments that are valid and reliable. Both forms of evidence for instruction must be integrated to be effective. To do this, teachers need to be skilled at critically appraising information and monitoring student progress.

Critical appraisal involves both sourcing reliable information and evaluating its relevance and value. This can be hard. You may not have been taught how to critically appraise information, or perhaps it's been a while since you had to exercise these skills. Regardless, becoming an informed consumer of research will help to ensure that your practices and routines are backed by rigorous evidence of effectiveness *with students like those you serve.*

We would be remiss not to acknowledge the barriers teachers face in accessing knowledge and high-quality instructional tools, paywalls being the most obvious barrier. Fortunately, increasingly more high-quality,

open access information and resources are available through reliable organizations. (For a list of a few such resources, see NAEYC.org/dap-focus-kindergarten.)

Evaluating student performance and monitoring progress is just as important to guiding your practice as understanding and using external evidence is. You must be skilled and engaged in ongoing progress monitoring of all the students in your classroom, including those whose first language or dialect is not General American English and those who have delays or disabilities. The individual progress monitoring data you collect is the starting point for providing equitable, differentiated instruction.

Literacy: The House That Oral Language Built

The human brain is hard wired for communication and language. This means that children do not require explicit teaching to learn language; rather, they acquire language through exposure in their environment. However, learning to read requires that new neural pathways be established. These pathways are most effectively established through explicit and systematic instruction. (Incidental language exposure, though often natural for adults, requires intentionality for maximum benefit for a child.) Foundational skill development for reading, spelling, and writing is a core academic purpose for the kindergarten year, and literacy acquisition is a difficult feat for many children regardless of background. For children whose first language or dialect varies from academic English—the language of print—learning to read can be especially taxing (Washington, Lee-James, & Stanford 2023).

When children enter kindergarten, they already possess a depth and breadth of knowledge in their first language or dialect. Unless a speech or language delay is present, by this age, children demonstrate language knowledge of rules that govern phonology, morphology, syntax, semantics, and pragmatics. Their early experiences and interactions have established them as competent language users of their speech community. This is a strength—not a deficit—irrespective of which language or dialect they speak.

If children's first dialect or language is not General American English, children must learn a new set of language rules to be successful at school. This "translation" that must happen between children's first language or dialect and academic English increases the brainwork or cognitive load, which means teachers must carefully consider how linguistic differences may affect their instruction (Washington & Seidenberg 2021). For example, children who speak African American English and Southern American English leave off final consonants as a rule governed feature. Given the speech-to-print and print-to-speech connections, children who speak these dialects may leave off a final consonant or sound when spelling words with final consonant clusters (e.g., *walking* spelled as "walkin'" or "walkn" or *cold* spelled

as "col"). In this case, it is essential to provide students with additional opportunities for phonemic awareness practice where teachers reinforce, through explicit instruction and routine practice, identifying word-final phonemes.

Importantly, final consonant deletion is one of many features of children's first language or dialect that may differ from academic English. As educators and leaders, we must be familiar with these features to be prepared to support all students. Remember to use affirming and strengths-based language as you respond to and talk about language differences. Students' language is closely tied to their identity. Therefore, it is critical to avoid deficit-based language that will be damaging to students.

Sample Language and Reading Routine: Phonemic Awareness

"Phonemic Awareness Routine" shows a sample literacy routine for bridging students' existing language knowledge to their learning of new skills.

Phonemic Awareness Routine

Routine	Phonemic awareness	
Target skill	Phoneme segmentation	
Instructional approach	Explicit instruction	
Format	Small group	
	Description	**Example**
Model	Show students how.	"The words we say are made up of individual sounds. We are going to play a game where we break the words apart. Breaking words apart is called *segmenting*. We will use our sound boxes to segment. Each box [Elkonin box] represents one sound. I am going to say a word and point to a box for each sound I hear. Watch me first. *Bold*: /b/ (point to the first box), /o/ (point to the second box), /l/ (point to the third box), /d/ (point to the fourth box). Now you try. First, repeat the word after me, then as you say the word, touch a box for each sound you hear."

(continues)

Phonemic Awareness Routine

	Description	Example
Specific praise	Give specific feedback about something the student did well.	Child answers "bol" and touches three sound boxes. "That was a really close try—you identified three sounds in the word! You're becoming a pretty good sound detective."
Corrective feedback	Provide feedback that is tailored to the student's needs so they understand what they did correctly and what they did incorrectly.	"But the word I said was *bold*. I heard you say *bol*, which was very close, but I didn't hear the final consonant sound, /d/. Repeat after me: *bold*. That's right! Now, separate the word *bold* by sliding a chip into each sound box for every sound that you hear."
Scaffolding	Provide targeted support to help a student access and master a skill.	(If the child needs more support) "The word I said was *bold*. I heard you say *bol*, which was very close, but I didn't hear the final sound. Repeat after me: *bold*. Let's tap out the sounds together." (If necessary, model and then encourage the student to repeat.) "What is the last sound you heard? That's right! The last sound was /d/. Now separate *bold* by sliding a counter into each sound box for every sound you hear."
Supports for executive function	Provide students with a pictorial checklist at the beginning of the lesson so they can organize and prepare their materials to participate. Repeat the activity multiple times, following a scope and sequence, to help students process and practice the skill with different words. Minimize environmental distractions to support attention.	
Considerations for accessibility and equity	Intentional pacing: slow down and/or speed up based on student need. Linguistic differences: final consonant deletion is a rule-governed feature of many dialects of English. When you ask students to segment words, they may struggle to perceive the final consonant and may require more time and practice to master the skill. You will need to bring students' attention to the final consonant in various ways (e.g., pausing to tap out the word; using mirrors to visualize and feel the movement of their mouth, teeth, tongue, lips [these are articulators]; and comparing similar words). Additional practice opportunities are critical. This practice will also support multilingual students.	
Considerations for joy and agency	Make space for student choice: students can choose their favorite manipulative (e.g., counting chip game piece) to segment words they select from a word bank.	

The Phonemic Awareness Routine is adapted from *The Reading Teacher's Top 10 Tools* and used with permission from 95 Percent Group.

It illustrates one way you might honor a student's language by affirming their responses and leveraging the student's existing language knowledge through explicit instruction to build awareness of sounds in word-final position. By focusing on phonemic awareness skills, this routine will contribute to automatic, fluent reading and reading comprehension (Scarborough 2001). (You can see a second sample literacy routine at NAEYC.org/dap-focus-kindergarten that focuses on language comprehension, which also supports fluent reading and comprehension.)

Creating a phonemic awareness routine in your classroom can include fun, play-based activities that allow for connections throughout the day. Provide multiple opportunities to practice the skill throughout the day. For example, circle time and transitions are opportunities to practice phoneme identification (e.g., "If your name starts with the /d/ sound, go to the round table"). Phonemic awareness practice can be fun and student led by allowing children to choose words to manipulate.

Conclusion

Integrating the three EBP components will prepare and support your implementation of equitable and joyful practices and learning materials. By honoring student and family values and perspectives, cultivating and utilizing your professional expertise, and relying on internal and external evidence to drive assessment and instruction, you will be well positioned to meet each student where they are and leverage their knowledge in ways that are culturally responsive and preserving while providing high-quality instruction. The focus of this chapter was on equitable and joyful literacy practices as a critical component of teaching and learning because literacy is the bedrock upon which all other learning stands. However, the information provided relative to EBP can be applied across disciplines and grade levels.

RYAN LEE-JAMES, PhD, CCC-SLP, is a speech-language pathologist, researcher, and implementation scientist. She currently serves as the chief academic officer and director of the Rollins Center for Language and Literacy and Cox Campus at the Atlanta Speech School. Dr. Lee-James believes that one day all children will be liberated through language and literacy.

STACEY WALLEN, PhD, CCC-SLP, is a speech-language pathologist and former clinical educator with expertise in early intervention, language development, and disorders in culturally and linguistically different populations and community-based clinical education. She currently serves as the director of field implementation for the Rollins Center for Language and Literacy.

CHAPTER 25

Adapting the Curriculum to Incorporate Student Inquiry Through Teachable Moments

Sabrina Burroughs

Series editor's note: Sabrina Burroughs, a kindergarten teacher at John Lewis Elementary School in Washington, DC, is the kind of teacher who makes me want to go back in time and be a kindergartner again. She describes a classroom full of joyful learning and hands-on exploration as she adapts the curriculum to incorporate children's interests and respond to their thought-provoking questions. She uses an interdisciplinary approach to curriculum planning, addressing several content areas such as literacy, math, science, and social studies and media literacy as children engage in studies anchored in questions they have asked. These questions—like "Who is John Lewis?" and "What is a planet?"—inspire Sabrina to adapt her plans and set the stage for deep exploration with the children of interesting, meaningful content. Social and emotional development are also intentionally woven into the daily routine. The following is adapted from an interview with Sabrina in which I asked her to describe how she goes about curriculum planning and how she incorporates hands-on learning, joyful play, and exploration into the kindergarten day.

—Susan Friedman

Describe your approach to curriculum planning.

As I plan for the day, I build in different questions for children, thinking about the specific children in my class as I do this. All students learn differently, so it's important to scaffold questioning. I use higher-order thinking questions, open-ended questions, and sometimes close- questions; "W" question words can stimulate parallel talk or prompt real-world connections to stimulate a child's background knowledge. This year, I have one student who is *so* into science. I've tried my best to consider that as I plan our literacy lessons and have books and stories on hand about some of the scientific topics he's interested in, like *Ada Twist, Scientist* (by Andrea Beaty, illus. by David Roberts) and *A Scientist Like Me* (by Dr. Shini Somara, illus. by Nadja Sarell).

Another student just moved to the United States from France, and she's learning about America. She asked me recently, "Mrs. Burroughs, who's John Lewis?" Not every question warrants a deep study, but since our school was recently renamed after John Lewis I had been thinking about how we would study him. This was a great time for me to work that into my planning. We were already talking about Black Americans during social studies. We read books and watched videos that described who John Lewis was. We talked about why a school would have been renamed to honor him and how we felt about being in a school named after him. We did some writing about what we had learned about John Lewis. Children described different things in their writing. Some described moments they had read about from his life. Others described how they felt about going to a school named after him. Others wrote about some of the things that he did. Some children described how they were going to change the world. All this was inspired by a single question from one student: "Who's John Lewis?"

Tell us little about how you address learning standards across content areas.

Now, I don't just change my lessons without also thinking about how they connect to the learning standards. When you have a big teachable moment, like when a child asks an intriguing question, you can adapt your plans and let your principal or administrator know. I have never had an issue changing and adapting my lessons and describing what I'm doing to the principal when I've shown how I am connecting and supporting the same learning goals related to literacy, math, social studies, science, and other content areas as well.

DAP Educators arrange firsthand, meaningful experiences that are cognitively and creatively stimulating, invite exploration and investigation, and engage children's active, sustained involvement.

What I want to emphasize to other teachers is that you can do this—you can go beyond rote approaches to address learning standards. You can connect different areas of the curriculum, ask engaging questions, and provide hands-on experiences to engage children in the learning. You just have to see the value and want to do it.

For example, I once had a student who wanted more information about the planets and stars in the sky. "I've never seen a planet. I don't know what planets are." This led me to ask all the children, "What planet do we live on?" and when they answered, "Washington DC," I thought of that as a teachable moment. The goal for kindergartners in learning about planets is really to build their background knowledge about planets and what they are. I looked through the learning standards and thought of many ways I could incorporate a study of planets. Here are some that I used:

> **Reading.** We read about different planets and stars. I filled our classroom library with books about planets like *If I Were an Astronaut* (by Eric Braun, illus. by Sharon Harmer). Other science books popular with my students are *Ada Twist, Scientist* (by Andrea Beaty, illus. by David Roberts) and *101 Cool Science Experiments* (by Helen Chapman and Glen Singleton).

> **Social studies and science.** We talked about the discoveries of the world and how the planets were discovered. We talked about where we live, how Earth is a planet, and how Earth is situated in a larger solar system. Science was embedded in everything we read and talked about.

> **Art.** We used materials to create our own galaxy filled with planets and stars. We called our classroom Planet 185.

> **Writing and creating.** We used a tool I like to use called Book Creator. The students used this app to write their own stories about planets. Some of these stories were factual stories based on what we had learned about planets. Other children focused on writing fantastical stories about their own planets or galaxies, giving them fantastical names. They imagined and described what their planets and galaxies were like, incorporating facts they had learned about our solar system into their writing.

> **Research and media literacy.** I asked each child to select a planet from our solar system and research it. Using iPads and computers, they were to find three credible sources that would provide different types of information. One might be as simple as a reference source they used to find the correct spelling for the planet. If they were learning about or "discovering" Jupiter, they could find a source where they could read about and learn about Jupiter or they could find something that was then read to them using an application like Epic. Or they might find images of Jupiter or a song about it.

Tell us more about media literacy.

Looking for information online and thinking about whether it is a credible source or not, like my students did during our study on planets, is media literacy. Children learn that there is a lot of content and information but that it's not all credible, and they need to be able to evaluate the source. I ask children to find sources they can understand and learn from. To help them find good sources, I ask them questions like "What do you think you might see to help you know that the information is real?," "Have you checked the author's name to find other books or articles they've written to make sure that the source is good?," and "If you find something that does not look or sound right, did you look for a picture, a video, or a kid source in your toolkit to help you?" When they sort through and determine that they have found useful sources—ones they can understand and that have good information—they're using media literacy.

Because New Jersey recently required media literacy as an area of study and exploration, I have been approached about how to motivate other teachers to incorporate media literacy. I was asked about this in an interview with NPR. My answer was that many teachers are already doing media literacy. They just don't know that's what they are doing, or they don't label it as such. We need to label this as media literacy when we implement it related to content being studied.

Young Children Benefit from Interdisciplinary Approaches to Teaching Content

by Douglas H. Clements and Tanya S. Wright

In many kindergarten classrooms, teaching addresses isolated content areas. However, children benefit from an *interdisciplinary* approach to content learning, in which rich connections are made across content areas and domains of development. When two or more domains are integrated, learning in each is strengthened.

Learning content in interconnected ways is beneficial in many ways. First, many real-world topics and phenomena are inherently interconnected. As children create a structure that does not fall over in the block area, they may discuss how many blocks they need on each side of the building, thus using mathematics understandings to support an engineering task. When they draw and label their observations of a plant growing in the classroom, they are using writing to collect data during a science investigation. Second, the content areas work synergistically, each one supporting learning in the other and promoting transfer of knowledge across content areas and contexts; children also learn to *apply* the knowledge they gain in this way to solve problems (Clements & Sarama 2021; Moore, Johnston, & Glancy 2020). For example, knowledge about the topic of a text supports text comprehension (Cervetti & Wright 2020). So a child who knows a lot about birds—perhaps she spends time with her grandfather watching a bird feeder and learning about the different birds who visit—is likely to better comprehend a text about birds than a child with more limited knowledge of this topic (e.g., Kaefer, Neuman, & Pinkham 2015).

Likewise, engagement in literacy can support engagement in other content areas. For example, when answering science questions, children may gain some understandings through firsthand investigations (e.g., observing the plant that is growing in their classroom) and obtain additional understandings as their teachers read aloud from science texts (e.g., learning about plants that grow in different habitats, such as in a rainforest or in a desert) (Cervetti et al. 2007; Wright & Gotwals 2017).

Using an interdisciplinary approach also addresses a common concern in early education—that content areas must compete for time in children's education (e.g., Berliner 2011). For example, when large blocks of time are spent on early literacy alone, science and social studies learning may be pushed out from the curriculum in the early years of school. This practice has negative consequences for children's literacy development and for their math, science, and social studies learning. It is critical, therefore, for early childhood educators to make time for all of the content areas and to understand the content areas as mutually supportive for children's learning. Using an interdisciplinary approach helps ensure these goals.

Adapted from D.H. Clements and T.S. Wright, "Teaching Content in Early Childhood Education," in *Developmentally Appropriate Practice in Early Childhood Programs Serving Children from Birth Through Age 8,* 4th ed., NAEYC (Washington, DC: NAEYC, 2022), 74–75.

What's an example of an experience where you brought families into the learning?

When our class took a virtual trip to a planetarium, I invited the families to join us. I was able to re-create an actual planetarium in our classroom. We darkened the room and watched images of the solar system and galaxy as we listened to narration from the planetarium website. That was the most fun you could ever ask for, because you could see the wonderment on the kids' faces. The adults' faces too. And I think learning should always include wonderment, at any age.

With all that you are required to do, how are you able to adapt the curriculum?

Sometimes teachers ask me how I can shift gears and fit in an area of study like planets. If the children say or do something that strikes me as being especially worthy of following up on, I modify my lesson plan for the next day slightly or even extensively. Sometimes I get asked, "How can you do this?" As long as I'm doing the "musts" of the learning standards, I feel that adjusting to incorporate something as rich as a study of planets—especially when it's something the children are very interested in—is worth it. I think this is just me. It's Sabrina's way of doing things is what I call it.

What about the children's supporting social and emotional development?

Kindergarten can be overwhelming for children. We have to remember that children are transitioning from pre-K, where they're napping and playing, to kindergarten, where they might get a five-minute social-emotional break. Or this may be their first time in any type of learning program. And if all we do as teachers is feed children words and writing and math and science and social studies, and then they go home, it can be very stressful for them.

So I created a space where children can have a moment to themselves to regroup or to relax, relate, reflect, and talk about something that happened with a friend—whatever they're going through at that moment. This space is a tent shaped like a giant rocket ship. Inside, there's a blanket with a cloud pattern, along with pillows and stuffies. I also have some learning materials in the rocket ship, like a number of words that start with the letter *r*, because maybe when the kids are taking a break, they will engage in that as well.

Have you ever seen a View-Master, where kids can slip a reel in the slot, push the lever, and look through the view finder to explore different pictures? I found some of these and put them in the tent. The children really like clicking through and looking at the images of planets, animals, birds, and flowers. I intentionally include images from nature so that as the children take a moment to themselves, they might be inspired by an image and want to find out more.

What are other ways you help children care for their emotions throughout the day?

I make sure to incorporate a few moments into the schedule each day to help children identify and address their emotions, starting when they come in. I'm a hugger, so we hug at the door as children enter (if they want a hug). I call it *crossing the threshold*. When they come in and cross the threshold, there is a poster on my door where the kids can tap a picture of how they feel, and if they are feeling sad or angry, we have a quick discussion about those feelings before we start the day. I also have a feeling poster in our Calming Corner. These posters are helpful for children who have a need to show you their feelings visually, and the process doesn't cause any disruption to other students' learning time.

After lunch and recess, we have a decompression/reflection time that might include meditation. It might include children selecting a feeling card, which has an image and a word such as *happy, sad, lonely,* or *content* on it, to let me know how they feel.

We also play a game called Emotion. It's like dominoes, but the pieces show different emotions instead of numbers. I also do a calming circle at any point in the day when the kids just need a moment. We take three minutes to reflect, calm, and regroup. I'll never forget that a previous supervisor once said to me, "The kids are young, but they are just like all of us. They need a break sometimes." I encourage students to take a break when they need one. If *you* need a break, take two or three minutes for yourself. We all need it!

We also have a mentor and peer mentors. A mentor is usually a responsible older student whom I recruit to work in my classroom for 20 minutes. The kids look up to them, causing a preplanned buddy system. The peer mentors are responsible same-age students who may be in my class or another kindergarten class. They model what other students should be doing without ridicule or judgment. At each table there is a captain who serves as the first line of inquiry when a peer needs support. If children need someone to talk to, there are several people that they can have a conversation with.

If there's a conflict at recess, kids can go back into the classroom and take a moment. We have five stuffies in the classroom, so the kids can choose to have a conversation with a stuffie rather than a person. I'll also let the kids record an audio or video message to someone they love if they're feeling a little blue. Taking care of ourselves and our well-being is part of our day. At the end of each day, we sing a clapping song to celebrate all the special little moments we had throughout the day.

How do you share important moments with families?

If a child records a message for a family member, I'll send it to their family. We also have sunshine messages or good news messages, so if someone is having a wonderful moment and a beautiful day we'll send a message home about that as well. Maybe a child's had a struggle in the morning, but by the end of the day, there's been a beautiful resurrection, so to speak, and they've heard an encouraging comment from me or from my coteacher that they want to share. We want to celebrate all of these moments and share them with families.

Do you have any other words to share with us?

Teaching is my gift, which gives me purpose, like those *aha!* moments that send you soaring with emotions when you see a child's face light up from learning. I feel as if every teacher should view this peek into a child's journey as life changing. I often feel guilty when I come home laughing at what one of my learners said or did, how they called me "silly" because I could not stop laughing or even crying. I am grateful for the opportunity to provide one child with one moment, hug, or smile to make their day. I have done talks, webinars, radio, television, interviews, panels, and professional development, and each time I present I still have the same joy as if it's my first day of school.

SABRINA BURROUGHS, an educator for nearly two decades, teaches kindergarten at John Lewis Elementary School in Washington, DC. As a former systems analyst, it is her goal to provide intentional developmentally appropriate early childhood media literacy in her curriculum design.

PART 6

Demonstrating Professionalism as an Early Childhood Educator

RECOMMENDATIONS FROM THE DAP POSITION STATEMENT

Developmentally appropriate practice serves as the hallmark of the early childhood education profession. Fully achieving these guidelines and effectively promoting all young children's development and learning depends on the establishment of a strong profession with which all early childhood educators, working across all settings, identify.

Professional early childhood educators are trained in and hold certifications and/or degrees in the field of education. Many have years of experience and have completed higher levels of education. Others are just beginning their professional journeys. Regardless of experience, all early childhood professionals have unique knowledge of their subject and display behaviors that are reflective of the ideals of the education profession.

Like other professional early childhood educators, kindergarten teachers are lifelong learners and reflective practitioners who embrace developmentally appropriate practice and strive to find a balance between effectively implementing mandated curricula and providing child-centered, playful, and joyful learning opportunities for each child. They participate in ongoing professional development and learning throughout their career, connect with other educators to share and learn together, and participate in the efforts of organizations that support early education. All of this is done for the purpose of becoming more effective in the craft of teaching young children, with the ultimate goal of "ensuring all students receive the rich, well-rounded education they need to be productive, engaged citizens" (Chenoweth & Theokas 2012, 24).

In the early education field, the connection between professionalism, developmentally appropriate practice, and equity is especially strong. "The work of professionalism is . . . fundamentally about seeking equity and justice as part [of] an effort to ensure access to high-quality early childhood education for all"

(NAEYC 2022, 253). Early childhood educators serve as "informed advocates for young children, families, and the profession" (NAEYC 2019b, 24) in early learning settings and at wider levels.

In the five preceding sections of the book, whose topics correspond to the first five guidelines of developmentally appropriate practice, you have seen the decision making that early childhood educators engage in to provide high-quality learning experiences for children and forge partnerships with families. The sixth guideline, professionalism, brings forward the knowledge, skills, and dispositions that enable educators to make such decisions and "exemplify ethical, intentional, and reflective professional judgment and practice" (NAEYC 2019a). Thus, professionalism does not stand alone from the other guidelines—it is woven throughout all of them. NAEYC's "Professional Standards and Competencies for Early Childhood Educators" position statement (NAEYC.org/resources/position-statements/professional-standards-competencies) outlines specific key competencies that constitute the expectations for professionalism in early childhood educators. There are many examples of professionalism throughout this book; following are just a few from various chapters that demonstrate key competencies 6a and 6b of professionalism in action.

Key competency 6a: [Early childhood educators] identify and involve themselves with the early childhood field and serve as informed advocates for young children, families, and the profession.

In her chapter "Adapting the Curriculum to Incorporate Student Inquiry Through Teachable Moments" (page 142), Sabrina Burroughs describes how she responds to teachable moments, adapts lessons, considers learning goals, and communicates with her school's principal. As she explains, "I don't just change my lessons [to respond to children's interest in a topic] without also thinking about how they connect to the learning standards. When you have a big teachable moment, like when a child asks an intriguing question, you can adapt your plans and let your principal or administrator know. I have never had an issue changing and adapting my lessons and describing what I'm doing to the principal when I've shown how I am connecting and supporting the same learning goals related to literacy, math, social studies, science, and other content areas as well." Her approach demonstrates how she identifies as part of the early childhood profession and considers the needs of the children and families while she also communicates with her school's principal about the teaching and learning that is happening in her classroom. This kind of advocacy for children and families within schools takes place daily in kindergarten classrooms across the country.

Jennifer Keys Adair and Shubhi Sachdeva describe a broader approach to advocating for social justice in "Agency and Power in Young Children's Lives: Five Ways to Advocate for Social Justice as an Early Childhood Educator" (page 154). Of key importance to kindergarten educators, they highlight an example that demonstrates what a social justice approach looks like in a classroom and the difference one team of educators made in the lives of a child and family and, indeed, an entire classroom of children. These authors illustrate the effort and thinking necessary for social justice work and how it begins in small and simple actions that educators can take themselves.

Key competency 6b: [Early childhood educators] know about and uphold ethical and other early childhood professional guidelines.

Amy Blessing, who wrote "Assessment in Kindergarten: Meeting Children Where They Are" (page 66), found herself considering how to better assess a child with emerging English language skills when a required assessment did not seem to show the full picture of what the child understood about the structure of a story. She shows how she integrated observational assessment of the child at play to broaden her understanding of what he understood from stories he had heard read aloud. Her chapter illustrates how, in this situation and others, Ms. Blessing acts on her professional and ethical responsibility to "minimize the adverse impact of inappropriate assessments on young children and on instructional practices" (NAEYC 2020, 19) by using authentic assessment tools and providing each child with different ways to demonstrate their understanding.

The chapters in Part 6 articulate the importance of staying abreast of current effective and equitable practices within kindergarten classrooms while emphasizing the critical need to advocate for equitable opportunities in your classroom, school, and community.

READ AND REFLECT

As you read these chapters, consider and evaluate your own practices using these reflection questions.

"Portraits of Teacher Leadership" explores four teachers' journeys in becoming strong teacher leaders in their schools and districts and at state and national levels. Their inspiring stories of growth and change over time will ignite a fire in you to strengthen your own leadership skills. **Consider:** In what ways are you already a leader in your setting? What strategies might you try to expand your leadership skills and opportunities? What supports will you need?

"Agency and Power in Young Children's Lives: Five Ways to Advocate for Social Justice as an Early Childhood Educator" shares strategies to support you in understanding, practicing, and advocating for social justice in your classroom, school, and community. **Consider:** In what ways do you already provide opportunities for your kindergartners to experience a safe, equitable environment for learning? What other ideas could you implement to support the development of social justice in your classroom and larger community?

NEXT STEPS

1. What are you passionate about when it comes to kindergarten children and their school experiences? What changes would you like to see? In what ways can you advocate for more appropriate practices in kindergarten? Who are the other people (educators, administrators, families, community members) in your community with whom you could partner in your advocacy efforts? What other resources are available to you?

2. Do some investigating to discover if your district or state provides a teacher leadership initiative similar to North Carolina's Power of K, mentioned in Chapter 26, or professional development in key topics in which you want to grow your knowledge. Who could you talk to in your district or state to advocate for professional development opportunities like this? What action(s) can you take *now*?

References for the chapters in this part can be accessed online at NAEYC.org/dap-focus-kindergarten.

Portraits of Teacher Leadership

Jessica Jackson, Samantha Mehrlich, Yolanda A. Sawyer, and Susan Choplin

Volume editor's note: The following is a conversation I had with four kindergarten teacher leaders from across North Carolina. Jessica, Samantha, Yolanda, and Susan teach in geographically and economically diverse settings and have varying years of experience teaching kindergarten. One commonality among these dedicated educators is their participation in a long-term comprehensive professional development experience. In the following conversation, they share their experiences in developing into strong teacher leaders and their own portraits of teacher leadership. Their individual journeys highlight the various ways in which teacher leadership grows and takes root.

—Eva Phillips

You are all considered to be teacher leaders in your schools, local districts, and across the state. What does teacher leadership mean to you?

When you think deeply about your work, you need other people to think and reflect alongside you. You need other teacher leaders. Teacher leadership is not necessarily the assigned role of a grade-level chair. It is not necessarily being a mentor to entry-level teachers. It is more of a state of mind, and it can occur at any time during a teaching career. Leaders embody humility, collaboration, and professionalism. A teacher leader constantly reflects on their practice, seeks new knowledge and solutions, shares resources, and models effective practices. This leadership benefits the students and families in the teacher's classroom as well as other teachers and the students and families in those classrooms.

A teacher leader inspires and effects positive change in the lives of other educators, students, families, and the community in which they serve by gaining knowledge and perfecting the craft of teaching through ongoing professional development, collaborating with others, providing and receiving feedback, listening, and cultivating an environment of efficacy.

How did each of you begin your teacher leadership journeys?

We all found that the first step in becoming a teacher leader was by following other leaders. Yolanda and Susan both applied to and participated in the Power of K, a North Carolina three-year kindergarten teacher leader development initiative. Susan became a demonstration teacher (demo teacher) after participating in the Power of K. Later on, Jessica, Samantha, and Yolanda became demonstration teachers as well.

Jessica found hope and inspiration in Stephanie, a 17-year career kindergarten teacher when Jessica joined the team in 2005:

> Stephanie was a master teacher, and we clicked like peanut butter and jelly. She took me in; stayed late in the afternoons and arrived early in the mornings; and taught me by bringing me along in planning, brainstorming, room arranging and rearranging, activity creating, all of it. We'd sit side by side with our computers and talk through each element of the day: morning meeting, shared reading (we called it "big book time"), choice time, math, science, small groups—she literally planned every part of the day with me. She explained what I was to accomplish and how to do it in a joyful way that would be meaningful and fun for our students. We taught together for seven years before I switched school districts to be closer to home, and those seven years laid such an amazing foundation for my understanding of how young children learn and how to teach them. The capacity that she invested in me—we in each other— was immensely impactful and carried me through all 16 years of my career.

Samantha found strength and purpose in working alongside and learning from Sandra, a kindergarten teacher:

Sandra was well loved by many and sought after by all the rest. She would become my "person" and the teacher I would strive to be. Sandra's kindergarten classroom was filled with love and a sense of family. She taught in a way that honored children and their abilities. She reminded me that every child was someone else's most prized possession and when they entered our classroom, we took on the role of loving them as their loved ones at home did. I learned from her what developmentally appropriate teaching looked like and how in teaching this way I would get the most from my children. I found that her opinion was not always the popular opinion, but it was always what was best for children. I also learned that her opinion was respected because it came from a place of caring and she was good at articulating what was best for her students. If nothing else, I have learned that being able to articulate your why and to show it through your students' growth, both academically and socially, is essential to being heard.

As teacher leaders, we found that our humility drove us to connect and learn from many possible sources. Again, finding other master teachers allowed us to reflect purposely on our practice. Susan, Jessica, and Yolanda all had the privilege of visiting master teachers Lee and Marylee in western North Carolina. Jessica recalls,

Little did we know how influential these women would become in our lives and careers. Watching them teach was like watching Michael Jordan in the slam dunk contests of his career. They were so masterful—and everything about the observation (the classrooms, their plans, their words, the way they interacted with children) was drenched in so many layers of intention. The children were reading, playing with each other, cooperating, leveraging every aspect of their environments (overflowing with materials for creative play and learning), singing the songs they had learned in their morning meeting. It was a powerful and inspirational experience.

Becoming intricately involved in a variety of state and local initiatives also allowed us to strengthen our own practices. As a young teacher in undergraduate school at Winston-Salem State University, Yolanda

found support and encouragement through her connection with the North Carolina Association of Educators (NCAE):

I had the opportunity to attend an NCAE convention with educators from across the state and listened to passionate pleas for educational reform. I saw firsthand what advocacy looked like and experienced a sense of unity. This led me to choose to be our school building's NCAE representative as a first-year hire in 1996. I continued to connect and grow from joining other organizations: ILA (International Literacy Association), NAEYC, NCCTM (North Carolina Council of Teachers of Mathematics), NCSS (National Council for the Social Studies), and NSTA (National Science Teachers Association). In addition, I found subjects that I was passionate about, like STEAM (Science, Technology, Engineering, the Arts, and Mathematics), and learned how to incorporate those interests into teaching in the classroom and volunteering to present at workshops.

We sought out professional growth opportunities to improve our practice, such as inclusion training and STEAM training, and pursued graduate degrees. Susan found motivation and renewed purpose by experiencing the cognitive dissonance that comes during the first few years of teaching:

While my background in the birth through kindergarten years helped me gain strong knowledge in working with families and using learning centers, I was missing key content knowledge and felt unsure how to teach kindergarteners to read and write. Likewise, I was disappointed in some of the common practices that relied heavily on worksheets and behaviorist classroom management strategies such as color charts. My reflections and personal drive led me back to school to pursue a master's degree. I believe this first step to find other like-minded thinkers created the snowball effect that allowed me to continue to find my people even now, after 22 years in the profession. I joined state-level early childhood task forces and work groups and was given opportunities to present at local and national conferences. I eagerly joined cross-sector work at the local level to better the lives of children and families in my local community.

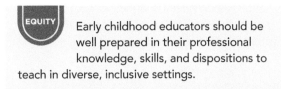

All of these amazing opportunities allowed us to continue connecting with others, to continue to fuel our professional fires, thus allowing us to become leaders in the field.

What suggestions do you have for teachers who want to strengthen their own leadership skills?

Step One: Be an articulate advocate

Become an advocate for change and continuous improvement. We found ourselves involved in initiatives such as Kindergarten Entry Assessment work, supervising student teachers, working with struggling teachers, participating in a state-level kindergarten teacher leadership initiative, and more. Look for opportunities in your area and join in! Speak confidently and with research in your back pocket about the needs of young learners.

Step Two: Connect with and visit other master teachers

We were all extremely fortunate to become kindergarten demonstration classroom teachers through our state department leadership initiative. It was in this phase of our careers where we had the most personal growth and were able to make an even stronger impact on others. Find other teachers to visit, in your own school, your district, and your state. Visiting other teachers during classroom instruction is making a commitment to each other's success. Both the observer and the one being observed gain valuable insight into effective practices as you reflect individually and together on the day. This can be done even without a formal demonstration program, and we strongly encourage you to find master teachers to visit and to invite others to visit your classroom as well. Teachers observing teachers is the ticket to growing capacity in the ability to hone their craft. We cannot teach in isolation!

Step Three: Find your people

Relationships with like-minded, self-driven people are critical factors for teacher leadership development. Seek out other passionate educators who want to uplift public education and make a difference in the lives of young children. Build relationships and strengthen your practices by discussing current research and practices in early learning, sharing and reading articles, blogs, and relevant websites about teaching young children. Develop a book study group and support each other through the good times and the challenging ones.

Step Four: Join in the work

Join committees and cross-sector work with passionate purposes. There are many opportunities to participate in enhancing the education profession and, at the same time, develop professionally. Teacher organizations (i.e., NSTA, NAEYC) invite educators to serve on committees that write position papers or give opportunities for teachers to serve in leadership capacities.

Moreover, NAEYC has an active online community and topical Interest Forums where members can ask and answer questions about various topics, gaining and providing support from fellow educators across the country. In addition, for educators in North Carolina there is the North Carolina Center for the Advancement of Teaching (NCCAT). NCCAT's mission statement is to "help North Carolina teachers grow in knowledge, skill, compassion, and professionalism so that students become engaged, self-motivated, and successful" (NCCAT, n.d.). Through NCCAT, educators choose professional development that interests them and provides opportunities for teachers to collaborate with like-minded individuals from across the state. We encourage you to search for similar opportunities in your states.

Step Five: Keep learning and growing

Continue your education and growth through attending graduate school, participating in professional development, and joining professional organizations such as NAEYC or ASCD. Keep up with the newest advances in the field to continue improving your own practice while sharing your new learning with others.

Conclusion

"Teacher leadership is at the heart of transformation in any school" (NEA, n.d., 32). True change can be made through the empowerment of teachers to model and advocate for effective practices for all young children. We encourage all teachers who read this chapter to truly reflect on your own leadership journeys and on the words below. Keeping these tenets in mind will guide your teacher leadership journey. We wish you well and thank you for your dedication to professional growth and development!

We close with the wording of standard 6 of NAEYC's professional standards and competencies:

> Early childhood educators (a) identify and participate as members of the early childhood profession. They serve as informed advocates for young children, for the families of the children in their care, and for the early childhood profession. They (b) know and use ethical guidelines and other early childhood professional guidelines. They (c) have professional communication skills that effectively support their relationships and work [with] young children, families, and colleagues. Early childhood educators (d) are continuous, collaborative learners who (e) develop and sustain the habit of reflective and intentional practice in their daily work with young children and as members of the early childhood profession. (NAEYC 2019b, 24)

JESSICA JACKSON, MEd, NBCT, is a retired kindergarten teacher in Asheville, North Carolina.

SAMANTHA MEHRLICH, MEd, teaches kindergarten in Denver, North Carolina. She is a National Board Certified teacher.

YOLANDA A. SAWYER, MAEd, MSA, is a kindergarten teacher in Rockingham, North Carolina. She is a National Board Certified teacher.

SUSAN CHOPLIN, MEd, a former kindergarten teacher, is the exceptional children and preschool coordinator for Stokes County Schools in North Carolina.

CHAPTER 27

Agency and Power in Young Children's Lives

Five Ways to Advocate for Social Justice as an Early Childhood Educator

Jennifer Keys Adair and Shubhi Sachdeva

Early childhood education is increasingly positioned as an important part of making societies more equitable and prosperous. Strong early childhood systems can be both a safety net and an accelerator for families experiencing poverty and other oppressive forces. However, there are also ways in which early childhood education can perpetuate social injustices through White-centric curriculum, deficit-oriented programs, and intense pressure (even if unintentional) on families of color and/or families experiencing poverty to behave as White, middle-class families to be seen as successful. Social justice in early childhood education therefore requires an "interrogation of power" (De Lissovoy 2019, 42) by all of us who work with and make policies for young children.

In this chapter, we describe how and why social justice education is important for early childhood education. We begin with a story that demonstrates what this approach can look like in a classroom. It illustrates the effort and thinking necessary for social justice work and how our collective effort can begin in small and simple ways. We then offer five ways to shift thinking and practice in your work with young children.

> In a kindergarten classroom in Texas, Gina often arrives at school irritated and tired. She struggles to make friends. She gets angry and hits her classmates when things don't go her way. The teachers have worked hard to create a meaningful and positive relationship with Gina's parents, who they first met when Gina's older brother was a student in their classroom. The teachers know that Gina has been living on relatives' sofas and changing apartments, sometimes in the middle of the night. Therefore, Gina does not get to have a regular schedule for sleeping, eating, or daily

hygiene. Instead of blaming the family or calling her behavior problematic, Gina's teachers understand that she needs care and understanding. When she is struggling, the teachers provide her space in the classroom where she can go to regroup, calm down, and sleep if needed. She usually returns to the classroom community feeling calm and ready to engage with her classmates.

The teachers intentionally use effective strategies to build and strengthen positive relationships among the children as well. With guidance from the teachers, the children, without knowing about Gina's specific hardships outside of school, have found ways to support her. They engage Gina in their play and entice her to be calmer and softer by gently reminding her to "Be soft, Gina!" Instead of changing Gina, they welcome her by considering her need for patience and sleep as something that requires support rather than judgment. The children figure out Gina's favorite activities and use them to motivate her. When they see her upset, they offer to "get the animals," the soft pillow-like animals in a basket in the reading area. They know her favorite book and encourage her to work with them by bringing the book to the table and calling out, "Look, Gina, we have your book!" Paying attention to her favorite activities, allowing her to sleep, and being patient when she is angry or tired are small but important ways to change the context rather than to blame or speak negatively about the child.

The children also do not hear teachers and other school staff speak negatively about Gina or her family. They only know that Gina does not get enough sleep at home sometimes. The children work to validate her situation through their inclusion efforts, all without specific teacher direction.

Social Justice Requires Belief and Effort

In this example, Gina's teachers valued equity and worked toward it, even when it was not convenient or comfortable. Social justice in early childhood education requires both belief and effort: a belief that everyone deserves equal economic, political, and social rights and opportunities *and* significant effort to transform the institutions and systems that sustain unequal relationships and realities. All of those involved with social justice education—including young children—are learning about how institutional racism and other social injustices impact their lives. Young children are not too young for social justice, because "young children can think about fairness and are deeply moved and highly motivated by the recognition of injustice" (Cowhey 2006, 18). In the next section, we offer examples and practical next steps for educators who want to center social justice in their classrooms.

We (the authors) believe that working for social justice in early childhood education requires at least two major shifts in our field. The first is that instead of trying to fix children and families, we must look collectively at the systems and institutions that continue to create inequitable opportunities, resource allocation, and experiences. That is, we must acknowledge *institutional racism* and *structural inequities*.

The second is that instead of insisting on only biological, normalized versions of child development, we also need to depend on political and cultural understandings of development. For a discussion of both elements of social justice, see a longer version of this chapter at NAEYC.org/dap-focus-kindergarten.

Five Ways We Can All Work Toward Social Justice in Early Childhood Settings

1. Reject Deficit Talk

Rejecting deficit talk in early childhood education means speaking positively about families and focusing on their assets, strengths, and everyday realities that go into their decision making and ways of seeing the world. It means speaking up when deficit talk is a part of the curriculum, teacher planning, or policies at the school, district, or state levels. Educators who reject deficit talk ask families and communities what they think about curriculum and pedagogical practices. This doesn't mean that educators have to agree with everything families do. Instead, social justice educators seek to understand and include families in addressing the underlying inequities that are responsible for so much trauma and suffering in people's lives. And social justice educators work to identify their own roles in perpetuating such inequities. Social justice educators operate under the assumption that everyone has a logic and rationale for the way they live, parent, and engage with the world. Just as there is danger in behaving as though there is only one best way of teaching children, there is also danger in believing that there is one way to parent or engage with one's family or larger community.

Deficit thinking justifies inequity and normalizes oppression. Deficit approaches dismiss and devalue practices that are meaningful and important to communities (Valencia 1997). Deficit thinking and approaches to teaching and learning view "the languages, literacies, and cultural ways of being of many students and communities of color as deficiencies to be overcome in learning the demanded and legitimized dominant language, literacy, and cultural ways of schooling" (Paris 2012, 93). Schools, classrooms, assessment companies, and community organizations can state upfront that deficit language will not be used to describe children or families. Educators who use deficit language should not *ever* be involved in assessing or teaching young children.

Deficit talk can include "at-risk" language ("We have a lot of at-risk children at our school, so we have behavior issues"); quick references to race and poverty without context ("Children don't get enough attention at home because their parents are urban poor"); assumptions about communities ("Immigrant parents don't care enough to learn English"); rationales for low expectations ("The children at our school cannot handle that curriculum"); and justifications for harsh discipline ("Children need to prove they are ready for more freedom"). See Brown (2016) for more examples.

Children cannot be described as *at risk* in the same way they can be described as *smart* or *young* or *capable*. *At risk* is not a label or an adjective, and it typically ignores the reality of children's lives. Young children are put at risk by larger, unjust societal systems that fail them and their families. Immigrant parents *do* care about their children, even if they show it in ways that teachers from different backgrounds don't understand because they expect something different. Young children deserve to explore, talk, move around, and connect regardless of circumstance. It is the environment that must shift to accommodate and make such experiences possible when children are dealing with the ongoing impact of historic injustices. Strengths-based observations and assumptions position young children, families, and communities as knowledgeable and capable.

2. De-Privilege White-Centric, Western Philosophies and Approaches

Social justice necessitates that we think deeply about the role our backgrounds, experiences, beliefs, and training play in how we interpret the actions of children and families and approach teaching and learning. Gutiérrez and Johnson (2017) call for us to check the lenses (e.g., curriculum, research, pedagogy models, materials, classroom management approaches) we look through and ask

> How can one *see* dignity in people's everyday lives when the operant analytical lens (e.g., urban, poor, English Learner, "gritless") has already defined the nature of possibility of people and their practices? (249)

If most of what guides our practice comes from White upper-middle-class researchers and educators, our knowledge base will be too narrow. Knowledge and learning need to be constantly redefined to be more representative of the voices that are silenced, erased, or unheard, rather than it being a prerogative of a few privileged ones. Educators can broaden the authors they read; the educators they consult for help; and the scientific ideas that come from various racial, linguistic, ethnic, LGBTQIA+, geographic, discipline, and cultural communities. By including these practices in their teaching and pedagogy, the teachers can begin to decenter whiteness and combat deficit thinking by centering the narratives and stories of groups that have been historically silenced (Sachdeva & Adair 2019). In classrooms, teachers can provide materials, books, decorations, and conversations that privilege historically underserved communities, including books focused on normalizing racial, cultural, linguistic, gender, economic, religious, and LGBTQIA+ diversity through everyday stories of empowered or nuanced characters told by anti-colonial authors and illustrators. Experiencing the normalization of diversity without colonizing deficit thinking serves young children from both privileged and marginalized communities (Beneke, Park, & Taitingfong 2019).

Often, important skills and knowledge normalized within marginalized communities go unrecognized or are devalued in larger institutions of schooling. Social justice means looking at the cultural variance in how young children learn and valuing a broad range of learning experiences and dispositions beyond following directions.

3. Prioritize Children's Agency Every Day

Creating socially just early childhood education classrooms and systems is as much (if not more) about how to teach as what is taught. Children need opportunities to use their *agency* every day to see themselves as leaders—those who can advocate, plan for, and make change for themselves and their communities.

Agency, a core recommendation in NAEYC's advancing equity position statement, is the ability to influence or make decisions about what and how something is learned to expand individual and collective capabilities (Adair, Colegrove, & McManus 2017;

NAEYC 2019a). Using their agency, children investigate ideas, relationships, or things around them that are meaningful to them, which expands their capabilities in broad and deep ways. Multiple studies have shown that when young children can use their agency, they use it to help others and work together (Colegrove & Adair 2014). A collective sense of effort and understanding is key to fighting social injustice.

EQUITY High-quality programs will look different in different settings because they reflect the values, beliefs, and practices of specific children, families, and communities.

The ways in which children use their agency vary across communities, so there are many ways to support agency. For example, children can

> Choose the topics to study or be free to wander the room to help friends; observe others' learning activities; or get materials to build, experiment, or explain something to a classmate

> Write books on their own topics or family stories with materials they determine from inside and outside of the classroom

> Handle conflict or make an experiment or share stories from home without constant adult control or disruption

> Create shared learning materials such as calendars, word walls, or letter and number posters instead of using commercially prepared ones

> Move and talk in all areas of the school and classroom instead of walking in prison-like lines

> Alter lessons, schedules, and plans when they have a rigorous idea to study

> Share knowledge in class and suggest ideas for study or ways of teaching and learning

> Move outside as well as engage with and care for the natural world in ways that expand their relationships and capabilities

If children's everyday learning experiences primarily involve following directions, completing tasks, taking individual assessments, following behavioralist checklists, and being quiet and still, then children will equate learning and being a learner with compliance, stillness, and quiet rather than with multimodal knowledge construction, problem solving, agency, collective work, and leadership (McManus 2019). Bang and colleagues (2012) argue that such low expectations, or "settled expectations," are a continuing colonizing idea that some children (those in marginalized groups) cannot handle the sophisticated learning experiences that others (those in the dominant group) can or are forced to learn ways that devalue their community knowledge. While children do not determine state or national standards for content, they and their families should have a significant role in how they learn such content.

4. Make Space for Children's Realities and Community Knowledge

Detangling from singular or White-normative ways of viewing children also means making space for children's stories and real lives as they are being lived. Children need time every day to share, play, and communicate what is going on and what they are thinking about. Social justice education in kindergarten means bringing children's knowledge into curriculum and pedagogical approaches.

Children are capable of having conversations about difficult subjects such as sexism, racism, and religious exclusion, especially if those conversations incorporate high-quality literature, children's questions, and a spoken commitment to being a learning community that welcomes and values diversity.

Teachers can make space for children's stories through active and ongoing discussions that inform projects while still being cognizant of the academic concerns many families have for their children. Classrooms that dismiss or ignore community realities and concerns, regardless of any progressive or high-quality teaching and learning practices, are not working toward social justice. Educators can begin by asking children and families to contribute their ideas about what should be studied and then actively creating opportunities for families and children to contribute their knowledge as well.

5. Create Healing Spaces

Childhood is often idealized and seen as a worry-free, innocent time. For some, this may be true; however, a significant number of children witness and experience traumatizing events. Trauma can be racial slurs aimed at their parents from someone in line at the grocery store; abuse or neglect at home; homelessness; media coverage of mass shootings; patterned violence; and/or bullying, mistreatment, or intimidation. Trauma and its effects look different across individuals, contexts, ages, and communities and continue across generations. Children's responses to trauma too often get mistaken for "bad behavior" or "learning difficulties" (Wright 2007, 2010, 2017). When teachers have bias or presume to understand children's lives without getting to know them or their families, attempts to discipline are unhelpful or, at worst, retraumatizing.

NAEYC's position statement on advancing equity (2019) recommends trauma-informed care to address issues of inequity. It recognizes the role of *historical and multigenerational trauma* (Fast & Collin-Vézina 2010) "inflicted through slavery, genocide, sexual exploitation, segregation, incarceration, exclusion, and forced relocation" (NAEYC 2019a, 14). These traumas often go unaddressed, furthering inequities by denying access to sources of healing. Spaces where young children exist should be comforting and supportive of their well-being. Creating healing classrooms often means veering slightly from the script of lesson plans, schedules, and even protocols to attend to the immediate needs of children.

Conclusion

Early education spaces can and should be one of the primary spaces where children feel safe and can heal. This healing process is where social justice begins for some children and their families as a way to compensate for, or at least hold off, the personal and structural violence children experience. Teachers can create safe, healing spaces by bravely listening to children's stories and acknowledging and validating the difficult circumstances children are going through. Just as with Gina in the first vignette, teachers who care for their students and their families as human beings worthy of dignity create opportunities for them to feel welcome and safe. They help young children engage in social justice activities by caring for one another through engagement and compassion.

JENNIFER KEYS ADAIR, PhD, is professor of early childhood education and director of the Agency and Young Children Research Collective at the University of Texas at Austin. She is the coauthor, with Kiyomi Sánchez-Suzuki Colegrove, of *Segregation by Experience: Agency, Racism and Learning in the Early Grades*.

SHUBHI SACHDEVA, PhD, is an assistant professor of child and adolescent development at San Francisco State University. Her research focuses on equity and justice issues in early education and development and global perspectives in early childhood education.

Index

Note: Page numbers followed by *f* and *t* indicate figures and tables, respectively.